HENRIK IBSEN

THREE PLAYS

IN TRANSLATIONS REVISED BY

WILLIAM ARCHER

THREE PLAYS OF

HENRIK IBSEN

AN ENEMY OF THE PEOPLE
THE WILD DUCK
HEDDA GABLER

WITH AN INTRODUCTION BY
JOHN GASSNER

ILLUSTRATED BY
FREDRIK MATHESON

The Heritage Press

NORWALK, CONNECTICUT

INTRODUCTION

IT MAY be idle to speak of Ibsen and Shakespeare in the same breath, but the comparison has been made with some aptness ever since Ibsen's reputation for iconoclasm started waning and his complexity came to be recognized. Although he retained an inquiring mind and remained a master of protest to the end (his dying words are reported to have been "On the contrary!"), he soon applied the yardstick of scepticism to himself and his own ideas or ideals. And becoming an iconoclast in reserve, so to speak, the propagandist gradually approached the high order of comprehensiveness we have long associated with Shakespeare and with perhaps no other dramatist since Sophocles earned a reputation for seeing life steadily and seeing it whole.

If Ibsen did not quite do the same, he did acquire without loss of intensity an almost classical perspective by comparison with most of his successors, and he did manifest an almost Shakespearian sense of life, which is chiefly a feeling for many-faceted characterization. Henry James well described this quality in Ibsen as "the artistic exercise of a mind saturated with the vision of human infirmities; saturated, above all, with a sense of the infinitude, for all its mortal savour, of *character,* finding that an endless romance and a perpetual challenge." If he was only a prose Shakespeare (and a prose Shakespeare is *no* Shakespeare), Ibsen, nevertheless, owes his singularity far more to this Shakespearian amplitude than to the modern attitudes with which he first invigorated the theatre. Ibsen became many men in one man and many dramatists in one dramatist, so that almost any statement concerning him—that he is, for instance, a realist or a symbolist, an idealist or a pragmatist, a paragon of clarity or a compounder of dramatic conundrums—will possess some validity.

The three plays with which Ibsen is represented in the present volume show him at various stages of this transformation into a universal playwright. In *An Enemy of the People* (1882) we find Ibsen firing parting shots at the enemies of his first important social dramas, *A Doll's House* and *Ghosts,* but diversifying his barrage until the target is virtually humanity as a whole. His subject is the moral inertia of the average unheroic men of high or low degree who constitute the mass of mankind. They are the habitual opportunists who in any final confrontation, if not always at the very start, consult only their self-interest and ignore or compound corruption for profit and convenience. Their "knowledge" is little more than the standardization of error, even as their "wisdom" is mere accommodation or compromise. The "majority is always *wrong*"; and the individual who is right will have to be strong, for he will stand alone. In putting these conclusions into the mouth of his hero Dr. Stockmann (whose remarks are intemperate, to be sure, but are sufficiently sustained by the action of the play) Ibsen is, moreover, already being many-sided and complicated. This viewpoint is being hurled at the public in the work of an author who was allied with Scandinavian liberalism and whom both admirers and detractors associated with the progressive movement for which the "majority" was distinctly more *right* than wrong.

It is noteworthy, finally, that a new complexity infiltrates the play once acclaimed—and normally still revered—as Ibsen's passionate advocacy of idealism. Ibsen not only whiplashes both conservatives and liberals in *An Enemy of the People,* but takes an amused view of Stockmann himself. Although entirely right in calling attention to the infectious waters of a provincial spa, which by symbolic extension becomes the whole of established society, Stockmann is almost childishly naive in expecting support for his project and in not taking the measure of his opponents and fair-weather supporters. He is, in contemporary parlance, a screwball as well as an honest man.

Perhaps Ibsen is also implying, with ironic ambivalence, that in order to remain an honest man in a dishonest society a man actually has to be a screwball. Although it is perfectly understandable that men of good will and liberal inclination should want to idealize Dr. Stockmann and take his crusade seriously, the fact remains that for Ibsen the play was a *comedy* and its spirited central character "a grotesque adolescent and hothead"—"*ein grotesker Bursche und ein Strudelkopf.*" In the 1950's, during the McCarthy episode in American history, Arthur Miller, in adapting the play, divested Stockmann of comic characteristics and circumstances, and the result, in two New York productions, was quite stirring. But Ibsen's play is, indisputably, a more complex and ironic work than the American adaptation.

The spirit of irony that hovered over Ibsen in 1882, when he completed *An Enemy of the People,* appeared to have been replaced by a veritable demon of contradiction when he came to write his next play. When *The Wild Duck* began to appear in the bookstalls in 1884, many a liberal must have been dismayed by the suspicion that his elected spokesman in the theatre had betrayed him. That in doing so the author had apparently also betrayed himself could hardly lessen the pain or soften the impeachment, for Ibsen had become a charismatic figure in advanced European circles and had been entrusted with some of their fondest hopes. Dismaying as were the sentiments of the mordant raisonneur Dr. Relling, who refused to distinguish between ideals and lies and who maintained that human frailty needed the support of "Life-illusions," it was even more disturbing to find Ibsen demonstrating this viewpoint with the main action and the central character. His hero or, shall we say, *anti-hero* Gregers Werle, an oedipally fixated neurotic and a downright simpleton in human relations, seemed to stalk through *The Wild Duck* as the prime caricature of would-be reformers. In the opinion of those who had persisted in wrapping a prophet's mantle around Ibsen, moreover, this portrait of a reformer as an inept meddler also seemed an unsettling self-portrait.

It would take some reflection to validate Ibsen's warning, if warning it was, that a private passion for reform could have its source in sickness rather than integrity. And it would take some understanding of the difference between an artist's role and a pedagogue's in literature to acknowledge the artist rather than the propagandist in Ibsen. Only then would one be reconciled to the artist's truth in *The Wild Duck,* which is equivalent to nothing less than the rich texture of the play itself; that is, Ibsen's presentation of life itself in its variety and complexity, its absurdity and its pathos. It would be difficult, in fact, to know where to start with a revision of popular estimates of Ibsen during the last third of the nineteenth century as either a revolutionary ogre (the conservative view) or revolutionary savior (the liberal view), without actually starting at the beginning.

Born in 1828 in the Norwegian shipping town of Skien, of a good family whose fortunes declined during his childhood, apprenticed in his sixteenth year to a provincial pharmacist, and involved with some radicalism and political journalism in his twenties, Ibsen was not particularly atypical in any of his circumstances or interests but for the fact that he became a poet. He was not an especially good one except in a few lyrics, but he gradually acquired a reputation as a dramatist and man of the theatre after becoming the stage manager and official playwright of a progressive little theatre in the city of Bergen in 1851. As a young writer of romantic plays in verse based on Scandinavian folklore and history he was also unremarkable, if by no means ineffective.

What is noteworthy, however, is that the more penetrative the plays were in characterization (as in the great historical drama *The Pretenders,* written in 1863) and the more abrasive in social criticism (as in *Brand* and *Peer Gynt,* published in 1865 and 1867 respectively), the richer they were in poetry as well as drama. Not even the topical success of the early prose plays of his middle period, starting with *Pillars of Society* in 1877, could cast any doubt on the fact that he was, first and last, an artist. He was not less the artist even when he appeared as a prose dramatist with *A Doll's House,* in 1879, and with *Ghosts* in 1881—both works being far richer in irony than in instruction, affording a more comprehensive view of human relations than had ever been provided by pamphleteering for feminine emancipation, and possessing a more shapely dramatic structure than any argument or demonstration. Each play also had its own special theatricality, tone, and atmosphere, and even a touch of the grotesque such as Nora's tarantella dance in *A Doll's House* and the burning down of the orphanage that Mrs. Alving had dedicated to the memory of a faithless husband in *Ghosts*—not to mention the *frisson* of family doom in the ghost-haunted house of Alving.

Only by overlooking these and other elements in Ibsen's so-called problem plays was it possible to see a retreat, rather than an advance, in *The Wild Duck*. To which one might have added the reflection that social reform could hardly be invalidated by the imbecile resolve and tactics of a Gregers Werle: the "call of the ideal" he hears is decidedly puritanical and retrogressive rather than progressive. By an odd coincidence, moreover, Ibsen's public conduct on his return to Scandinavia within a year of the publication of the play amounted to a total repudiation of any middle-aged retreat to conservatism. It was no "tired radical" who left Rome for his homeland in 1885, promptly attacked the conservative leadership of the Norwegian Students' Union, became an honorary member of its radical wing, and called for more rapid progress toward the liberalization of the Norwegian state.

Ibsen in the podium, however, did not commit Ibsen in the study; and the playwright, still bent upon investigating men and women in states of crisis, went ahead with such unvarnished representations of human complexity that his plays could have been misconstrued as the recantations of a reformed radical rather than as the incisive qualifications of a student of human nature. This was apparent in his perturbing tragedy of a "free woman" and an emancipated clergyman, *Rosmersholm,* published two years after *The Wild Duck,* and in the most powerful of his realistic dramas, *Hedda Gabler,* published in 1890.

With its devastating portrait of an "unwomanly woman," whose urbane sophistication masks provincial narrowness and whose upper-class pistol-firing bravado conceals cowardice, *Hedda Gabler* is a profound character study. The play represented a radical revision of the role of feminist champion into which history had cast the author of *A Doll's House,* whose disenchanted *womanly* heroine had left the shelter of Victorian marriage in order to become a self-reliant adult. Within a dozen years of the publication of that drama of feminist revolt, Ibsen was dramatizing the failure of an *unwomanly* woman and giving what emotional and spiritual victory there is in *Hedda Gabler* to her ultrawomanly foil, Mrs. Elvsted.

"All in the service of a realistic view of character," Ibsen could have said, in replying to both doctrinaire feminists disappointed with his portrait of Hedda and to August Strindberg, his junior colleague from neighboring Sweden, who congratulated himself upon having cured Ibsen of feminism with the antifeminist tirades of *Comrades, The Father, Miss Julie* and *Creditors!* "All for the sake of obtaining a balanced view of life," Ibsen might have countered, refusing to commit himself to anything as neurotically compulsive as Strindberg's misogynistic tirades. And he could have pointed, as we must, to the rich texture of *Hedda Gabler* as a self-contained play. He did not offer it as a tract but as a human document, and whatever the relevance of his character analysis of Hedda to the emotional incapacities of twentieth-century "career women," he himself supplied no generalization on the subject.

Instead, he concentrated on an individual case, verging indeed on a case history but not actually crossing the borderline between a psychological drama and a mere clinical report in dramatic form. Giving due attention to Hedda's environmental and parental conditioning as well as to her present tensions, including her ennui and her distaste for pregnancy, Ibsen brought her crisis to the pitch of destructive diabolism without stinting on her humanity. He went even further and with the sure instinct of a serious dramatist set a seal of distinction on her that few actresses have succeeded in bringing to the role. There is a touch of integrity and self-respect commingled with her baser elements that increases the distance between Hedda, the creature or character-creation of a poet-realist, and her ordinary sisters in life.

There is a noteworthy singularity of temperament in Hedda's perversity, and her very frigidity freezes her in attitudes that would be rather heroic but for her small-town dread of a scandal. She is a sort of suburban Brunnhilde with a "tragic flaw" as well as a run-of-the-couch neurosis. She cannot abide fatuity even when it is wrapped in sentiment or coated with goodness. She yielded once to necessity when she married the placid mediocrity Tesman; but she does not pretend to like, she barely tolerates, her marriage. She also scorns the pinchbeck substitute of an affair with the mediocre man-of-the-world Judge Brack, and refuses to submit to his attentions, at the end of the drama, as the price of his silence concerning her part in Løvborg's scandalous death in a brothel. To want Løvborg to wear vine-leaves in his hair and kill himself "beautifully" after he has disgraced himself, a wish she carries out in her own desperate case after his death, is undoubtedly romantic nonsense. But in this, as in other matters, there is undoubtedly a sort of élan in General Gabler's daughter that graces her folly. Reality, as she herself comes to realize, mocks her aspirations at every point; but unless we brush her off as a complete fool, which she is not, we can credit her with a half-redeeming discontent with mediocrity in her life and environment.

It is not at all certain either that Mrs. Elvsted, Hedda's warm-hearted foil, offers a glowing alternative. It is doubtful that this "good" woman is not at least as possessive as Hedda. There is perhaps no small amount of egotism in her devotion to the unstable young genius Løvborg whose rehabilitation became her mission in life. It is indeed a question whether Mrs. Elvsted, who has just left her husband and her stepchildren in order to watch over Løvborg, is constitutionally less ruthless than Hedda proves to be in a fit of jealousy when she burns Løvborg's manuscript. One may even wonder whether Ibsen the habitual ironist did not intend some irony in this soft "womanly" woman's first taking charge of Hedda's former lover Løvborg and then, when she sits down with Tesman to reconstruct Løvborg's book from his notes, promptly possessing herself of Hedda's husband. In fine, Ibsen did not use Hedda to sound a warning to modern women and her foil to set them a good example, but to demonstrate the sometimes horrifying, sometimes amusing, and nearly always tantalizing game of life. It is no wonder he came to be considered an enigmatic or "obscure" author even by so ambiguous a writer himself as Henry James.

This does not, however, mean that Ibsen had renounced his vocation of iconoclasm. In *Hedda Gabler* he did, in effect, smash the idol of pseudo feminism, which also passed in the late nineteenth century for Ibsenism; and he did characterize, in some anticipatory manner, a species of woman that began to proliferate wherever feminine emancipation was under way. Hedda may be regarded as the prototype of the modern woman who substitutes self-assertion and egotism for the passiveness and self-effacement that once passed for true and fruitful femininity. It is essential only to realize that if Ibsen smashed any sort of idol in this play, he left the pedestal vacant for a multifaceted character called Hedda whose *dramatic worth* is beyond question.

In the interest of truth and genuine self-realization Ibsen continued to oppose idolatry to the end of his creative life, which unfortunately terminated (as a result of a paralytic stroke) half a decade before his death at the age of seventy-eight on May 23, 1906. Various forms of false worship, including self-worship, fell under his assault in the more or less poetic or symbolist plays he wrote after 1890—in *The Master Builder* (1892), *Little Eyolf* (1894), and the relentless tragedy of a business tycoon, *John Gabriel Borkman* (1896).

Finally, in *When We Dead Awaken* (1899), deploring the immolation of life and love even in the service of one's art, Ibsen the dedicated artist assailed the idolatry of art itself. He apparently felt that there was one more idol to be toppled before he closed his account with his vocation. And so, with a final rally of failing talent, the dour old master smashed his own special idol and called it a long day since the dawn of his private passion for art half a century before, when he had turned from pharmacy to poetry and published his first tentative play, *Catiline,* at the age of twenty-two. It is an ironic detail of literary history that *When We Dead Awaken* should have been extravagantly acclaimed shortly after publication by a seventeen-year-old Dublin collegian, James Joyce, who was soon to become the culture hero of a new, twentieth-century, art-for-art's sake generation.

JOHN GASSNER

AN ENEMY OF THE PEOPLE

TRANSLATED BY
ELEANOR MARX-AVELING

CHARACTERS

DOCTOR THOMAS STOCKMANN
Medical officer of the Baths

MRS. STOCKMANN
His wife

PETRA
Their daughter, a teacher

EILIF   MORTEN
Their sons, thirteen and ten years old respectively

PETER STOCKMANN
*The doctor's elder brother, Burgomaster and chief of
police, chairman of the Baths Committee, etc.*

MORTEN KIIL*
Owner of a tannery, Mrs. Stockmann's foster-father

HOVSTAD
Editor of the "People's Messenger"

BILLING
On the staff of the paper

HORSTER
A ship's captain

ASLAKSEN
A printer

*Participants in a meeting of citizens: all sorts and conditions
of men, some women, and a band of schoolboys*

The action passes in a town on the South Coast of Norway

* Pronounced *Keel*

ACT FIRST

Evening. Dr. Stockmann's sitting-room; simply but neatly decorated and furnished. In the wall to the right are two doors, the further one leading to the hall, the nearer one to the Doctor's study. In the opposite wall, facing the hall door, a door leading to the other rooms of the house. Against the middle of this wall stands the stove; further forward a sofa with a mirror above it, and in front of it an oval table with a cover. On the table a lighted lamp, with a shade. In the back wall an open door leading to the dining-room, in which is seen a supper-table, with a lamp on it.

Billing is seated at the supper-table, with a napkin under his chin. Mrs. Stockmann is standing by the table and placing before him a dish with a large joint of roast beef. The other seats round the table are empty; the table is in disorder, as after a meal.

MRS. STOCKMANN. If you come an hour late, Mr. Billing, you must put up with a cold supper.

BILLING *(eating)*. It is excellent—really first rate.

MRS. STOCKMANN. You know how Stockmann insists on regular meal-hours . . .

BILLING. Oh, I don't mind at all. I almost think I enjoy my supper more when I can sit down to it like this, alone and undisturbed.

MRS. STOCKMANN. Oh, well, if you enjoy it . . . *(Listening in the direction of the hall.)* I believe this is Mr. Hovstad coming too.

BILLING. Very likely.

(Burgomaster Stockmann enters, wearing an overcoat and an official gold-laced cap, and carrying a stick.)

BURGOMASTER. Good evening, sister-in-law.

MRS. STOCKMANN *(coming forward into the sitting-room)*. Oh, good evening; is it you? It is good of you to look in.

BURGOMASTER. I was just passing, and so . . . *(Looks towards the drawing-room.)* Ah, I see you have company.

MRS. STOCKMANN *(rather embarrassed)*. Oh no, not at all; it's the merest chance. *(Hurriedly.)* Won't you sit down and have a little supper?

BURGOMASTER. I? No, thank you. Good gracious! hot meat in the evening! That wouldn't suit my digestion.

MRS. STOCKMANN. Oh, for once in a way . . .

BURGOMASTER. No, no,—much obliged to you. I stick to tea and bread and butter. It's more wholesome in the long run—and rather more economical, too.

MRS. STOCKMANN *(smiling)*. You mustn't think Thomas and I are mere spendthrifts, either.

BURGOMASTER. You are not, sister-in-law; far be it from me to say that. *(Pointing to the Doctor's study.)* Is he not at home?

MRS. STOCKMANN. No, he has gone for a little turn after supper—with the boys.

BURGOMASTER. I wonder if that is a good thing to do? *(Listening.)* There he is, no doubt.

MRS. STOCKMANN. No, that is not he. *(A knock.)* Come in!

(Hovstad enters from the hall.)

MRS. STOCKMANN. Ah, it's Mr. Hovstad . . .

HOVSTAD. You must excuse me; I was detained at the printer's. Good evening, Burgomaster.

BURGOMASTER *(bowing rather stiffly)*. Mr. Hovstad? You come on business, I presume?

HOVSTAD. Partly. About an article for the paper.

BURGOMASTER. So I supposed. I hear my brother is an extremely prolific contributor to the *People's Messenger.*

HOVSTAD. Yes, when he wants to unburden his mind on one thing or another, he gives the *Messenger* the benefit.

MRS. STOCKMANN *(to Hovstad).* But will you not...? *(Points to the dining-room.)*

BURGOMASTER. Well, well, I am far from blaming him for writing for the class of readers he finds most in sympathy with him. And, personally, I have no reason to bear your paper any ill-will, Mr. Hovstad.

HOVSTAD. No, I should think not.

BURGOMASTER. One may say, on the whole, that a fine spirit of mutual tolerance prevails in our town—an excellent public spirit. And that is because we have a great common interest to hold us together—an interest in which all right-minded citizens are equally concerned...

HOVSTAD. Yes—the Baths.

BURGOMASTER. Just so. We have our magnificent new Baths. Mark my words! The whole life of the town will centre around the Baths, Mr. Hovstad. There can be no doubt of it!

MRS. STOCKMANN. That is just what Thomas says.

BURGOMASTER. How marvellously the place has developed, even in this couple of years! Money has come into circulation, and brought life and movement with it. Houses and ground-rents rise in value every day.

HOVSTAD. And there are fewer people out of work.

BURGOMASTER. That is true. There is a gratifying diminution in the burden imposed on the well-to-do classes by the poor-rates; and they will be still further lightened if only we have a really good summer this year—a rush of visitors—plenty of invalids, to give the Baths a reputation.

HOVSTAD. I hear there is every prospect of that.

BURGOMASTER. Things look most promising. Inquiries about apartments and so forth keep on pouring in.

HOVSTAD. Then the Doctor's paper will come in very opportunely.

BURGOMASTER. Has he been writing again?

HOVSTAD. This is a thing he wrote in the winter; enlarging on the virtues of the Baths, and on the excellent sanitary conditions of the town. But at that time I held it over.

BURGOMASTER. Ah—I suppose there was something not quite judicious about it?

HOVSTAD. Not at all. But I thought it better to keep it till the spring, when people are beginning to look about them, and think of their summer quarters . . .

BURGOMASTER. You were right, quite right, Mr. Hovstad.

MRS. STOCKMANN. Yes, Thomas is really indefatigable where the Baths are concerned.

BURGOMASTER. It is his duty as one of the staff.

HOVSTAD. And of course he was really their creator.

BURGOMASTER. Was he? Indeed! I gather that certain persons are of that opinion. But I should have thought that I, too, had a modest share in that undertaking.

MRS. STOCKMANN. Yes, that is what Thomas is always saying.

HOVSTAD. No one dreams of denying it, Burgomaster. You set the thing going, and put it on a practical basis; everybody knows that. I only meant that the original idea was the doctor's.

BURGOMASTER. Yes, my brother has certainly had ideas enough in his time—worse luck! But when it comes to realising them, Mr. Hovstad, we want men of another stamp. I should have thought that in this house at any rate . . .

MRS. STOCKMANN. Why, my dear brother-in-law . . .

HOVSTAD. Burgomaster, how can you . . . ?

MRS. STOCKMANN. Do go in and have some supper, Mr. Hovstad; my husband is sure to be home directly.

HOVSTAD. Thanks; just a mouthful, perhaps.

(He goes into the dining-room.)

BURGOMASTER *(speaking in a low voice)*. It is extraordinary how people who spring direct from the peasant class never can get over their want of tact.

MRS. STOCKMANN. But why should you care? Surely you and Thomas can share the honour, like brothers.

BURGOMASTER. Yes, one would suppose so; but it seems a share of the honour is not enough for some persons.

MRS. STOCKMANN. What nonsense! You and Thomas always get on so well together. *(Listening.)* There, I think I hear him. *(Goes and opens the door to the hall.)*

DR. STOCKMANN *(laughing and talking loudly, without)*. Here's another visitor for you, Katrina. Isn't it capital, eh? Come in, Captain Horster. Hang your coat on the peg. What! you don't wear an overcoat? Fancy, Katrina, I caught him in the street, and I could hardly get him to come in.

(Captain Horster enters and bows to Mrs. Stockmann.)

DR. STOCKMANN *(in the doorway)*. In with you, boys. They're famishing again! Come along, Captain Horster; you must try our roast beef . . .

(He forces Horster into the dining-room. Eilif and Morten follow them.)

MRS. STOCKMANN. But, Thomas, don't you see . . .

DR. STOCKMANN *(turning round in the doorway)*. Oh, is that you, Peter! *(Goes up to him and holds out his hand.)* Now this is really capital.

BURGOMASTER. Unfortunately, I have only a moment to spare . . .

DR. STOCKMANN. Nonsense! We shall have some toddy in a minute. You're not forgetting the toddy, Katrina?

MRS. STOCKMANN. Of course not; the water's boiling. *(She goes into the dining-room.)*

BURGOMASTER. Toddy too . . . !

DR. STOCKMANN. Yes; sit down, and let's make ourselves comfortable.

BURGOMASTER. Thanks; I never join in drinking parties.

DR. STOCKMANN. But this isn't a party.

BURGOMASTER. I don't know what else . . . *(Looks towards the dining-room.)* It's extraordinary how they can get through all that food.

DR. STOCKMANN *(rubbing his hands)*. Yes, doesn't it do one good to see young people eat? Always hungry! That's as it should be. They need good, solid meat to put stamina into them! It is they that have got to whip up the ferment of the future, Peter.

BURGOMASTER. May I ask what there is to be "whipped up," as you call it?

DR. STOCKMANN. You'll have to ask the young people that—when the time comes. We shan't see it, of course. Two old fogies like you and me . . .

BURGOMASTER. Come, come! Surely that is a very extraordinary expression to use . . .

DR. STOCKMANN. Oh, you mustn't mind my nonsense, Peter. I'm in such glorious spirits, you see. I feel so unspeakable happy in the midst of all this growing, germinating life. Isn't it a marvellous time we live in! It seems as though a whole new world were springing up around us.

BURGOMASTER. Do you really think so?

DR. STOCKMANN. Of course, you can't see it as clearly as I do. You have passed your life in the midst of it all; and that deadens the impression. But I who had to vegetate all those years in that little hole in the north, hardly ever seeing a soul that could speak a stimulating word to me—all this affects me as if I had suddenly dropped into the heart of some teeming metropolis.

BURGOMASTER. Well, metropolis . . .

DR. STOCKMANN. Oh, I know well enough that things are on a small scale here, compared with many other places. But there's life here— there's promise—there's an infinity of things to work and strive for; and that is the main point. *(Calling.)* Katrina, haven't there been any letters?

MRS. STOCKMANN *(in the dining-room)*. No, none at all.

DR. STOCKMANN. And then a good income, Peter! That's a thing one learns to appreciate when one has lived on starvation wages . . .

BURGOMASTER. Good heavens . . . !

DR. STOCKMANN. Oh yes, I can tell you we often had hard times of it up there. And now we can live like princes! To-day, for example, we had roast beef for dinner; and we've had some of it for supper too. Won't you have some? Come along—just look at it, at any rate . . .

BURGOMASTER. No, no; certainly not . . .

DR. STOCKMANN. Well then, look here—do you see we've bought a table-cover?

BURGOMASTER. Yes, so I observed.

DR. STOCKMANN. And a lamp-shade, too. Do you see? Katrina has been saving up for them. They make the room look comfortable, don't they? Come over here. No, no, no, not there. So—yes! Now you see how it concentrates the light . . . I really think it has quite an artistic effect. Eh?

BURGOMASTER. Yes, when one can afford such luxuries . . .

DR. STOCKMANN. Oh, I can afford it now. Katrina says I make almost as much as we spend.

BURGOMASTER. Ah—almost!

DR. STOCKMANN. Besides, a man of science must live in some style. Why, I believe a mere sheriff[1] spends much more a year than I do.

BURGOMASTER. Yes, I should think so! A member of the superior magistracy . . .

DR. STOCKMANN. Well, then, even a common shipowner! A man of that sort will get through many times as much . . .

BURGOMASTER. That is natural, in your relative positions.

DR. STOCKMANN. And after all, Peter, I really don't squander any money. But I can't deny myself the delight of having people about me. I must have them. After living so long out of the world, I find it a necessity of life to have bright, cheerful, freedom-loving, hard-working young fellows around me—and that's what they are, all of them, that are sitting there eating so heartily. I wish you knew more of Hovstad . . .

BURGOMASTER. Ah, that reminds me—Hovstad was telling me that he is going to publish another article of yours.

---

[1] *Amtmand,* the chief magistrate of an *Amt* or county; consequently a high dignitary in the official hierarchy. Peter Stockmann's title is *Byfogd,* which also has the meaning of "judge of a town court."

DR. STOCKMANN. An article of mine?

BURGOMASTER. Yes, about the Baths. An article you wrote last winter

DR. STOCKMANN. Oh, that one! But I don't want that to appear for the present.

BURGOMASTER. Why not? It seems to me this is the very time for it.

DR. STOCKMANN. Very likely—under ordinary circumstances—

(Crosses the room.)

BURGOMASTER *(following him with his eyes)*. And what is unusual in the circumstances now?

DR. STOCKMANN *(standing still)*. The fact is, Peter, I really cannot tell you just now; not this evening, at all events. There may prove to be a great deal that is unusual in the circumstances. On the other hand, there may be nothing at all. Very likely it's only my fancy.

BURGOMASTER. Upon my word, you are very enigmatical. Is there anything in the wind? Anything I am to be kept in the dark about? I should think, as Chairman of the Bath Committee . . .

DR. STOCKMANN. And I should think that I . . . Well, well, don't let us get our backs up, Peter.

BURGOMASTER. God forbid! I am not in the habit of "getting my back up," as you express it. But I must absolutely insist that all arrangements shall be made and carried out in a businesslike manner, and through the properly constituted authorities. I cannot be a party to crooked or underhand courses.

DR. STOCKMANN. Have *I* ever been given to crooked or underhand courses?

BURGOMASTER. At any rate you have an ingrained propensity to taking your own course. And that, in a well-ordered community is almost as inadmissible. The individual must subordinate himself to society, or, more precisely, to the authorities whose business it is to watch over the welfare of society.

DR. STOCKMANN. Maybe. But what the devil has that to do with me?

BURGOMASTER. Why this is the very thing, my dear Thomas, that it seems you will never learn. But take care; you will have to pay for it—sooner or later. Now I have warned you. Good-bye.

DR. STOCKMANN. Are you stark mad? You're on a totally wrong track . . .

BURGOMASTER. I am not often on the wrong track. Moreover, I must protest against . . . (*Bowing towards dining-room.*) Good-bye, sister-in-law; good-day to you, gentlemen.

MRS. STOCKMANN (*entering the sitting-room*). Has he gone?

DR. STOCKMANN. Yes, and in a fine temper, too.

MRS. STOCKMANN. Why, my dear Thomas, what have you been doing to him now?

DR. STOCKMANN. Nothing at all. He can't possibly expect me to account to him for everything—before the time comes.

MRS. STOCKMANN. What have you to account to him for?

DR. STOCKMANN. H'm;—never mind about that, Katrina.—It's very odd the postman doesn't come.

(*Hovstad, Billing, and Horster have risen from table and come forward into the sitting-room. Eilif and Morten presently follow.*)

BILLING (*stretching himself*). Ah! Strike me dead if one doesn't feel a new man after such a meal.

HOVSTAD. The Burgomaster didn't seem in the best of tempers this evening.

DR. STOCKMANN. That's his stomach. He has a very poor digestion.

HOVSTAD. I fancy it's the staff of the *Messenger* he finds it hardest to stomach.

MRS. STOCKMANN. I thought you got on well enough with him.

HOVSTAD. Oh, yes; but it's only a sort of armistice between us.

BILLING. That's it. That word sums up the situation.

DR. STOCKMANN. We must remember that Peter is a lonely bachelor, poor devil! He has no home to be happy in; only business, business. And then all that cursed weak tea he goes and pours down his throat! Now then, chairs round the table, boys! Katrina, shan't we have the toddy now?

MRS. STOCKMANN (*going towards the dining-room*). I am just getting it.

DR. STOCKMANN. And you, Captain Horster, sit beside me on the sofa. So rare a guest as you . . . Sit down, gentlemen, sit down.

(The men sit round the table; Mrs. Stockmann brings in a tray with kettle, glasses, decanters, etc.)

MRS. STOCKMANN. Here you have it: here's arrak, and this is rum, and this cognac. Now, help yourselves.

DR. STOCKMANN *(taking a glass)*. So we will. *(While the toddy is being mixed.)* And now out with the cigars. Eilif, I think you know where the box is. And Morten, you may fetch my pipe. *(The boys go into the room on the right.)* I have a suspicion that Eilif sneaks a cigar now and then, but I pretend not to notice. *(Calls.)* And my smoking-cap, Morten! Katrina, can't you tell him where I left it. Ah, he's got it. *(The boys bring in the things.)* Now, friends, help yourselves. I stick to my pipe, you know;—this one has been on many a stormy journey with me, up there in the north. *(They clink glasses.)* Your health! Ah, I can tell you it's better fun to sit cosily here, safe from wind and weather.

MRS. STOCKMANN *(who sits down and starts to knit)*. Do you sail soon, Captain Horster?

HORSTER. I hope to be ready for a start by next week.

MRS. STOCKMANN. And you're going to America?

HORSTER. Yes, that's the intention.

BILLING. But then you'll miss the election of the new Town Council.

HORSTER. Is there to be an election again?

BILLING. Didn't you know?

HORSTER. No, I don't trouble myself about those things.

BILLING. But I suppose you take an interest in public affairs?

HORSTER. No, I don't understand anything about them.

BILLING. All the same, one ought at least to vote.

HORSTER. Even those who don't understand anything about it?

BILLING. Understand? Why, what do you mean by that? Society is like a ship: every man must put his hand to the helm.

HORSTER. That may be all right on shore; but at sea it wouldn't do at all.

HOVSTAD. It's remarkable how little sailors care about public affairs as a rule.

BILLING. Most extraordinary.

DR. STOCKMANN. Sailors are like birds of passage; they are at home both in the south and in the north. So it behoves the rest of us to be all the more energetic, Mr. Hovstad. Will there be anything of public interest in the *People's Messenger* to-morrow?

HOVSTAD. Nothing of local interest. But the day after to-morrow I think of printing your article . . .

DR. STOCKMANN. Oh confound it, that article! No, you'll have to hold it over.

HOVSTAD. Really? We happen to have plenty of space, and I should say this was the very time for it . . .

DR. STOCKMANN. Yes, yes, you may be right; but you must hold it over all the same. I shall explain to you by-and-by.

(Petra, wearing a hat and cloak, and with a number of exercise-books under her arm, enters from the hall.)

PETRA. Good evening.

DR. STOCKMANN. Good evening, Petra. Is that you?

(General greetings. Petra puts her cloak, hat, and books on a chair by the door.)

PETRA. Here you all are, enjoying yourselves, while I've been out slaving.

DR. STOCKMANN. Well then, you come and enjoy yourself too.

BILLING. May I mix you a little . . . ?

PETRA *(coming towards the table).* Thank you, I'd rather help myself —you always make it too strong. By the way, father, I have a letter for you. *(Goes to the chair where her things are lying.)*

DR. STOCKMANN. A letter! From whom?

PETRA *(searching in the pocket of her cloak).* I got it from the postman just as I was going out . . .

DR. STOCKMANN *(rising and going towards her).* And you only bring it me now?

PETRA. I really hadn't time to run up again. Here it is.

DR. STOCKMANN *(seizing the letter).* Let me see, let me see, child. *(Reads the address.)* Yes; this is it . . . !

MRS. STOCKMANN. Is it the one you have been so anxious about, Thomas?

DR. STOCKMANN. Yes it is. I must go at once. Where shall I find a light, Katrina? Is there no lamp in my study again!

MRS. STOCKMANN. Yes—the lamp is lighted. It's on the writing-table.

DR. STOCKMANN. Good, good. Excuse me one moment... *(He goes into the room on the right.)*

PETRA. What can it be, mother?

MRS. STOCKMANN. I don't know. For the last few days he has been continually on the look-out for the postman.

BILLING. Probably a country patient...

PETRA. Poor father! He'll soon have far too much to do. *(Mixes her toddy.)* Ah, this will taste good!

HOVSTAD. Have you been teaching in the night school as well to-day?

PETRA *(sipping from her glass)*. Two hours.

BILLING. And four hours in the morning at the institute...

PETRA *(sitting down by the table)*. Five hours.

MRS. STOCKMANN. And I see you have exercises to correct this evening.

PETRA. Yes, a heap of them.

HORSTER. It seems to me you have plenty to do, too.

PETRA. Yes; but I like it. You feel so delightfully tired after it.

BILLING. Do you like that?

PETRA. Yes, for then you sleep so well.

MORTEN. I say, Petra, you must be a great sinner.

PETRA. A sinner?

MORTEN. Yes, if you work so hard. Mr. Rørlund says work is a punishment for our sins.

EILIF *(contemptuously)*. Bosh! What a silly you are, to believe such stuff as that.

MRS. STOCKMANN. Come come, Eilif.

BILLING *(laughing)*. Capital, capital!

HOVSTAD. Should you not like to work so hard, Morten?

MORTEN. No, I shouldn't.

HOVSTAD. Then what will you do with yourself in the world?

MORTEN. I should like to be a Viking.

EILIF. But then you'd have to be a heathen.

MORTEN. Well, so I would.

BILLING. There I agree with you, Morten! I say just the same thing.

MRS. STOCKMANN *(making a sign to him)*. No, no, Mr. Billing, I'm sure
you don't.

BILLING. Strike me dead but I do, though. I am a heathen, and I'm
proud of it. You'll see we shall all be heathens soon.

MORTEN. And shall we be able to do anything we like then?

BILLING. Well, you see, Morten . . .

MRS. STOCKMANN. Now run away, boys; I'm sure you have lessons to
prepare for to-morrow.

EILIF. You might let me stay just a little longer . . .

MRS. STOCKMANN. No, you must go too. Be off, both of you. *(The boys
say good-night and go into the room on the left.)*

HOVSTAD. Do you really think it can hurt the boys to hear these things?

MRS. STOCKMANN. Well, I don't know; I don't like it.

PETRA. Really, mother, I think you are quite wrong there.

MRS. STOCKMANN. Perhaps. But I don't like it—not here, at home.

PETRA. There's no end of hypocrisy both at home and at school. At home you must hold your tongue, and at school you have to stand up and tell lies to the children.

HORSTER. Have you to tell lies?

PETRA. Yes; do you think we don't have to tell them many and many a thing we don't believe ourselves?

BILLING. Ah, that's too true.

PETRA. If only I could afford it, I should start a school myself, and things should be very different there.

BILLING. Oh, afford it . . . !

HORSTER. If you really think of doing *that,* Miss Stockmann, I shall be delighted to let you have a room at my place. You know my father's old house is nearly empty; there's a great big dining-room on the ground floor . . .

PETRA *(laughing).* Oh, thank you very much—but I'm afraid it won't come to anything.

HOVSTAD. No, I fancy Miss Petra is more likely to go over to journalism. By the way, have you had time to look into the English novel you promised to translate for us?

PETRA. Not yet. But you shall have it in good time.

(Dr. Stockmann enters from his room, with the letter open in his hand.)

DR. STOCKMANN *(flourishing the letter).* Here's news, I can tell you, that will waken up the town!

BILLING. News?

MRS. STOCKMANN. What news?

DR. STOCKMANN. A great discovery, Katrina!

HOVSTAD. Indeed?

MRS. STOCKMANN. Made by you?

DR. STOCKMANN. Precisely—by me! *(Walks up and down.) Now* let them go on accusing me of fads and crackbrained notions. But they won't dare to! Ha-ha! I tell you they won't dare!

PETRA. Do tell us what it is, father.

DR. STOCKMANN. Well, well, give me time, and you shall hear all about it. If only I had Peter here now! This just shows how we men can go about forming judgments like the blindest moles . . .

HOVSTAD. What do you mean, doctor?

DR. STOCKMANN *(stopping beside the table).* Isn't it the general opinion that our town is a healthy place?

HOVSTAD. Of course.

DR. STOCKMANN. A quite exceptionally healthy place, indeed—a place to be warmly recommended, both to invalids and people in health . . .

MRS. STOCKMANN. My dear Thomas . . .

DR. STOCKMANN. And assuredly we haven't failed to recommend and belaud it. I've sung its praises again and again, both in the *Messenger* and in pamphlets . . .

HOVSTAD. Well, what then?

DR. STOCKMANN. These Baths, that we have called the pulse of the town, its vital nerve, and—and the devil knows what else . . .

BILLING. "Our city's palpitating heart," I once ventured to call them in a convivial moment . . .

DR. STOCKMANN. Yes, I daresay. Well—do you know what they really are, these mighty, magnificent, belauded Baths, that have cost so much money—do you know what they are?

HOVSTAD. No, what are they?

MRS. STOCKMANN. Do tell us.

DR. STOCKMANN. Simply a pestiferous hole.

PETRA. The Baths, father?

MRS. STOCKMANN *(at the same time).* Our Baths!

HOVSTAD *(also at the same time).* But, Doctor . . . !

BILLING. Oh, it's incredible!

DR. STOCKMANN. I tell you the whole place is a poisonous whited-sepulchre; noxious in the highest degree! All that filth up there in the Mill Dale—the stuff that smells so horribly—taints the water in the feed-pipes of the Pump-Room; and the same accursed poisonous refuse oozes out by the beach . . .

HOVSTAD. Where the sea-baths are?

DR. STOCKMANN. Exactly.

HOVSTAD. But how are you so sure of all this, Doctor?

DR. STOCKMANN. I've investigated the whole thing as conscientiously as possible. I've long had my suspicions about it. Last year we had some extraordinary cases of illness among the patients—both typhoid and gastric attacks . . .

MRS. STOCKMANN. Yes, I remember.

DR. STOCKMANN. We thought at the time that the visitors had brought the infection with them; but afterwards—last winter—I began to question that. So I set about testing the water as well as I could.

MRS. STOCKMANN. It was *that* you were working so hard at!

DR. STOCKMANN. Yes, you may well say I've worked, Katrina. But here, you know, I hadn't the necessary scientific appliances; so I sent samples both of our drinking-water and of our sea-water to the University, for exact analysis by a chemist.

HOVSTAD. And you have received his report?

DR. STOCKMANN *(showing letter)*. Here it is! And it proves beyond dispute the presence of putrefying organic matter in the water—millions of infusoria. It's absolutely pernicious to health, whether used internally or externally.

MRS. STOCKMANN. What a blessing you found it out in time.

DR. STOCKMANN. Yes, you may well say that.

HOVSTAD. And what do you intend to do now, Doctor?

DR. STOCKMANN. Why, to set things right, of course.

HOVSTAD. You think it can be done, then?

DR. STOCKMANN. It *must* be done. Else the whole Baths are useless, ruined. But there's no fear. I am quite clear as to what is required.

MRS. STOCKMANN. But, my dear Thomas, why should you have made such a secret of all this?

DR. STOCKMANN. Would you have had me rush all over the town and chatter about it, before I was quite certain? No, thank you; I'm not so mad as that.

PETRA. But to us at home . . .

DR. STOCKMANN. I couldn't say a word to a living soul. But to-morrow you may look in at the Badger's . . .

MRS. STOCKMANN. Oh, Thomas!

DR. STOCKMANN. Well well, at your grandfather's. The old fellow *will* be astonished! He thinks I'm not quite right in my head—yes, and plenty of others think the same, I've noticed. But now these good people shall see—yes, they shall see now! *(Walks up and down rubbing his hands.)* What a stir there will be in the town, Katrina! Just think of it! All the water-pipes will have to be relaid.

HOVSTAD *(rising)*. All the water-pipes . . . ?

DR. STOCKMANN. Why, of course. The intake is too low down; it must be moved much higher up.

PETRA. So you were right, after all.

DR. STOCKMANN. Yes, do you remember, Petra? I wrote against it when they were beginning the works. But no one would listen to me then. Now, you may be sure, I shall give them my full broadside—for of course I've prepared a statement for the Directors; it has been lying ready a whole week; I've only been waiting for this report. *(Points to letter.)* But now they shall have it at once. *(Goes into his room and returns with a MS. in his hand.)* See! Four closely-written sheets! And I'll enclose the report. A newspaper, Katrina! Get me something to wrap them up in. There—that's it. Give it to—to—*(Stamps.)*—what the devil's her name? Give it to the girl, I mean, and tell her to take it at once to the Burgomaster.

(Mrs. Stockmann goes out with the packet through the dining-room.)

PETRA. What do you think Uncle Peter will say, father?

DR. STOCKMANN. What should he say? He can't possibly be otherwise than pleased that so important a fact has been brought to light.

HOVSTAD. I suppose you will let me put a short announcement of your discovery in the *Messenger*.

DR. STOCKMANN. Yes, I shall be much obliged if you will.

HOVSTAD. It is highly desirable that the public should know about it as soon as possible.

DR. STOCKMANN. Yes, certainly.

MRS. STOCKMANN *(returning)*. She's gone with it.

BILLING. Strike me dead if you won't be the first man in the town, Doctor!

DR. STOCKMANN *(walks up and down in high glee)*. Oh, nonsense! After all, I have done no more than my duty. I've been a lucky treasure-hunter, that's all. But all the same . . .

BILLING. Hovstad, don't you think the town ought to get up a torch-light procession in honour of Dr. Stockmann?

HOVSTAD. I shall certainly propose it.

BILLING. And I'll talk it over with Aslaksen.

DR. STOCKMANN. No, my dear friends; let all such claptrap alone. I won't hear of anything of the sort. And if the Directors should want to raise my salary, I won't accept it. I tell you, Katrina, I will not accept it.

MRS. STOCKMANN. You are quite right, Thomas.

PETRA *(raising her glass)*. Your health, father!

HOVSTAD *and* BILLING. Your health, your health, Doctor!

HORSTER *(clinking glasses with the Doctor)*. I hope you may have nothing but joy of your discovery.

DR. STOCKMANN. Thanks, thanks, my dear friends! I can't tell you how happy I am . . . ! Oh, what a blessing it is to feel that you have deserved well of your native town and your fellow citizens. Hurrah, Katrina! *(He puts both his arms around her neck, and whirls her round with him. Mrs. Stockmann screams and struggles. A burst of laughter, applause, and cheers for the Doctor. The boys thrust their heads in at the door.)*

ACT SECOND

The Doctor's sitting-room. The dining-room door is closed. Morning.

MRS. STOCKMANN *(enters from the dining-room with a sealed letter in her hand, goes to the foremost door on the right, and peeps in).* Are you there, Thomas?

DR. STOCKMANN *(within).* Yes, I have just come in. *(Enters.)* What is it?

MRS. STOCKMANN. A letter from your brother. *(Hands it to him.)*

DR. STOCKMANN. Aha, let us see. *(Opens the envelope and reads.)* "The MS. sent me is returned herewith . . ." *(Reads on, mumbling to himself.)* H'm . . .

MRS. STOCKMANN. Well, what does he say?

DR. STOCKMANN *(putting the paper in his pocket).* Nothing; only that he'll come up himself about midday.

MRS. STOCKMANN. Then be sure you remember to stay at home.

DR. STOCKMANN. Oh, I can easily manage that; I've finished my morning's visits.

MRS. STOCKMANN. I am very curious to know how he takes it.

DR. STOCKMANN. You'll see he won't be over-pleased that it is I that have made the discovery, and not he himself.

MRS. STOCKMANN. Ah, that's just what I'm afraid of.

DR. STOCKMANN. Of course at bottom he'll be glad. But still—Peter is damnably unwilling that any one but himself should do anything for the good of the town.

MRS. STOCKMANN. Do you know, Thomas, I think you might stretch a point, and share the honour with him. Couldn't it appear that it was he that put you on the track . . . ?

DR. STOCKMANN. By all means, for aught I care. If only I can get things put straight . . .

(Old Morten Kiil puts his head in at the hall door, and asks slyly.)

MORTEN KIIL. Is it—is it true?

MRS. STOCKMANN *(going towards him)*. Father—is that you?

DR. STOCKMANN. Hallo, father-in-law! Good morning, good morning.

MRS. STOCKMANN. Do come in.

MORTEN KIIL. Yes, if it's true; if not, I'm off again.

DR. STOCKMANN. If what is true?

MORTEN KIIL. This crazy business about the water-works. Now, is it true?

DR. STOCKMANN. Why, of course it is. But how came *you* to hear of it?

MORTEN KIIL *(coming in)*. Petra looked in on her way to the school . . .

DR. STOCKMANN. Oh, did she?

MORTEN KIIL. Ay ay—and she told me . . . I thought she was only making game of me; but that's not like Petra either.

DR. STOCKMANN. No, indeed; how could you think so?

MORTEN KIIL. Oh, you can never be sure of anybody. You may be made a fool of before you know where you are. So it is true, after all?

DR. STOCKMANN. Most certainly it is. Do sit down, father-in-law. *(Forces him down on the sofa.)* Now isn't it a real blessing for the town . . . ?

MORTEN KIIL *(suppressing his laughter)*. A blessing for the town?

DR. STOCKMANN. Yes, that I made this discovery in time . . .

MORTEN KIIL *(as before)*. Ay, ay, ay!—Well, I could never have believed that you would play monkey-tricks with your very own brother.

DR. STOCKMANN. Monkey-tricks!

MRS. STOCKMANN. Why, father dear . . .

MORTEN KIIL *(resting his hands and chin on the top of his stick and blinking slyly at the Doctor)*. What was it again? Wasn't it that some animals had got into the water-pipes?

DR. STOCKMANN. Yes; infusorial animals.

MORTEN KIIL. And any number of these animals had got in, Petra said —whole swarms of them.

DR. STOCKMANN. Certainly; hundreds of thousands.

MORTEN KIIL. But no one can see them—isn't that it?

DR. STOCKMANN. Quite right; no one can see them.

MORTEN KIIL *(with a quiet, chuckling laugh)*. I'll be damned if that isn't the best thing I've heard of you yet.

DR. STOCKMANN. What do you mean?

MORTEN KIIL. But you'll never in this world make the Burgomaster take in anything of the sort.

DR. STOCKMANN. Well, that we shall see.

MORTEN KIIL. Do you really think he'll be so crazy?

DR. STOCKMANN. I hope the whole town will be so crazy.

MORTEN KIIL. The whole town! Well, I don't say but it may. But it serves them right; it'll teach them a lesson. They wanted to be so much cleverer than we old fellows. They hounded me out of the Town Council. Yes; I tell you they hounded me out like a dog, that they did. But now it's their turn. Just you keep up the game with them, Stockmann.

DR. STOCKMANN. Yes, but, father-in-law . . .

MORTEN KIIL. Keep it up, I say. *(Rising.)* If you can make the Burgomaster and his gang eat humble pie, I'll give a hundred crowns straight away to the poor.

DR. STOCKMANN. Come, that's good of you.

MORTEN KIIL. Of course I've little enough to throw away; but if you can manage that, I shall certainly remember the poor at Christmas-time, to the tune of fifty crowns.

(Hovstad enters from hall.)

HOVSTAD. Good morning! *(Pausing.)* Oh! I beg your pardon . . .

DR. STOCKMANN. Not at all. Come in, come in.

MORTEN KIIL (*chuckling again*). He! Is he in it too?

HOVSTAD. What do you mean?

DR. STOCKMANN. Yes, of course he is.

MORTEN KIIL. I might have known it! It's to go into the papers. Ah, you're the one, Stockmann! Do you two lay your heads together; I'm off.

DR. STOCKMANN. Oh no; don't go yet, father-in-law.

MORTEN KIIL. No, I'm off now. Play them all the monkey-tricks you can think of. Deuce take me but you shan't lose by it.

(*He goes, Mrs. Stockmann accompanying him.*)

DR. STOCKMANN (*laughing*). What do you think . . . ? The old fellow doesn't believe a word of all this about the water-works.

HOVSTAD. Was that what he . . . ?

DR. STOCKMANN. Yes; that was what we were talking about. And I daresay you have come on the same business?

HOVSTAD. Yes. Have you a moment to spare, Doctor?

DR. STOCKMANN. As many as you like, my dear fellow.

HOVSTAD. Have you heard anything from the Burgomaster?

DR. STOCKMANN. Not yet. He'll be here presently.

HOVSTAD. I have been thinking the matter over since last evening.

DR. STOCKMANN. Well?

HOVSTAD. To you, as a doctor and a man of science, this business of the water-works appears an isolated affair. I daresay it hasn't occurred to you that a good many other things are bound up with it?

DR. STOCKMANN. Indeed! In what way? Let us sit down, my dear fellow.—No; there, on the sofa.

(*Hovstad sits on sofa; the Doctor in an easy-chair on the other side of the table.*)

DR. STOCKMANN. Well, so you think . . . ?

HOVSTAD. You said yesterday that the water is polluted by impurities in the soil.

DR. STOCKMANN. Yes, undoubtedly; the mischief comes from that poisonous swamp up in the Mill Dale.

HOVSTAD. Excuse me, Doctor, but I think it comes from a very different swamp.

DR. STOCKMANN. What swamp may that be?

HOVSTAD. The swamp in which our whole municipal life is rotting.

DR. STOCKMANN. The devil, Mr. Hovstad! What notion is this you've got hold of?

HOVSTAD. All the affairs of the town have gradually drifted into the hands of a pack of bureaucrats . . .

DR. STOCKMANN. Come now, they're not all bureaucrats.

HOVSTAD. No; but those who are not are the friends and adherents of those who are. We are entirely under the thumb of a ring of wealthy men, men of old family and position in the town.

DR. STOCKMANN. Yes, but they are also men of ability and insight.

HOVSTAD. Did they show ability and insight when they laid the water-pipes where they are?

DR. STOCKMANN. No; that, of course, was a piece of stupidity. But that will be set right now.

HOVSTAD. Do you think it will go so smoothly?

DR. STOCKMANN. Well, smoothly or not, it will have to be done.

HOVSTAD. Yes, if the press exerts its influence.

DR. STOCKMANN. Not at all necessary, my dear fellow; I am sure my brother . . .

HOVSTAD. Excuse me, Doctor, but I must tell you that I think of taking the matter up.

DR. STOCKMANN. In the paper?

HOVSTAD. Yes. When I took over the *People's Messenger,* I was determined to break up the ring of obstinate old blockheads who held everything in their hands.

DR. STOCKMANN. But you told me yourself what came of it. You nearly ruined the paper.

HOVSTAD. Yes, at that time we had to draw in our horns, that's true enough. The whole Bath scheme might have fallen through if these men had been sent about their business. But now the Baths are an accomplished fact, and we can get on without these august personages.

DR. STOCKMANN. Get on without them, yes; but still we owe them a great deal.

HOVSTAD. The debt shall be duly acknowledged. But a journalist of my democratic tendencies cannot let such an opportunity slip through his fingers. We must explode the tradition of official infallibility. That rubbish must be got rid of, like every other superstition.

DR. STOCKMANN. There I am with you with all my heart, Mr. Hovstad. If it's a superstition, away with it!

HOVSTAD. I should be sorry to attack the Burgomaster, as he is your brother. But I know you think with me—the truth before all other considerations.

DR. STOCKMANN. Why, of course. *(Vehemently.)* But still ... ! but still ... !

HOVSTAD. You mustn't think ill of me. I am neither more self-interested nor more ambitious than other men.

DR. STOCKMANN. Why, my dear fellow—who says you are?

HOVSTAD. I come of humble folk, as you know; and I have had ample opportunities of seeing what the lower classes really require. And that is to have a share in the direction of public affairs, Doctor. That is what develops ability and knowledge and self-respect ...

DR. STOCKMANN. I understand that perfectly.

HOVSTAD. Yes; and I think a journalist incurs a heavy responsibility if he lets slip a chance of helping to emancipate the downtrodden masses. I know well enough that our oligarchy will denounce me as an agitator, and so forth; but what do I care? If only my conscience is clear, I ...

DR. STOCKMANN. Just so, just so, my dear Mr. Hovstad. But still— deuce take it ... ! *(A knock at the door.)* Come in!

(Aslaksen, the printer, appears at the door leading to the hall. He is humbly but respectably dressed in black, wears a white necktie, slightly crumpled, and has a silk hat and gloves in his hand.)

ASLAKSEN *(bowing)*. I beg pardon, Doctor, for making so bold ...

DR. STOCKMANN *(rising)*. Hallo! If it isn't Mr. Aslaksen!

ASLAKSEN. Yes, it's me, Doctor.

HOVSTAD *(rising)*. Is it me you want, Aslaksen?

ASLAKSEN. No, not at all. I didn't know you were here. No, it's the Doctor himself . . .

DR. STOCKMANN. Well, what can I do for you?

ASLAKSEN. Is it true, what Mr. Billing tells me, that you're going to get us a better set of water-works?

DR. STOCKMANN. Yes, for the Baths.

ASLAKSEN. Of course, of course. Then I just looked in to say that I'll back up the movement with all my might.

HOVSTAD *(to the Doctor)*. You see!

DR. STOCKMANN. I'm sure I thank you heartily; but . . .

ASLAKSEN. You may find it no such bad thing to have us lower-middle-class men at your back. We form what you may call a compact majority in the town—when we really make up our minds, that's to say. And it's always well to have the majority with you, Doctor.

DR. STOCKMANN. No doubt, no doubt; but I can't conceive that any special measures will be necessary in this case. I should think in so clear and straightforward a matter . . .

ASLAKSEN. Yes, but all the same, it can do no harm. I know the local authorities very well—the powers that be are not over ready to adopt suggestions from outsiders. So I think it wouldn't be amiss if we made some sort of a demonstration.

HOVSTAD. Precisely my opinion.

DR. STOCKMANN. A demonstration, you say? But in what way would you demonstrate?

ASLAKSEN. Of course with great moderation, Doctor. I always insist upon moderation; for moderation is a citizen's first virtue—at least that's my way of thinking.

DR. STOCKMANN. We all know that, Mr. Aslaksen.

ASLAKSEN. Yes, I think my moderation is generally recognised. And this affair of the water-works is very important for us lower-middle-class men. The Baths bid fair to become, as you might say, a little gold-mine for the town. We shall all have to live by the Baths, especially we house-owners. So we want to support the Baths all we can; and as I am Chairman of the House-owners' Association . . .

DR. STOCKMANN. Well . . . ?

ASLAKSEN. And as I'm an active worker for the Temperance Society— of course you know, Doctor, that I'm a temperance man?

DR. STOCKMANN. To be sure, to be sure.

ASLAKSEN. Well, you'll understand that I come in contact with a great many people. And as I'm known to be a prudent and law-abiding citizen, as you yourself remarked, Doctor, I have a certain influence in the town, and hold some power in my hands—though I say it that shouldn't.

DR. STOCKMANN. I know that very well, Mr. Aslaksen.

ASLAKSEN. Well then, you see—it would be easy for me to get up an address, if it came to a pinch.

DR. STOCKMANN. An address?

ASLAKSEN. Yes, a kind of vote of thanks to you, from the citizens of the town, for your action in a matter of such general concern. Of course it will have to be drawn up with all fitting moderation, so as to give no offence to the authorities and parties in power. But so long as we're careful about that, no one can take it ill, I should think.

HOVSTAD. Well, even if they didn't particularly like it . . .

ASLAKSEN. No, no, no; no offence to the powers that be, Mr. Hovstad. No opposition to people that can take it out of us again so easily. I've had enough of that in my time; no good ever comes of it. But no one can object to the free but temperate expression of a citizen's opinion.

DR. STOCKMANN (*shaking his hand*). I can't tell you, my dear Mr. Aslaksen, how heartily it delights me to find so much support among my fellow townsmen. I'm so happy—so happy! Come, you'll have a glass of sherry? Eh?

ASLAKSEN. No, thank you; I never touch spirituous liquors.

DR. STOCKMANN. Well, then, a glass of beer—what do you say to that?

ASLAKSEN. Thanks, not that either, Doctor. I never take anything so early in the day. And now I'll be off round the town, and talk to some of the house-owners, and prepare public opinion.

DR. STOCKMANN. It's extremely kind of you, Mr. Aslaksen; but I really cannot get it into my head that all these preparations are necessary. The affair seems to me so simple and self-evident.

ASLAKSEN. The authorities always move slowly, Doctor—God forbid I should blame them for it . . .

HOVSTAD. We'll stir them up in the paper to-morrow, Aslaksen.

ASLAKSEN. No violence, Mr. Hovstad. Proceed with moderation, or you'll do nothing with them. Take my advice; I've picked up experience in the school of life.—And now I'll say good morning, Doctor. You know now that at least you have us lower-middle-class men behind you, solid as a wall. You have the compact majority on your side, Doctor.

DR. STOCKMANN. Many thanks, my dear Mr. Aslaksen. *(Holds out his hand.)* Good-bye, good-bye.

ASLAKSEN. Are you coming to the office, Mr. Hovstad?

HOVSTAD. I shall come on presently. I have still one or two things to arrange.

ASLAKSEN. Very vell. *(Bows and goes. Dr. Stockmann accompanies him into the hall.)*

HOVSTAD *(as the Doctor re-enters).* Well, what do you say to that, Doctor? Don't you think it is high time we should give all this weak-kneed, half-hearted cowardice a good shaking up?

DR. STOCKMANN. Are you speaking of Aslaksen?

HOVSTAD. Yes, I am. He's a decent enough fellow, but he's one of those who are sunk in the swamp. And most people here are just like him; they are for ever wavering and wobbling from side to side; what with scruples and misgivings, they never dare advance a step.

DR. STOCKMANN. Yes, but Aslaksen seems to me thoroughly well-intentioned.

HOVSTAD. There is one thing I value more than good intentions, and that is an attitude of manly self-reliance.

DR. STOCKMANN. There I am quite with you.

HOVSTAD. So I am going to seize this opportunity, and try whether I can't for once put a little grit into their good intentions. The worship of authority must be rooted up in this town. This gross, inexcusable blunder of the water-works must be brought home clearly to every voter.

DR. STOCKMANN. Very well. If you think it's for the good of the community, so be it; but not till I have spoken to my brother.

HOVSTAD. At all events, I shall be writing my leader in the meantime. And if the Burgomaster won't take the matter up . . .

DR. STOCKMANN. But how can you conceive his refusing?

HOVSTAD. Oh, it's not inconceivable. And then . . .

DR. STOCKMANN. Well then, I promise you . . . ; look here—in that case you may print my paper—put it in just as it is.

HOVSTAD. May I? Is that a promise?

DR. STOCKMANN (handing him the manuscript). There it is; take it with you. You may as well read it in any case; you can return it to me afterwards.

HOVSTAD. Very good; I shall do so. And now, good-bye, Doctor.

DR. STOCKMANN. Good-bye, good-bye. You'll see it will all go smoothly, Mr. Hovstad—as smoothly as possible.

HOVSTAD. H'm—we shall see. (Bows and goes out through the hall.)

DR. STOCKMANN (going to the dining-room door and looking in). Katrina! Hallo! are you back, Petra?

PETRA (entering). Yes, I've just got back from school.

MRS. STOCKMANN (entering). Hasn't he been here yet?

DR. STOCKMANN. Peter? No; but I have been having a long talk with Hovstad. He's quite enthusiastic about my discovery. It turns out to be of much wider import than I thought at first. So he has placed his paper at my disposal, if I should require it.

MRS. STOCKMANN. Do you think you will?

DR. STOCKMANN. Not I! But at the same time, one cannot but be proud to know that the enlightened, independent press is on one's side. And what do you think? I have had a visit from the Chairman of the House-owners' Association too.

MRS. STOCKMANN. Really? What did he want?

DR. STOCKMANN. To assure me of his support. They will all stand by me at a pinch. Katrina, do you know what I have behind me?

MRS. STOCKMANN. Behind you? No. What have you behind you?

DR. STOCKMANN. The compact majority!

MRS. STOCKMANN. Oh! Is that good for you, Thomas?

DR. STOCKMANN. Yes, indeed; I should think it was good. *(Rubbing his hands as he walks up and down.)* Great God! what a delight it is to feel oneself in such brotherly unison with one's fellow townsmen!

PETRA. And to do so much that's good and useful, father!

DR. STOCKMANN. And all for one's native town, too!

MRS. STOCKMANN. There's the bell.

DR. STOCKMANN. That must be he. *(Knock at the door.)* Come in!

(Enter Burgomaster Stockmann from the hall.)

BURGOMASTER. Good morning.

DR. STOCKMANN. I'm glad to see you, Peter.

MRS. STOCKMANN. Good morning, brother-in-law. How are you?

BURGOMASTER. Oh, thanks, so-so. *(To the Doctor.)* Yesterday evening, after office hours, I received from you a dissertation upon the state of the water at the Baths.

DR. STOCKMANN. Yes. Have you read it?

BURGOMASTER. I have.

DR. STOCKMANN. And what do you think of the affair?

BURGOMASTER. H'm ... *(With a sidelong glance.)*

MRS. STOCKMANN. Come, Petra.

(She and Petra go into the room on the left.)

BURGOMASTER *(after a pause)*. Was it necessary to make all these investigations behind my back?

DR. STOCKMANN. Yes, till I was absolutely certain, I ...

BURGOMASTER. And are you absolutely certain now?

DR. STOCKMANN. My paper must surely have convinced you of that.

BURGOMASTER. Is it your intention to submit this statement to the Board of Directors, as a sort of official document?

DR. STOCKMANN. Of course. Something must be done in the matter, and that promptly.

BURGOMASTER. As usual, you use very strong expressions in your statement. Amongst other things, you say that what we offer our visitors
is a slow poison.

DR. STOCKMANN. Why, Peter, what else can it be called? Only think—
poisoned water both internally and externally! And that to poor
invalids who come to us in all confidence, and pay us handsomely
to cure them!

BURGOMASTER. And then you announce as your conclusion that we must
build a sewer to carry off the alleged impurities from the Mill Dale,
and must re-lay all the water-pipes.

DR. STOCKMANN. Yes. Can you suggest any other plan?—I know of
none.

BURGOMASTER. I found a pretext for looking in at the town engineer's
this morning, and—in a half-jesting way—I mentioned these alterations as things we might possibly have to consider, at some future
time.

DR. STOCKMANN. At some future time!

BURGOMASTER. Of course he smiled at what he thought my extrav-
agance. Have you taken the trouble to think what your proposed
alterations would cost? From what the engineer said, I gathered that
the expenses would probably mount up to several hundred thousand
crowns.

DR. STOCKMANN. So much as that?

BURGOMASTER. Yes. But that is not the worst. The work would take at
least two years.

DR. STOCKMANN. Two years! Do you mean to say two whole years?

BURGOMASTER. At least. And what are we to do with the Baths in the
meanwhile? Are we to close them? We should have no alternative.
Do you think any one would come here, if it got abroad that the
water was pestilential?

DR. STOCKMANN. But, Peter, that's precisely what it is.

BURGOMASTER. And all this now, just now, when the Baths are doing
so well! Neighbouring towns, too, are not without their claims to
rank as health-resorts. Do you think they would not at once set to

work to divert the full stream of visitors to themselves? Undoubtedly they would; and we should be left stranded. We should probably have to give up the whole costly undertaking; and so you would have ruined your native town.

DR. STOCKMANN. I—ruined . . . !

BURGOMASTER. It is only through the Baths that the town has any future worth speaking of. You surely know that as well as I do.

DR. STOCKMANN. Then what do you think should be done?

BURGOMASTER. I have not succeeded in convincing myself that the condition of the water at the Baths is as serious as your statement represents.

DR. STOCKMANN. I tell you it's if anything worse—or will be in the summer, when the hot weather sets in.

BURGOMASTER. I repeat that I believe you exaggerate greatly. A competent physician should know what measures to take—he should be able to obviate deleterious influences, and to counteract them in case they should make themselves unmistakably felt.

DR. STOCKMANN. Indeed . . . ? And then . . . ?

BURGOMASTER. The existing water-works are, once for all, a fact, and must naturally be treated as such. But when the time comes, the Directors will probably not be indisposed to consider whether it may not be possible, without unreasonable pecuniary sacrifices, to introduce certain improvements.

DR. STOCKMANN. And do you imagine I could ever be a party to such dishonesty?

BURGOMASTER. Dishonesty?

DR. STOCKMANN. Yes, it would be dishonesty—a fraud, a lie, an absolute crime against the public, against society as a whole!

BURGOMASTER. I have not, as I before remarked, been able to convince myself that there is really any such imminent danger.

DR. STOCKMANN. You have! You must have! I know that my demonstration is absolutely clear and convincing. And you understand it perfectly, Peter, only you won't admit it. It was you who insisted that both the Bath-buildings and the water-works should be placed where they now are; and it's *that*—it's that damned blunder that you won't confess. Pshaw! Do you think I don't see through you?

BURGOMASTER. And even if it were so? If I do watch over my reputation with a certain anxiety, I do it for the good of the town. Without moral authority I cannot guide and direct affairs in the way I consider most conducive to the general welfare. Therefore—and on various other grounds—it is of great moment to me that your statement should not be submitted to the Board of Directors. It must be kept back, for the good of the community. Later on I will bring up the matter for discussion, and we will do the best we can, quietly; but not a word, not a whisper, of this unfortunate business must come to the public ears.

DR. STOCKMANN. But it can't be prevented now, my dear Peter.

BURGOMASTER. It must and shall be prevented.

DR. STOCKMANN. It can't be, I tell you; far too many people know about it already.

BURGOMASTER. Know about it! Who? Surely not those fellows on the *People's Messenger* . . . ?

DR. STOCKMANN. Oh yes; they know. The liberal, independent press will take good care that you do your duty.

BURGOMASTER (*after a short pause*). You are an amazingly reckless man, Thomas. Have not you reflected what the consequences of this may be to yourself?

DR. STOCKMANN. Consequences?—Consequences to me?

BURGOMASTER. Yes—to you and yours.

DR. STOCKMANN. What the devil do you mean?

BURGOMASTER. I believe I have always shown myself ready and willing to lend you a helping hand.

DR. STOCKMANN. Yes, you have, and I thank you for it.

BURGOMASTER. I ask for no thanks. Indeed, I was in some measure forced to act as I did—for my own sake. I always hoped I should be able to keep you a little in check, if I helped to improve your pecuniary position.

DR. STOCKMANN. What! So it was only for your own sake . . . !

BURGOMASTER. In a measure, I say. It is painful for a man in an official position, when his nearest relative goes and compromises himself time after time.

DR. STOCKMANN. And you think I do that?

BURGOMASTER. Yes, unfortunately, you do, without knowing it. Yours is a turbulent, unruly, rebellious spirit. And then you have an unhappy propensity for rushing into print upon every possible and impossible occasion. You no sooner hit upon an idea than you must needs write a newspaper article or a whole pamphet about it.

DR. STOCKMANN. Isn't it a citizen's duty, when he has conceived a new idea, to communicate it to the public!

BURGOMASTER. Oh, the public has no need for new ideas. The public gets on best with the good old recognised ideas it has already.

DR. STOCKMANN. You say that right out!

BURGOMASTER. Yes, I must speak frankly to you for once. Hitherto I have tried to avoid it, for I know how irritable you are; but now I must tell you the truth, Thomas. You have no conception how much you injure yourself by your officiousness. You complain of the authorities, ay, of the Government itself—you cry them down and maintain that you have been slighted, persecuted. But what else can you expect, with your impossible disposition?

DR. STOCKMANN. Oh, indeed! So I am impossible, am I?

BURGOMASTER. Yes, Thomas, you are an impossible man to work with. I know that from experience. You have no consideration for any one or any thing; you seem quite to forget that you have me to thank for your position as medical officer of the Baths . . .

DR. STOCKMANN. It was mine by right! Mine, and no one else's! I was the first to discover the town's capabilities as a watering-place; I saw them, and, at that time, I alone. For years I fought single-handed for this idea of mine; I wrote and wrote . . .

BURGOMASTER. No doubt; but then the right time had not come. Of course, in that out-of-the-world corner, you could not judge of that. As soon as the propitious moment arrived, I—and others—took the matter in hand . . .

DR. STOCKMANN. Yes, and you went and bungled the whole of my glorious plan. Oh, we see now what a set of wiseacres you were!

BURGOMASTER. All *I* can see is that you are again seeking an outlet for your pugnacity. You want to make an onslaught on your superiors—that is an old habit of yours. You cannot endure any authority over you; you look askance at any one who holds a higher post than your own; you regard him as a personal enemy—and then you care nothing what kind of weapon you use against him. But now I have shown you how much is at stake for the town, and consequently for me too. And therefore I warn you, Thomas, that I am inexorable in the demand I am about to make of you!

DR. STOCKMANN. What demand?

BURGOMASTER. As you have not had the sense to refrain from chattering to outsiders about this delicate business, which should have been kept an official secret, of course it cannot now be hushed up. All sorts of rumours will get abroad, and evil-disposed persons will invent all sorts of additions to them. It will therefore be necessary for you publicly to contradict these rumours.

DR. STOCKMANN. I! How? I don't understand you?

BURGOMASTER. We expect that, after further investigation, you will come to the conclusion that the affair is not nearly so serious or pressing as you had at first imagined.

DR. STOCKMANN. Aha! So you expect that?

BURGOMASTER. Furthermore, we expect you to express your confidence that the Board of Directors will thoroughly and conscientiously carry out all measures for the remedying of any possible defects.

DR. STOCKMANN. Yes, but that you'll never be able to do, so long as you go on tinkering and patching. I tell you that, Peter; and it's my deepest, sincerest conviction . . .

BURGOMASTER. As an official, you have no right to hold any individual conviction.

DR. STOCKMANN *(starting)*. No right to . . . ?

BURGOMASTER. As an official, I say. In your private capacity, of course, it is another matter. But as a subordinate official of the Baths, you have no right to express any conviction at issue with that of your superiors.

DR. STOCKMANN. This is too much! I, a doctor, a man of science, have no right to . . . !

BURGOMASTER. The matter in question is not a purely scientific one; it is a complex affair; it has both a technical and an economic side.

DR. STOCKMANN. What the devil do I care what it is! I will be free to speak my mind upon any subject under the sun!

BURGOMASTER. As you please—so long as it does not concern the Baths. With them we forbid you to meddle.

DR. STOCKMANN (*shouts*). You forbid . . . ! You! A set of . . .

BURGOMASTER. *I* forbid it—*I*, your chief; and when I issue an order, you have simply to obey.

DR. STOCKMANN (*controlling himself*). Upon my word, Peter, if you weren't my brother . . .

PETRA (*tears open the door*). Father, you shan't submit to this!

MRS. STOCKMANN *(following her)*. Petra, Petra!

BURGOMASTER. Ah! So we have been listening!

MRS. STOCKMANN. The partition is so thin, we couldn't help . . .

PETRA. I stood and listened on purpose.

BURGOMASTER. Well, on the whole, I am not sorry . . .

DR. STOCKMANN *(coming nearer to him)*. You spoke to me of forbidding and obeying . . .

BURGOMASTER. You have forced me to adopt that tone.

DR. STOCKMANN. And am I to give myself the lie, in a public declaration?

BURGOMASTER. We consider it absolutely necessary that you should issue a statement in the terms indicated.

DR. STOCKMANN. And if I do not obey?

BURGOMASTER. Then we shall ourselves put forth a statement to reassure the public.

DR. STOCKMANN. Well and good; then I shall write against you. I shall stick to my point and prove that *I* am right, and you wrong. And what will you do then?

BURGOMASTER. Then I shall be unable to prevent your dismissal.

DR. STOCKMANN. What . . . ?

PETRA. Father! Dismissal!

MRS. STOCKMANN. Dismissal!

BURGOMASTER. Your dismissal from the Baths. I shall be compelled to move that notice be given you at once, and that you have henceforth no connection whatever with the Baths.

DR. STOCKMANN. You would dare to do that!

BURGOMASTER. It is you who are playing the daring game.

PETRA. Uncle, this is a shameful way to treat a man like father!

MRS. STOCKMANN. Do be quiet, Petra!

BURGOMASTER *(looking at Petra)*. Aha! We have opinions of our own already, eh? To be sure, to be sure! *(To Mrs. Stockmann.)* Sister-in-law, you are presumably the most rational member of this household. Use all your influence with your husband; try to make him realise what all this will involve both for his family . . .

DR. STOCKMANN. My family concerns myself alone!

BURGOMASTER. . . . both for his family, I say, and for the town he lives in.

DR. STOCKMANN. It is I that have the real good of the town at heart! I want to lay bare the evils that, sooner or later, must come to light. Ah! You shall see whether I love my native town.

BURGOMASTER. You, who, in your blind obstinacy, want to cut off the town's chief source of prosperity!

DR. STOCKMANN. That source is poisoned, man! Are you mad? We live by trafficking in filth and corruption! The whole of our flourishing social life is rooted in a lie!

BURGOMASTER. Idle fancies—or worse. The man who scatters broadcast such offensive insinuations against his native place must be an enemy of society.

DR. STOCKMANN *(going towards him)*. You dare to . . . !

MRS. STOCKMANN *(throwing herself between them)*. Thomas!

PETRA *(seizing her father's arm)*. Keep calm, father!

BURGOMASTER. I will not expose myself to violence. You have had your warning now. Reflect upon what is due to yourself and to your family. Good-bye. *(He goes.)*

DR. STOCKMANN *(walking up and down)*. And I must put up with such treatment! In my own house, Katrina! What do you say to that!

MRS. STOCKMANN. Indeed, it's a shame and a disgrace, Thomas . . .

PETRA. Oh, if I could only get hold of uncle . . . !

DR. STOCKMANN. It's my own fault. I ought to have stood up against them long ago—to have shown my teeth—and used them too!—And to be called an enemy of society! Me! I won't bear it; by Heaven, I won't!

MRS. STOCKMANN. But my dear Thomas, after all, your brother has the power . . .

DR. STOCKMANN. Yes, but I have the right.

MRS. STOCKMANN. Ah yes, right, right! What good does it do to have the right, if you haven't any might?

PETRA. Oh, mother—how can you talk so?

DR. STOCKMANN. What! No good, in a free community, to have right on your side? What an absurd idea, Katrina! And besides—haven't I the free and independent press before me—and the compact majority at my back? That is might enough, I should think!

MRS. STOCKMANN. Why, good heavens, Thomas! you're surely not thinking of . . . ?

DR. STOCKMANN. What am I not thinking of?

MRS. STOCKMANN. . . . of setting yourself up against your brother, I mean.

DR. STOCKMANN. What the devil would you have me do, if not stick to what is right and true?

PETRA. Yes, that's what I should like to know?

MRS. STOCKMANN. But it will be of no earthly use. If they won't, they won't.

DR. STOCKMANN. Ho-ho, Katrina! just wait a while, and you shall see whether I can fight my battles to the end.

MRS. STOCKMANN. Yes, to the end of getting your dismissal; that is what will happen.

DR. STOCKMANN. Well then, I shall at any rate have done my duty towards the public, towards society—I who am called an enemy of society!

MRS. STOCKMANN. But towards your family, Thomas? Towards us at home? Do you think *that* is doing your duty towards those who are dependent on you?

PETRA. Oh, mother, don't always think first of us.

MRS. STOCKMANN. Yes, it's easy for you to talk; you can stand alone if need be.—But remember the boys, Thomas; and think a little of yourself too, and of me . . .

DR. STOCKMANN. You're surely out of your senses, Katrina! If I were to be such a pitiful coward as to knuckle under to this Peter and his confounded crew—should I ever have another happy hour in all my life?

MRS. STOCKMANN. I don't know about *that;* but God preserve us from the happiness we shall all of us have if you persist in defying them.

There you will be again, with nothing to live on, with no regular income. I should have thought we had had enough of that in the old days. Remember them, Thomas; think of what it all means.

DR. STOCKMANN *(struggling with himself and clenching his hands).* And this is what these jacks-in-office can bring upon a free and honest man! Isn't it revolting, Katrina?

MRS. STOCKMANN. Yes, no doubt they are treating you shamefully. But God knows there's plenty of injustice one must just submit to in this world.—Here are the boys, Thomas. Look at them! What is to become of them? Oh no, no! you can never have the heart . . .

(Eilif and Morten, with school-books, have meanwhile entered.)

DR. STOCKMANN. The boys . . . ! *(With a sudden access of firmness and decision.)* Never, though the whole earth should crumble, will I bow my neck beneath the yoke. *(Goes towards his room.)*

MRS. STOCKMANN *(following him).* Thomas—what are you going to do?

DR. STOCKMANN *(at the door).* I must have the right to look my boys in the face when they have grown into free men.

(Goes into his room.)

MRS. STOCKMANN *(bursts into tears).* Ah, God help us all!

PETRA. Father is true to the core. He will never give in!

(The boys ask wonderingly what it all means; Petra signs to them to be quiet.)

ACT THIRD

The Editor's Room of the "People's Messenger." In the background, to the left, an entrance-door; to the right another door, with glass panes, through which can be seen the composing-room. A door in the right-hand wall. In the middle of the room a large table covered with papers, newspapers, and books. In front, on the left, a window, and by it a desk with a high stool. A couple of arm-chairs beside the table; some other chairs along the walls. The room is dingy and cheerless, the furniture shabby, the arm-chairs dirty and torn. In the composing-room are seen a few compositors at work; further back, a hand-press in operation.

Hovstad is seated at the desk, writing. Presently Billing enters from the right, with the Doctor's manuscript in his hand.

BILLING. Well, I must say . . . !

HOVSTAD *(writing)*. Have you read it through?

BILLING *(laying the MS. on the desk)*. Yes, I should think I had.

HOVSTAD. Don't you think the Doctor comes out strong?

BILLING. Strong! Why, strike me dead if he isn't crushing! Every word falls like a—well, like a sledge-hammer.

HOVSTAD. Yes, but these fellows won't collapse at the first blow.

BILLING. True enough; but we'll keep on hammering away, blow after blow, till the whole officialdom comes crashing down. As I sat there reading that article, I seemed to hear the revolution thundering afar.

HOVSTAD *(turning round)*. Hush! Don't let Aslaksen hear that.

BILLING *(in a lower voice)*. Aslaksen's a white-livered, cowardly fellow, without a spark of manhood in him. But this time you'll surely carry your point? Eh? You'll print the Doctor's paper?

HOVSTAD. Yes, if only the Burgomaster doesn't give in . . .

BILLING. That would be deuced annoying.

HOVSTAD. Well, whatever happens, fortunately we can turn the situation to account. If the Burgomaster won't agree to the Doctor's proposal, he'll have all the lower middle-class down upon him—all the House-owners' Association, and the rest of them. And if he does agree to it, he'll fall out with the whole crew of big shareholders in the Baths, who have hitherto been his main support . . .

BILLING. Yes, of course; for no doubt they'll have to fork out a lot of money . . .

HOVSTAD. You may take your oath on that. And then, don't you see, when the ring is broken up, we'll din it into the public day by day that the Burgomaster is incompetent in every respect, and that all responsible positions in the town, the whole municipal government in short, must be entrusted to men of liberal ideas.

BILLING. Strike me dead if that isn't the square truth! I see it—I see it: we are on the eve of a revolution!

(A knock at the door.)

HOVSTAD. Hush! *(Calls.)* Come in!

(Dr. Stockmann enters from the back, left.)

HOVSTAD *(going towards him)*. Ah, here is the Doctor. Well?

DR. STOCKMANN. Print away, Mr. Hovstad!

HOVSTAD. So it has come to that?

BILLING. Hurrah!

DR. STOCKMANN. Print away, I tell you. To be sure it has come to that. Since they will have it so, they must. War is declared, Mr. Billing!

BILLING. War to the knife, say I! War to the death, Doctor!

DR. STOCKMANN. This article is only the beginning. I have four or five others sketched out in my head already. But where do you keep Aslaksen?

BILLING *(calling into the printing-room)*. Aslaksen! just come here a moment.

HOVSTAD. Four or five more articles, eh? On the same subject?

DR. STOCKMANN. Oh no—not at all, my dear fellow. No; they will deal with quite different matters. But they're all of a piece with the water-works and sewer question. One thing leads to another. It's just like beginning to pick at an old house, don't you know?

BILLING. Strike me dead, but that's true! You feel you can't leave off till you've pulled the whole lumber-heap to pieces.

ASLAKSEN. *(enters from the printing-room)*. Pulled to pieces! Surely the Doctor isn't thinking of pulling the Baths to pieces?

HOVSTAD. Not at all. Don't be alarmed.

DR. STOCKMANN. No, we were talking of something quite different. Well, what do you think of my article, Mr. Hovstad?

HOVSTAD. I think it's simply a masterpiece . . .

DR. STOCKMANN. Yes, isn't it? I'm glad you think so—very glad.

HOVSTAD. It's so clear and to the point. One doesn't in the least need to be a specialist to understand the gist of it. I am certain every intelligent man will be on your side.

ASLAKSEN. And all the prudent ones too, I hope?

BILLING. Both the prudent and imprudent—in fact, almost the whole town.

ASLAKSEN. Then I suppose we may venture to print it.

DR. STOCKMANN. I should think so!

HOVSTAD. It shall go in to-morrow.

DR. STOCKMANN. Yes, plague take it, not a day must be lost. Look here, Mr. Aslaksen, this is what I wanted to ask you: won't you take personal charge of the article?

ASLAKSEN. Certainly I will.

DR. STOCKMANN. Be as careful as if it were gold. No printers' errors; every word is important. I shall look in again presently; perhaps you'll be able to let me see a proof.—Ah! I can't tell you how I long to have the thing in print—to see it launched . . .

BILLING. Yes, like a thunderbolt!

DR. STOCKMANN. . . . and submitted to the judgment of every intelligent citizen. Oh, you have no idea what I have had to put up with to-day. I've been threatened with all sorts of things. I was to be robbed of my clearest rights as a human being . . .

BILLING. What! Your rights as a human being!

DR. STOCKMANN. . . . I was to humble myself, and eat the dust; I was to set my personal interests above my deepest, holiest convictions . . .

BILLING. Strike me dead, but that's too outrageous.

HOVSTAD. Oh, what can you expect from that quarter?

DR. STOCKMANN. But they shall find they were mistaken in me; they shall learn that in black and white, I promise them! I shall throw myself into the breach every day in the *Messenger,* bombard them with one explosive article after another . . .

ASLAKSEN. Yes, but look here . . .

BILLING. Hurrah! It's war! War!

DR. STOCKMANN. I shall smite them to the earth, I shall crush them, I shall level their entrenchments to the ground in the eyes of all right-thinking men! That's what I shall do!

ASLAKSEN. But above all things be temperate, Doctor; bombard with moderation . . .

BILLING. Not at all, not at all! Don't spare the dynamite!

DR. STOCKMANN *(going on imperturbably).* For now it's no mere question of water-works and sewers, you see. No, the whole community must be purged, disinfected . . .

BILLING. *There* sounds the word of salvation!

DR. STOCKMANN. All the old bunglers must be sent packing, you understand. And that in every possible department! Such endless vistas have opened out before me to-day. I am not quite clear about everything yet, but I shall see my way presently. It's young and vigorous standard-bearers we must look for, my friends; we must have new captains at all the outposts.

BILLING. Hear, hear!

DR. STOCKMANN. And if only we hold together, it will go so smoothly, so smoothly! The whole revolution will glide off the stocks just like a ship. Don't you think so?

HOVSTAD. For my part, I believe we have now every prospect of placing our municipal affairs in the right hands.

ASLAKSEN. And if only we proceed with moderation, I really don't think there can be any danger.

DR. STOCKMANN. Who the devil cares whether there's danger or not! What I do, I do in the name of truth and for conscience' sake.

HOVSTAD. You are a man to be backed up, Doctor.

ASLAKSEN. Yes, there's no doubt the Doctor is a true friend to the town; he's what I call a friend of society.

BILLING. Strike me dead if Dr. Stockmann isn't a Friend of the People, Aslaksen!

ASLAKSEN. I have no doubt the House-owners' Association will soon adopt that expression.

DR. STOCKMANN (*shaking their hands, deeply moved*). Thanks, thanks, my dear, faithful friends; it does me good to hear you. My respected brother called me something very different. Never mind! Trust me to pay him back with interest! But I must be off now to see a poor devil of a patient. I shall look in again, though. Be sure you look after the article, Mr. Aslaksen; and, whatever you do, don't leave out any of my notes of exclamation! Rather put in a few more! Well, good-bye for the present, good-bye, good-bye.

(*Mutual salutations while they accompany him to the door. He goes out.*)

HOVSTAD. He will be invaluable to us.

ASLAKSEN. Yes, so long as he confines himself to this matter of the Baths. But if he goes further, it will scarcely be advisable to follow him.

HOVSTAD. H'm—that entirely depends on . . .

BILLING. You're always so confoundedly timid, Aslaksen.

ASLAKSEN. Timid? Yes, when it's a question of attacking local authori-

ties, I *am* timid, Mr. Billing; I have learnt caution in the school
of experience, let me tell you. But start me on the higher politics, confront me with the Government itself, and then see if I'm
timid.

BILLING. No, you're not; but that's just where your inconsistency comes
in.

ASLAKSEN. The fact is, I am keenly alive to my responsibilities. If you
attack the Government, you at least do society no harm; for the men
attacked don't care a straw, you see—they stay where they are all the
same. But *local* authorities can be turned out; and then we might get
some incompetent set into power, to the irreparable injury both of
house-owners and other people.

HOVSTAD. But the education of citizens by self-government—do you
never think of *that?*

ASLAKSEN. When a man has solid interests to protect, he can't think of
everything, Mr. Hovstad.

HOVSTAD. Then I hope I may never have solid interests to protect.

BILLING. Hear, hear!

ASLAKSEN *(smiling)*. H'm! *(Points to the desk.)* Governor Stensgård
sat in that editorial chair before you.

BILLING *(spitting)*. Pooh! A turncoat like that!

HOVSTAD. I am no weathercock—and never will be.

ASLAKSEN. A politician should never be too sure of anything on earth,
Mr. Hovstad. And as for you, Mr. Billing, you ought to take in a
reef or two, I should say, now that you are applying for the secretaryship to the Town Council.

BILLING. I . . . !

HOVSTAD. Is it so, Billing?

BILLING. Well, yes—but, deuce take it, you understand, I'm only doing
it to spite their high-mightinesses.

ASLAKSEN. Well, that has nothing to do with me. But if I am to be
accused of cowardice and inconsistency, I should just like to point
out *this:* My political record is open to every one. I have not changed
at all, except in becoming more moderate. My heart still belongs to

the people; but I don't deny that my reason inclines somewhat towards the authorities—the local ones, I mean.

(Goes into the printing-room.)

BILLING. Don't you think we should try to get rid of him, Hovstad?

HOVSTAD. Do you know of any one else that will pay for our paper and printing?

BILLING. What a confounded nuisance it is to have no capital!

HOVSTAD *(sitting down by the desk)*. Yes, if we only had that . . .

BILLING. Suppose you applied to Dr. Stockmann?

HOVSTAD *(turning over his papers)*. What would be the good? He hasn't a rap.

BILLING. No; but he has a good man behind him—old Morten Kiil —"The Badger," as they call him.

HOVSTAD *(writing)*. Are you so sure he has money?

BILLING. Yes, strike me dead if he hasn't! And part of it must certainly go to Stockmann's family. He's bound to provide for—for the children at any rate.

HOVSTAD *(half turning)*. Are you counting on *that?*

BILLING. Counting? How should I be counting on it?

HOVSTAD. Best not! And that secretaryship you shouldn't count on either; for I can assure you you won't get it.

BILLING. Do you think I don't know *that?* A refusal is the very thing I want. Such a rebuff fires the spirit of opposition in you, gives you a fresh supply of gall, as it were; and that's just what you need in a god-forsaken hole like this, where anything really stimulating so seldom happens.

HOVSTAD *(writing)*. Yes, yes.

BILLING. Well—they shall soon hear from me!—Now I'll go and write the appeal to the House-owners' Association.

(Goes into the room on the right.)

HOVSTAD *(sits at his desk, biting his penholder, and says slowly):* H'm —so that's the way of it.—*(A knock at the door.)* Come in.

(Petra enters from the back, left.)

HOVSTAD *(rising)*. What! Is it you? Here?

PETRA. Yes; please excuse me . . .

HOVSTAD *(offering her an arm-chair)*. Won't you sit down?

PETRA. No, thanks; I must go again directly.

HOVSTAD. Perhaps you bring a message from your father . . . ?

PETRA. No, I have come on my own account. *(Takes a book from the pocket of her cloak.)* Here is that English story.

HOVSTAD. Why have you brought it back?

PETRA. Because I won't translate it.

HOVSTAD. But you promised . . .

PETRA. Yes; but then I hadn't read it. I suppose you have not read it either?

HOVSTAD. No; you know I can't read English; but . . .

PETRA. Exactly; and that's why I wanted to tell you that you must find something else. *(Putting the book on the table.)* This will never do for the *Messenger*.

HOVSTAD. Why not?

PETRA. Because it flies in the face of all your convictions.

HOVSTAD. Well, for that matter . . .

PETRA. You don't understand me. It makes out that a supernatural power looks after the so-called good people in this world, and turns everything to their advantage at last; while all the so-called bad people are punished.

HOVSTAD. Yes, but that's all right. That's the very thing the public like.

PETRA. And would *you* supply the public with such stuff? You don't believe a word of it yourself. You know well enough that things do not really happen like that.

HOVSTAD. Of course not; but an editor can't always do as he likes. He has often to humour people's fancies in minor matters. After all, politics is the chief thing in life—at any rate for a newspaper; and if I want the people to follow me along the path of emancipation and progress, I mustn't scare them away. If they find a moral story like this down in the cellar,[1] they are all the more ready to take in what we tell them above—they feel themselves safer.

---

[1] The reference is to the continental *feuilleton* at the foot of the page.

PETRA. For shame! You're not such a hypocrite as to set traps like that for your readers. You're not a spider.

HOVSTAD *(smiling)*. Thanks for your good opinion. It's true that the idea is Billing's, not mine.

PETRA. Mr. Billing's!

HOVSTAD. Yes, at least he was talking in that strain the other day. It was Billing that was so anxious to get the story into the paper; I don't even know the book.

PETRA. But how can Mr. Billing, with his advanced views . . .

HOVSTAD. Well, Billing is many-sided. He's applying for the secretaryship to the Town Council, I hear.

PETRA. I don't believe that, Mr. Hovstad. How could he descend to such a thing?

HOVSTAD. That you must ask *him*.

PETRA. I could never have thought it of Billing!

HOVSTAD *(looking more closely at her)*. No? Is it such a surprise to you?

PETRA. Yes. And yet—perhaps not. Oh, I don't know . . .

HOVSTAD. We journalists are not worth much, Miss Petra.

PETRA. Do you really say that?

HOVSTAD. I think so, now and then.

PETRA. Yes, in the little every-day squabbles—that I can understand. But now that you have taken up a great cause . . .

HOVSTAD. You mean this affair of your father's?

PETRA. Of course. I should think you must feel yourself worth more than the general run of people now.

HOVSTAD. Yes, to-day I do feel something of the sort.

PETRA. Yes, surely you must. Oh, it's a glorious career you have chosen! To be the pioneer of unrecognised truths and new and daring ways of thought!—even, if that were all, to stand forth fearlessly in support of an injured man . . .

HOVSTAD. Especially when the injured man is—I hardly know how to put it . . .

PETRA. You mean when he is so upright and true?

HOVSTAD (*in a low voice*). I mean—especially when he is your father.

PETRA (*suddenly taken aback*). That?

HOVSTAD. Yes, Petra—Miss Petra.

PETRA. So that is your chief thought, is it? Not the cause itself? Not the truth? Not father's great, warm heart?

HOVSTAD. Oh, that too, of course.

PETRA. No, thank you; you said too much that time, Mr. Hovstad. Now I shall never trust you again, in anything.

HOVSTAD. Can you be so hard on me because it's mainly for your sake . . . ?

PETRA. What I blame you for is that you have not acted straightforwardly towards father. You have talked to him as if you cared only for the truth and the good of the community. You have trifled with both father and me. You are not the man you pretended to be. And that I will never forgive you—never.

HOVSTAD. You shouldn't say that so bitterly, Miss Petra—least of all now.

PETRA. Why not now?

HOVSTAD. Because your father cannot do without my help.

PETRA (*measuring him from head to foot*). So you are capable of *that*, too? Oh, shame!

HOVSTAD. No, no. I spoke without thinking. You mustn't believe that of me.

PETRA. I know what to believe. Good-bye.

(*Aslaksen enters from printing-room, hurriedly and mysteriously.*)

ASLAKSEN. What do you think, Mr. Hovstad—(*Seeing Petra.*) Ow, that's awkward . . .

PETRA. Well, there is the book. You must give it to some one else. (*Going towards the main door.*)

HOVSTAD (*following her*). But, Miss Petra . . .

PETRA. Good-bye. (*She goes.*)

ASLAKSEN. I say, Mr. Hovstad!

HOVSTAD. Well, well; what is it?

ASLAKSEN. The Burgomaster's out there, in the printing-office.

HOVSTAD. The Burgomaster?

ASLAKSEN. Yes. He wants to speak to you; he came in by the back way—he didn't want to be seen, you understand.

HOVSTAD. What can be the meaning of this? Stop, I'll go myself . . . *(Goes towards the printing-room, opens the door, bows and invites the Burgomaster to enter.)*

HOVSTAD. Keep a look-out, Aslaksen, that no one . . .

ASLAKSEN. I understand. *(Goes into the printing-room.)*

BURGOMASTER. You didn't expect to see me here, Mr. Hovstad.

HOVSTAD. No, I cannot say that I did.

BURGOMASTER *(looking about him)*. You are comfortably installed here—very nice quarters.

HOVSTAD. Oh . . .

BURGOMASTER. And here have I come, without with your leave or by your leave, to take up your time . . .

HOVSTAD. You are very welcome, Burgomaster; I am at your service. Let me take your cap and stick. *(He does so, and puts them on a chair.)* And won't you be seated?

BURGOMASTER *(sitting down by the table)*. Thanks. *(Hovstad also sits by the table.)* I have been much—very much worried to-day, Mr. Hovstad.

HOVSTAD. Really? Well, I suppose with all your various duties, Burgomaster . . .

BURGOMASTER. It is the Doctor that has been causing me annoyance to-day.

HOVSTAD. Indeed! The Doctor?

BURGOMASTER. He has written a sort of memorandum to the Directors about some alleged shortcomings in the Baths.

HOVSTAD. Has he really?

BURGOMASTER. Yes; hasn't he told you? I thought he said . . .

HOVSTAD. Oh yes, by-the-bye, he did mention something . . .

ASLAKSEN *(from the printing-office)*. I've just come for the manuscript . . .

HOVSTAD *(in a tone of vexation)*. Oh!—there it is on the desk.

ASLAKSEN *(finding it)*. All right.

BURGOMASTER. Why, *that* is the very thing . . .

ASLAKSEN. Yes, this is the Doctor's article, Burgomaster.

HOVSTAD. Oh, is *that* what you were speaking of?

BURGOMASTER. Precisely. What do you think of it?

HOVSTAD. I have no technical knowledge of the matter, and I've only glanced through it.

BURGOMASTER. And yet you are going to print it!

HOVSTAD. I can't very well refuse a signed communication . . .

ASLAKSEN. I have nothing to do with the editing of the paper, Burgomaster . . .

BURGOMASTER. Of course not.

ASLAKSEN. I merely print what is placed in my hands.

BURGOMASTER. Quite right, quite right.

ASLAKSEN. So I must . . . *(Goes towards the printing-room.)*

BURGOMASTER. No, stop a moment, Mr. Aslaksen. With your permission, Mr. Hovstad . . .

HOVSTAD. By all means, Burgomaster.

BURGOMASTER. You are a discreet and thoughtful man, Mr. Aslaksen.

ASLAKSEN. I am glad you think so, Burgomaster.

BURGOMASTER. And a man of very wide influence.

ASLAKSEN. Well—chiefly among the lower middle-class.

BURGOMASTER. The small taxpayers form the majority—here as everywhere.

ASLAKSEN. That's very true.

BURGOMASTER. And I have no doubt that you know the general feeling among them. Am I right?

ASLAKSEN. Yes, I think I may say that I do, Burgomaster.

BURGOMASTER. Well—since our townsfolk of the poorer class appear to be so heroically eager to make sacrifices . . .

ASLAKSEN. How so?

HOVSTAD. Sacrifices?

BURGOMASTER. It is a pleasing evidence of public spirit—a most pleasing evidence. I admit it is more than I should quite have expected. But, of course, you know public feeling better than I do.

ASLAKSEN. Yes but, Burgomaster . . .

BURGOMASTER. And assuredly it is no small sacrifice the town will have to make.

HOVSTAD. The town?

ASLAKSEN. But I don't understand . . . It's the Baths . . .

BURGOMASTER. At a rough provisional estimate, the alterations the Doctor thinks desirable will come to two or three hundred thousand crowns.

ASLAKSEN. That's a lot of money; but . . .

BURGOMASTER. Of course we shall be obliged to raise a municipal loan.

HOVSTAD (rising). You surely can't mean that the town . . . ?

ASLAKSEN. Would you come upon the rates? Upon the scanty savings of the lower middle-class?

BURGOMASTER. Why, my dear Mr. Aslaksen, where else are the funds to come from?

ASLAKSEN. The proprietors of the Baths must see to that.

BURGOMASTER. The proprietors are not in a position to go to any further expense.

ASLAKSEN. Are you quite sure of that, Burgomaster?

BURGOMASTER. I have positive information. So if these extensive alterations are called for, the town itself will have to bear the cost.

ASLAKSEN. Oh, plague take it all—I beg your pardon!—but this is quite another matter, Mr. Hovstad.

HOVSTAD. Yes, it certainly is.

BURGOMASTER. The worst of it is, that we shall be obliged to close the establishment for a couple of years.

HOVSTAD. To close it? Completely?

ASLAKSEN. For two years!

BURGOMASTER. Yes, the work will require that time—at least.

ASLAKSEN. But, damn it all! we can't stand that, Burgomaster. What are we house-owners to live on in the meantime?

BURGOMASTER. It's extremely difficult to say, Mr. Aslaksen. But what would you have us do? Do you think a single visitor will come here if we go about making them fancy that the water is poisoned, that the place is pestilential, that the whole town . . .

ASLAKSEN. And it's all nothing but fancy?

BURGOMASTER. With the best will in the world, I have failed to convince myself that it is anything else.

ASLAKSEN. In that case it's simply inexcusable of Dr. Stockmann—I beg your pardon, Burgomaster, but . . .

BURGOMASTER. I'm sorry to say you are only speaking the truth, Mr. Aslaksen. Unfortunately, my brother has always been noted for his rashness.

ASLAKSEN. And yet you want to back him up in this, Mr. Hovstad!

HOVSTAD. But who could possibly imagine that . . . ?

BURGOMASTER. I have drawn up a short statement of the facts, as they appear from a sober-minded standpoint; and I have intimated that any drawbacks that may possibly exist can no doubt be remedied by measures compatible with the finances of the Baths.

HOVSTAD. Have you the article with you, Burgomaster?

BURGOMASTER *(feeling in his pockets)*. Yes; I brought it with me, in case you . . .

ASLAKSEN *(quickly)*. Plague take it, there he is!

BURGOMASTER. Who? My brother?

HOVSTAD. Where? where?

ASLAKSEN. He's coming through the composing-room.

BURGOMASTER. Most unfortunate! I don't want to meet him here, and yet there are several things I want to talk to you about.

HOVSTAD *(pointing to the door on the right)*. Go in there for a moment.

BURGOMASTER. But . . . ?

HOVSTAD. You'll find nobody but Billing there.

ASLAKSEN. Quick, quick, Burgomaster; he's just coming.

BURGOMASTER. Very well, then. But try to get rid of him quickly.

(He goes out by the door on the right, which Aslaksen opens, and closes behind him.)

HOVSTAD. Pretend to be busy, Aslaksen.

(He sits down and writes. Aslaksen turns over a heap of newspapers on a chair, right.)

DR. STOCKMANN *(entering from the composing-room)*. Here I am, back again. *(Puts down his hat and stick.)*

HOVSTAD *(writing)*. Already, Doctor? Make haste with what we were speaking of, Aslaksen. We've no time to lose to-day.

DR. STOCKMANN *(to Aslaksen)*. No proof yet, I hear.

ASLAKSEN *(without turning round)*. No; how could you expect it?

DR. STOCKMANN. Of course not; but you understand my impatience. I can have no rest or peace until I see the thing in print.

HOVSTAD. H'm; it will take a good while yet. Don't you think so, Aslaksen?

ASLAKSEN. I'm afraid it will.

DR. STOCKMANN. All right, all right, my good friend; then I shall look in again. I'll look in twice if necessary. With so much at stake —the welfare of the whole town—one mustn't grudge a little trouble. *(Is on the point of going but stops and comes back.)* Oh, by the way—there's one other thing I must speak to you about.

HOVSTAD. Excuse me; wouldn't some other time . . . ?

DR. STOCKMANN. I can tell you in two words. You see it's this: when people read my article in the paper to-morrow, and find I have spent the whole winter working quietly for the good of the town . . .

HOVSTAD. Yes but, Doctor . . .

DR. STOCKMANN. I know what you're going to say. You don't think it was a bit more than my duty—my simple duty as a citizen. Of course I know that, as well as you do. But you see, my fellow towns-men—good Lord! the poor souls think so much of me . . .

ASLAKSEN. Yes, the townspeople have hitherto thought very highly of you, Doctor.

DR. STOCKMANN. That's exactly why I'm afraid that—. What I wanted to say was this: when all this comes to them—especially to the poorer classes—as a summons to take the affairs of the town into their own hands for the future . . .

HOVSTAD *(rising)*. H'm, Doctor, I won't conceal from you . . .

DR. STOCKMANN. Aha! I thought there was something brewing! But I won't hear of it. If they are getting up anything of that sort . . .

HOVSTAD. Of what sort?

DR. STOCKMANN. Well, anything of any sort—a procession with banners, or a banquet, or a subscription for a testimonial, or whatever it may be—you must give me your solemn promise to put a stop to it. And you too, Mr. Aslaksen; do you hear?

HOVSTAD. Excuse me, Doctor; we may as well tell you the whole truth first as last . . .

(Mrs. Stockmann enters from the back, left.)

MRS. STOCKMANN *(seeing the Doctor)*. Ah! just as I thought.

HOVSTAD *(going towards her)*. Mrs. Stockmann, too?

DR. STOCKMANN. What the devil do *you* want here, Katrina?

MRS. STOCKMANN. You know very well what I want.

HOVSTAD. Won't you sit down? Or perhaps . . .

MRS. STOCKMANN. Thanks, please don't trouble. And you must forgive my following my husband here; remember, I am the mother of three children.

DR. STOCKMANN. Stuff and nonsense! We all know that well enough.

MRS. STOCKMANN. Well, it doesn't look as if you thought very much about your wife and children to-day, or you wouldn't be so ready to plunge us all into ruin.

DR. STOCKMANN. Are you quite mad, Katrina! Has a man with a wife and children no right to proclaim the truth? Has he no right to be an active and useful citizen? Has he no right to do his duty by the town he lives in?

MRS. STOCKMANN. Everything in moderation, Thomas!

ASLAKSEN. That's just what I say. Moderation in everything.

MRS. STOCKMANN. You are doing us a great wrong, Mr. Hovstad, in enticing my husband away from house and home, and befooling him in this way.

HOVSTAD. I am not befooling any one . . .

DR. STOCKMANN. Befooling! Do you think I should let myself be befooled?

MRS. STOCKMANN. Yes, that's just what you do. I know very well that you are the cleverest man in the town; but you're very easily made a fool of, Thomas. *(To Hovstad.)* Remember that he loses his post at the Baths if you print what he has written . . .

ASLAKSEN. What!

HOVSTAD. Well now, really, Doctor . . .

DR. STOCKMANN *(laughing)*. Ha ha! just let them try—! No no, my dear, they'll think twice about that. I have the compact majority behind me, you see!

MRS. STOCKMANN. That's just the misfortune, that you should have such a horrid thing behind you.

DR. STOCKMANN. Nonsense, Katrina;—you go home and look after your house, and let me take care of society. How can you be in such a fright when you see me so confident and happy? *(Rubbing his hands and walking up and down.)* Truth and the People must win the day; you may be perfectly sure of that. Oh! I can see all our free-souled citizens standing shoulder to shoulder like a conquering army . . . ! *(Stopping by a chair.)* Why, what the devil is *that?*

ASLAKSEN *(looking at it)*. Oh Lord!

HOVSTAD *(the same)*. H'm—

DR. STOCKMANN. Why, here's the top-knot of authority!

(He takes the Burgomaster's official cap carefully between the tips of his fingers and holds it up.)

MRS. STOCKMANN. The Burgomaster's cap!

DR. STOCKMANN. And here's the staff of office, too! But how in the devil's name did they . . . ?

HOVSTAD. Well then . . .

DR. STOCKMANN. Ah, I understand! He has been here to talk you over. Ha, ha! He reckoned without his host that time! And when he caught sight of me in the printing-room—*(bursts out laughing)*—he took to his heels, eh, Mr. Aslaksen?

ASLAKSEN *(hurriedly)*. Exactly; he took to his heels, Doctor.

DR. STOCKMANN. Made off without his stick and . . . No, *that* won't do! Peter never left anything behind him. But where the devil have you stowed him? Ah—in here, of course. Now you shall see, Katrina!

MRS. STOCKMANN. Thomas—I implore you . . . !

ASLAKSEN. Take care, Doctor!

(Dr. Stockmann has put on the Burgomaster's cap and grasped his stick; he now goes up to the door, throws it open, and makes a

military salute. The Burgomaster enters, red with anger. Behind him comes Billing.)

BURGOMASTER. What is the meaning of these antics?

DR. STOCKMANN. Respect, my good Peter! Now, it's I that am in power in this town. *(He struts up and down.)*

MRS. STOCKMANN *(almost in tears)*. Oh, Thomas!

BURGOMASTER *(following him)*. Give me my cap and stick!

DR. STOCKMANN *(as before)*. You may be Chief of Police, but I am Burgomaster. I am master of the whole town, I tell you!

BURGOMASTER. Put down my cap, I say. Remember it is an official cap, as by law prescribed!

DR. STOCKMANN. Pshaw! Do you think the awakening lion of the democracy will let itself be scared by a gold-laced cap? There's to be a revolution in the town to-morrow, let me tell you. You threatened me with dismissal; but now *I* dismiss *you*—dismiss you from all your offices of trust—. You think I can't do it?—Oh, yes, I can! I have the irresistible forces of society on my side. Hovstad and Billing will thunder in the *People's Messenger,* and Aslaksen will take the field at the head of the House-owners' Association . . .

ASLAKSEN. No, Doctor, I shall not.

DR. STOCKMANN. Why, of course you will . . .

BURGOMASTER. Aha! Perhaps Mr. Hovstad would like to join the agitation after all?

HOVSTAD. No, Burgomaster.

ASLAKSEN. No, Mr. Hovstad isn't such a fool as to ruin both himself and the paper for the sake of a delusion.

DR. STOCKMANN *(looking about him).* What does all this mean?

HOVSTAD. You have presented your case in a false light, Doctor; therefore I am unable to give you my support.

BILLING. And after what the Burgomaster has been so kind as to explain to me, I . . .

DR. STOCKMANN. In a false light! Well, I am responsible for that. Just you print my article, and I promise you I shall prove it up to the hilt.

HOVSTAD. I shall not print it. I cannot, and will not, and dare not print it.

DR. STOCKMANN. You dare not? What nonsense is this? You are editor; and I suppose it's the editor that controls a paper.

ASLAKSEN. No, it's the subscribers, Doctor.

BURGOMASTER. Fortunately.

ASLAKSEN. It's public opinion, the enlightened majority, the house-owners and all the rest. It's *they* who control a paper.

DR. STOCKMANN *(calmly)*. And all these powers I have against me?

ASLAKSEN. Yes, you have. It would mean absolute ruin for the town if your article were inserted.

DR. STOCKMANN. So *that* is the way of it!

BURGOMASTER. My hat and stick!

(Dr. Stockmann takes off the cap and lays it on the table along with the stick.)

BURGOMASTER *(taking them both)*. Your term of office has come to an untimely end.

DR. STOCKMANN. The end is not yet. *(To Hovstad.)* So you are quite determined not to print my article in the *Messenger?*

HOVSTAD. Quite; for the sake of your family, if for no other reason.

MRS. STOCKMANN. Oh, be kind enough to leave his family out of the question, Mr. Hovstad.

BURGOMASTER *(takes a manuscript from his pocket)*. When this appears, the public will be in possession of all necessary information; it is an authentic statement. I place it in your hands.

HOVSTAD *(taking the MS.)*. Good. It shall appear in due course.

DR. STOCKMANN. And not mine! You imagine you can kill me and the truth by a conspiracy of silence! But it won't be so easy as you think. Mr. Aslaksen, will you be good enough to print my article at once, as a pamphlet? I'll pay for it myself, and be my own publisher. I'll have four hundred copies—no, five—six hundred.

ASLAKSEN. No. If you offered me its weight in gold, I dare not lend my press to such a purpose, Doctor. I daren't fly in the face of public opinion. You won't get it printed anywhere in the whole town.

DR. STOCKMANN. Then give it me back.

HOVSTAD *(handing him the MS.)*. By all means.

DR. STOCKMANN *(taking up his hat and cane)*. It shall be made public all the same. I shall read it at a great mass meeting; all my fellow citizens shall hear the voice of truth!

BURGOMASTER. Not a single society in the town would let you their hall for such a purpose.

ASLAKSEN. Not one, I'm quite certain.

BILLING. No, strike me dead if they would!

MRS. STOCKMANN. That would be too disgraceful! Why do they turn against you like this, every one of them?

DR. STOCKMANN (*irritated*). I'll tell you why. It's because in this town all the men are old women—like you. They all think of nothing but their families, not of the general good.

MRS. STOCKMANN (*taking his arm*). Then I'll show them that an— an old woman can be a man for once in a way. For *now* I'll stand by you, Thomas.

DR. STOCKMANN. Bravely said, Katrina! I swear by my soul and conscience the truth shall out! If they won't let me a hall, I'll hire a drum and march through the town with it; and I'll read my paper at every street corner.

BURGOMASTER. You can scarcely be such a raving lunatic as that?

DR. STOCKMANN. I am.

ASLAKSEN. You would not get a single man in the whole town to go with you.

BILLING. No, strike me dead if you would!

MRS. STOCKMANN. Don't give in, Thomas. I'll ask the boys to go with you.

DR. STOCKMANN. That's a splendid idea!

MRS. STOCKMANN. Morten will be delighted; and Eilif will go too, I daresay.

DR. STOCKMANN. Yes, and so will Petra! And you yourself, Katrina!

MRS. STOCKMANN. No no, not I. But I'll stand at the window and watch you—that I will.

DR. STOCKMANN (*throwing his arms about her and kissing her*). Thank you for that! Now, my good sirs, we're ready for the fight! Now we shall see whether your despicable tactics can stop the mouth of the patriot who wants to purge society!

(*He and his wife go out together by the door in the back, left.*)

BURGOMASTER (*shaking his head dubiously*). Now he has turned *her* head too!

ACT FOURTH

A large old-fashioned room in Captain Horster's house. An open folding-door in the background leads to an anteroom. In the wall on the left are three windows. About the middle of the opposite wall is a platform, and on it a small table, two candles, a water-bottle and glass, and a bell. For the rest, the room is lighted by sconces placed between the windows. In front, on the left, is a table with a candle on it, and by it a chair. In front, to the right, a door, and near it a few chairs. Large assemblage of all classes of townsfolk. In the crowd are a few women and schoolboys. More and more people gradually stream in from the back until the room is quite full.

FIRST CITIZEN *(to another standing near him)*. So you're here too, Lamstad?

SECOND CITIZEN. I never miss a public meeting.

A BYSTANDER. I suppose you've brought your whistle?

SECOND CITIZEN. Of course I have; haven't you?

THIRD CITIZEN. I should think so. And Skipper Evensen said he'd bring a thumping big horn.

SECOND CITIZEN. He's a good 'un, is Evensen!

(Laughter in the group.)

A FOURTH CITIZEN *(joining them)*. I say, what's it all about? What's going on here to-night?

SECOND CITIZEN. Why, it's Dr. Stockmann that's going to lecture against the Burgomaster.

FOURTH CITIZEN. But the Burgomaster's his brother.

FIRST CITIZEN. That makes no difference. Dr. Stockmann's not afraid of him.

THIRD CITIZEN. But he's all wrong; the *People's Messenger* says so.

SECOND CITIZEN. Yes, he must be wrong this time; for neither the House-owners' Association nor the Citizens' Club would let him have a hall.

FIRST CITIZEN. They wouldn't even lend him the hall at the Baths.

SECOND CITIZEN. No, you may be sure they wouldn't.

A MAN *(in another group)*. Now, who's the one to follow in this business, eh?

ANOTHER MAN *(in the same group)*. Just keep your eye on Aslaksen, and do as he does.

BILLING *(with a portfolio under his arm, makes his way through the crowd)*. Excuse me, gentlemen. Will you allow me to pass? I'm here to report for the *People's Messenger*. Many thanks. *(Sits by the table on the left.)*

A WORKING-MAN. Who's he?

ANOTHER WORKING-MAN. Don't you know him? It's that fellow Billing, that writes for Aslaksen's paper.

(Captain Horster enters by the door in front on the right, escorting Mrs. Stockmann and Petra. Eilif and Morten follow them.)

HORSTER. This is where I thought you might sit; you can so easily slip out if anything should happen.

MRS. STOCKMANN. Do you think there will be any disturbance?

HORSTER. One can never tell—with such a crowd. But there's no occasion for anxiety.

MRS. STOCKMANN *(sitting down)*. How kind it was of you to offer Stockmann this room.

HORSTER. Since no one else would, I . . .

PETRA *(who has also seated herself)*. And it was brave too, Captain Horster.

HORSTER. Oh, I don't see where the bravery comes in.

(Hovstad and Aslaksen enter at the same moment, but make their way through the crowd separately.)

ASLAKSEN *(going up to Horster)*. Hasn't the Doctor come yet?

HORSTER. He's waiting in there. *(A movement at the door in the background.)*

HOVSTAD *(to Billing)*. There's the Burgomaster! Look!

BILLING. Yes, strike me dead if he hasn't put in an appearance after all!

(Burgomaster Stockmann makes his way blandly through the meeting, bowing politely to both sides, and takes his stand by the wall on the left. Soon afterwards, Dr. Stockmann enters by the door on the right. He wears a black frock-coat and white necktie. Faint applause, met by a subdued hissing. Then silence.)

DR. STOCKMANN *(in a low tone)*. How do you feel, Katrina?

MRS. STOCKMANN. Quite comfortable, thank you. *(In a low voice.)* Now do keep your temper, Thomas.

DR. STOCKMANN. Oh, I shall keep myself well in hand. *(Looks at his watch, ascends the platform, and bows.)* It's a quarter past the hour, so I shall begin . . . *(Takes out his MS.)*

ASLAKSEN. But surely a chairman must be elected first.

DR. STOCKMANN. No, that's not at all necessary.

SEVERAL GENTLEMEN *(shouting)*. Yes, yes.

BURGOMASTER. I should certainly say that a chairman ought to be elected.

DR. STOCKMANN. But I've called this meeting to give a lecture, Peter!

BURGOMASTER. Dr. Stockmann's lecture may possibly lead to differences of opinion.

SEVERAL VOICES IN THE CROWD. A chairman! A chairman!

HOVSTAD. The general voice of the meeting seems to be for a chairman!

DR. STOCKMANN *(controlling himself)*. Very well then; let the meeting have its way.

ASLAKSEN. Will not the Burgomaster take the chair?

THREE GENTLEMEN *(clapping)*. Bravo! Bravo!

BURGOMASTER. For reasons you will easily understand, I must decline. But, fortunately, we have among us one whom I think we can all accept. I allude to the president of the House-owners' Association, Mr. Aslaksen.

MANY VOICES. Yes, yes! Bravo Aslaksen! Hurrah for Aslaksen!

(Dr. Stockmann takes his MS. and descends from the platform.)

ASLAKSEN. Since my fellow citizens repose this trust in me, I cannot refuse . . .

(Applause and cheers. Aslaksen ascends the platform.)

BILLING *(writing)*. So—"Mr. Aslaksen was elected by acclamation . . ."

ASLAKSEN. And now, as I have been called to the chair, I take the liberty of saying a few brief words. I am a quiet, peace-loving man; I am in favour of discreet moderation, and of—and of moderate discretion. Every one who knows me, knows that.

MANY VOICES. Yes, yes, Aslaksen!

ASLAKSEN. I have learnt in the school of life and of experience that moderation is the virtue in which the individual citizen finds his best advantage . . .

BURGOMASTER. Hear, hear!

ASLAKSEN. . . . and it is discretion and moderation, too, that best serve the community. I could therefore suggest to our respected fellow citizen, who has called this meeting, that he should endeavour to keep within the bounds of moderation.

A MAN *(by the door)*. Three cheers for the Temperance Society!

A VOICE. Go to the devil!

VOICES. Hush! hush!

ASLAKSEN. No interruptions, gentlemen!—Does any one wish to offer any observations?

BURGOMASTER. Mr. Chairman!

ASLAKSEN. Burgomaster Stockmann will address the meeting.

BURGOMASTER. On account of my close relationship—of which you are probably aware—to the present medical officer of the Baths, I should have preferred not to speak here this evening. But my position as chairman of the Baths, and my care for the vital interests of this town, force me to move a resolution. I may doubtless assume that not a single citizen here present thinks it desirable that untrustworthy and exaggerated statements should get abroad as to the sanitary condition of the Baths and of our town.

MANY VOICES. No, no, no! Certainly not! We protest!

BURGOMASTER. I therefore beg to move, "That this meeting declines to hear the proposed lecture or speech on the subject by the medical officer of the Baths."

DR. STOCKMANN *(flaring up)*. Declines to hear . . . ! What do you mean?

MRS. STOCKMANN *(coughing)*. H'm! h'm!

DR. STOCKMANN *(controlling himself)*. So I am not to be heard?

BURGOMASTER. In my statement in the *People's Messenger* I have made the public acquainted with the essential facts, so that all well-disposed citizens can easily form their own judgment. From that statement it will be seen that the medical officer's proposal—besides amounting to a vote of censure upon the leading men of the town —at bottom only means saddling the ratepayers with an unnecessary outlay of at least a hundred thousand crowns.

(Sounds of protest and some hissing.)

ASLAKSEN *(ringing the bell)*. Order, gentlemen! I must beg leave to support the Burgomaster's resolution. I quite agree with him that there is something beneath the surface of the Doctor's agitation. In all his talk about the Baths, it is really a revolution he is aiming at; he wants to effect a redistribution of power. No one doubts the excellence of Dr. Stockmann's intentions—of course there cannot be two opinions as to that. I, too, am in favour of self-government by the people, if only it doesn't cost the ratepayers too much. But in this case it would do so; and therefore I'll be hanged if—excuse me— in short, I cannot go with Dr. Stockmann upon this occasion. You can buy even gold too dear; that's my opinion.

(Loud applause on all sides.)

HOVSTAD. I, too, feel bound to explain my attitude. Dr. Stockmann's agitation seemed at first to find favour in several quarters, and I supported it as impartially as I could. But it presently appeared that we had been misled by a false representation of the facts . . .

DR. STOCKMANN. False . . . !

HOVSTAD. Well then, an untrustworthy representation. This the Burgomaster's report has proved. I trust no one here present doubts my liberal principles; the attitude of the *Messenger* on all great political questions is well known to you all. But I have learned from men of judgment and experience that in purely local matters a paper must observe a certain amount of caution.

ASLAKSEN. I entirely agree with the speaker.

HOVSTAD. And in the matter under discussion it is quite evident that Dr. Stockmann has public opinion against him. But, gentlemen, what is an editor's clearest and most imperative duty? Is it not to work in harmony with his readers? Has he not in some sort received a tacit mandate to further assiduously and unweariedly the interests of his constituents? Or am I mistaken in this?

MANY VOICES. No, no, no! Hovstad is right!

HOVSTAD. It has cost me a bitter struggle to break with a man in whose house I have of late been a frequent guest—with a man who, up to this day, has enjoyed the unqualified goodwill of his fellow citizens—with a man whose only, or, at any rate, whose chief fault is that he consults his heart rather than his head.

A FEW SCATTERED VOICES. That's true! Hurrah for Dr. Stockmann!

HOVSTAD. But my duty towards the community has constrained me to break with him. Then, too, there is another consideration that impels me to oppose him, and, if possible, to block the ill-omened path upon which he is entering: consideration for his family . . .

DR. STOCKMANN. Keep to the water-works and sewers!

HOVSTAD. . . . consideration for his wife and his helpless children.

MORTEN. Is that us, mother?

MRS. STOCKMANN. Hush!

ASLAKSEN. I will now put the Burgomaster's resolution to the vote.

DR. STOCKMANN. You need not. I have no intention of saying anything this evening of all the filth at the Baths. No! You shall hear something quite different.

BURGOMASTER *(half aloud)*. What next, I wonder?

A DRUNKEN MAN *(at the main entrance)*. I'm a ratepayer, so I've a right to my opinion! And it's my full, firm, incomprehensible opinion that . . .

SEVERAL VOICES. Silence up there!

OTHERS. He's drunk! Turn him out!

(The drunken man is turned out.)

DR. STOCKMANN. Can I speak?

ASLAKSEN *(ringing the bell)*. Dr. Stockmann will address the meeting.

DR. STOCKMANN. A few days ago, I should have liked to see any one venture upon such an attempt to gag me as has been made here to-night! I would have fought like a lion for my sacred rights! But now I care little enough; for now I have more important things to speak of.

(The people crowd closer round him. Morten Kiil comes in sight among the bystanders.)

DR. STOCKMANN *(continuing)*. I have been pondering a great many things during these last days—thinking such a multitude of thoughts, that at last my head was positively in a whirl . . .

BURGOMASTER *(coughing)*. H'm . . . !

DR. STOCKMANN. But presently things seemed to straighten themselves out, and I saw them clearly in all their bearings. That is why I stand here this evening. I am about to make great revelations, my fellow citizens! I am going to announce to you a far-reaching discovery, beside which the trifling fact that our water-works are poisoned, and that our health-resort is built on pestilential ground, sinks into insignificance.

MANY VOICES *(shouting)*. Don't speak about the Baths! We won't listen to that! No more of that!

DR. STOCKMANN. I have said I would speak of the great discovery I have made within the last few days—the discovery that all our sources of spiritual life are poisoned, and that our whole society rests upon a pestilential basis of falsehood.

SEVERAL VOICES *(in astonishment and half aloud)*. What's he saying?

BURGOMASTER. Such an insinuation . . . !

ASLAKSEN *(with his hand on the bell)*. I must call upon the speaker to moderate his expressions.

DR. STOCKMANN. I have loved my native town as dearly as any man can love the home of his childhood. I was young when I left our town, and distance, homesickness and memory threw, as it were, a glamour over the place and its people.

(Some applause and cries of approval.)

DR. STOCKMANN. Then for years I was imprisoned in a horrible hole, far away in the north. As I went about among the people scattered here and there over the stony wilderness, it seemed to me, many a time, that it would have been better for these poor famishing creatures to have had a cattle-doctor to attend them, instead of a man like me. *(Murmurs in the room.)*

BILLING *(laying down his pen)*. Strike me dead if I've ever heard . . . !

HOVSTAD. What an insult to an estimable peasantry!

DR. STOCKMANN. Wait a moment!—I don't think any one can reproach me with forgetting my native town up there. I sat brooding like an eider duck, and what I hatched was—the plan of the Baths.

(Applause and expressions of dissent.)

DR. STOCKMANN. And when, at last, fate ordered things so happily that I could come home again—then, fellow citizens, it seemed to me that I hadn't another desire in the world. Yes, one desire I had: an eager, constant, burning desire to be of service to my birthplace, and to its people.

BURGOMASTER *(gazing into vacancy)*. A strange method to select . . . !

DR. STOCKMANN. So I went about revelling in my happy illusions. But yesterday morning—no, it was really two nights ago—my mind's eyes were opened wide, and the first thing I saw was the colossal stupidity of the authorities . . .

(Noise, cries, and laughter. Mrs. Stockmann coughs repeatedly.)

BURGOMASTER. Mr. Chairman!

ASLAKSEN *(ringing his bell)*. In virtue of my position . . . !

DR. STOCKMANN. It's petty to catch me up on a word, Mr. Aslaksen!
I only mean that I became alive to the extraordinary muddle our
leading men had been guilty of, down at the Baths. I cannot for
the life of me abide leading men—I've seen enough of them in my
time. They are like goats in a young plantation: they do harm at

every point; they block the path of a free man wherever he turns
—and I should be glad if we could exterminate them like other
noxious animals . . .

(Uproar in the room.)

BURGOMASTER. Mr. Chairman, are such expressions permissible?

ASLAKSEN *(with his hand on the bell)*. Dr. Stockmann . . .

DR. STOCKMANN. I can't conceive how it is that I have only now seen
through these gentry; for haven't I had a magnificent example before
my eyes here every day—my brother Peter—slow of understanding,
tenacious in prejudice . . .

(Laughter, noise, and whistling. Mrs. Stockmann coughs. Aslaksen rings violently.)

THE DRUNKEN MAN *(who has come in again)*. Is it me you're alluding to? Sure enough, my name's Petersen; but devil take me if . . .

ANGRY VOICES. Out with the drunken man! Turn him out!

(The man is again turned out.)

BURGOMASTER. Who is that person?

A BYSTANDER. I don't know him, Burgomaster.

ANOTHER. He doesn't belong to the town.

A THIRD. I believe he's a timber-dealer from . . . *(The rest is inaudible.)*

ASLAKSEN. The man was evidently intoxicated.—Continue, Dr. Stockmann; but pray endeavour to be moderate.

DR. STOCKMANN. Well, fellow citizens, I shall say no more about our leading men. If any one imagines, from what I have just said, that it's these gentlemen I want to make short work of to-night, he is mistaken—altogether mistaken. For I cherish the comfortable conviction that these laggards, these relics of a decaying order of thought, are diligently cutting their own throats. They need no doctor to hasten their end. And it is not people of *that* sort that constitute the real danger to society; it is not they who are most active in poisoning the sources of our spiritual life and making a plague-spot of the ground beneath our feet; it is not *they* who are the most dangerous enemies of truth and freedom in our society.

CRIES FROM ALL SIDES. Who, then? Who is it? Name, name!

DR. STOCKMANN. Yes, you may be sure I shall name them! For *this* is the great discovery I made yesterday: *(In a louder tone.)* The most dangerous foe to truth and freedom in our midst is the compact majority. Yes, it's the confounded, compact, liberal majority—that, and nothing else! There, I've told you.

(Immense disturbance in the room. Most of the audience are shouting, stamping, and whistling. Several elderly gentlemen exchange furtive glances and seem to be enjoying the scene. Mrs. Stockmann rises in alarm. Eilif and Morten advance threateningly towards the

schoolboys, who are making noises. Aslaksen rings the bell and calls for order. Hovstad and Billing both speak, but nothing can be heard. At last quiet is restored.)

ASLAKSEN. I must request the speaker to withdraw his ill-considered expressions.

DR. STOCKMANN. Never, Mr. Aslaksen! For it's this very majority that robs me of my freedom, and wants to forbid me to speak the truth.

HOVSTAD. The majority always has right on its side.

BILLING. Yes, and truth too, strike me dead!

DR. STOCKMANN. The majority never has right on its side. Never I say! That is one of the social lies that a free, thinking man is bound to rebel against. Who make up the majority in any given country? Is it the wise men or the fools? I think we must agree that the fools are in a terrible, overwhelming majority, all the wide world over. But how in the devil's name can it ever be right for the fools to rule over the wise men?

(Uproar and yells.)

DR. STOCKMANN. Yes, yes, you can shout me down, but you cannot gainsay me. The majority has *might*—unhappily—but *right* it has not. It is I, and the few, the individuals, that are in the right. The minority is always right.

(Renewed uproar.)

HOVSTAD. Ha ha! Dr. Stockmann has turned aristocrat since the day before yesterday!

DR. STOCKMANN. I have said that I have no words to waste on the little, narrow-chested, short-winded crew that lie in our wake. Pulsating life has nothing more to do with them. I am speaking of the few, the individuals among us, who have made all the new, germinating truths their own. These men stand, as it were, at the outposts, so far in the van that the compact majority has not yet reached them—and *there* they fight for truths that are too lately born into the world's consciousness to have won over the majority.

HOVSTAD. So the Doctor's a revolutionist now!

DR. STOCKMANN. Yes, by Heaven, I am, Mr. Hovstad! I am going to revolt against the lie that truth belongs exclusively to the majority. What sort of truths do the majority rally round? Truths so stricken in years that they are sinking into decrepitude. When a truth is so old as that, gentlemen, it's in a fair way to become a lie.

(Laughter and jeers.)

DR. STOCKMANN. Yes, yes, you may believe me or not, as you please; but truths are by no means the wiry Methusalehs some people think them. A normally-constituted truth lives—let us say—as a rule, seventeen or eighteen years; at the outside twenty; very seldom more. And truths so patriarchal as that are always shockingly emaciated; yet it's not till then that the majority takes them up and recommends them to society as wholesome food. I can assure you there's not much nutriment in that sort of fare; you may take my word as a doctor for that. All these majority-truths are like last year's salt pork; they're like rancid, mouldy ham, producing all the moral scurvy that devastates society.

ASLAKSEN. It seems to me that the honourable speaker is wandering rather far from the subject.

BURGOMASTER. I beg to endorse the Chairman's remark.

DR. STOCKMANN. Why you're surely mad, Peter! I'm keeping as closely to my text as I possibly can; for my text is precisely this—that the masses, the majority, this devil's own compact majority—it's that, I say, that's poisoning the sources of our spiritual life, and making a plague-spot of the ground beneath our feet.

HOVSTAD. And you make this charge against the great, independent majority, just because they have the sense to accept only certain and acknowledged truths?

DR. STOCKMANN. Ah, my dear Mr. Hovstad, don't talk about certain truths! The truths acknowledged by the masses, the multitude, were certain truths to the vanguard in our grandfather's days. We, the vanguard of to-day, don't acknowledge them any longer; and I don't believe there exists any other certain truth but this—that no society can live a healthy life upon truths so old and marrowless.

HOVSTAD. But instead of all this vague talk, suppose you were to give us some specimens of these old marrowless truths that we are living upon.

(Approval from several quarters.)

DR. STOCKMANN. Oh, I could give you no end of samples from the rubbish-heap; but, for the present, I shall keep to one acknowledged truth, which is a hideous lie at bottom, but which Mr. Hovstad, and the *Messenger,* and all adherents of the *Messenger,* live on all the same.

HOVSTAD. And that is . . . ?

DR. STOCKMANN. That is the doctrine you have inherited from your forefathers, and go on thoughtlessly proclaiming far and wide— the doctrine that the multitude, the vulgar herd, the masses, are the pith of the people—that they *are* the people—that the common man, the ignorant, undeveloped member of society, has the same right to sanction and to condemn, to counsel and to govern, as the intellectually distinguished few.

BILLING. Well, now, strike me dead . . . !

HOVSTAD *(shouting at the same time).* Citizens, please note this!

ANGRY VOICES. Ho-ho! Aren't we the people? Is it only the grand folks that are to govern?

A WORKING-MAN. Out with the fellow that talks like that!

OTHERS. Turn him out!

A CITIZEN *(shouting).* Blow your horn, Evensen.

(The deep notes of a horn are heard; whistling, and terrific noise in the room.)

DR. STOCKMANN *(when the noise has somewhat subsided).* Now do be reasonable! Can't you bear even for once in a way to hear the voice of truth? I don't ask you all to agree with me on the instant. But I certainly should have expected Mr. Hovstad to back me up, as soon as he had collected himself a bit. Mr. Hovstad sets up to be a freethinker . . .

SEVERAL VOICES *(subdued and wondering).* Freethinker, did he say? What? Mr. Hovstad a freethinker?

HOVSTAD *(shouting)*. Prove it, Dr. Stockmann. When have I said so in print?

DR. STOCKMANN *(reflecting)*. No, upon my soul, you're right there; you've never had the frankness to do that. Well, well, I won't put you on the rack, Mr. Hovstad. Let me be the freethinker then. And now I'll make it clear to you all, and on scientific grounds too, that the *Messenger* is leading you shamefully by the nose, when it tells you that you, the masses, the crowd, are the true pith of the people. I tell you that's only a newspaper lie. The masses are nothing but the raw material that must be fashioned into a People.

(Murmurs, laughter, and disturbance in the room.)

DR. STOCKMANN. Is it not so with all other living creatures? What a difference between a cultivated and an uncultivated breed of animals! Just look at a common barn-door hen. What meat do you get from such a skinny carcase? Not much, I can tell you! And what sort of eggs does she lay? A decent crow or raven can lay nearly as good. Then take a cultivated Spanish or Japanese hen, or take a fine pheasant or turkey—ah! then you'll see the difference! And now look at the dog, our near relation. Think first of an ordinary vulgar cur—I mean one of those wretched, ragged, plebeian mongrels that haunt the gutters, and soil the sidewalks. Then place such a mongrel by the side of a poodle-dog, descended through many generations from an aristocratic stock, who have lived on delicate food, and heard harmonious voices and music. Do you think the brain of the poodle isn't very differently developed from that of the mongrel? Yes, you may be sure it is! It's well-bred poodle-pups like this that jugglers train to perform the most marvellous tricks. A common peasant-cur could never learn anything of the sort—not if he tried till doomsday.

(Noise and laughter are heard all round.)

A CITIZEN *(shouting)*. Do you want to make dogs of us now?

ANOTHER MAN. We're not animals, Doctor!

DR. STOCKMANN. Yes, on my soul, but we *are* animals, my good sir! We're one and all of us animals, whether we like it or not. But truly there are few enough aristocratic animals among us. Oh, there's a terrible difference between poodle-men and mongrel-men! And the ridiculous part of it is, that Mr. Hovstad quite agrees with me so long as it's four-legged animals we're talking of . . .

HOVSTAD. Oh, beasts are only beasts.

DR. STOCKMANN. Well and good—but no sooner do I apply the law to two-legged animals, than Mr. Hovstad stops short; *then* he daren't hold his own opinions, or think out his own thoughts; then he turns the whole principle upside down, and proclaims in the *People's Messenger* that the barn-door hen and the gutter-mongrel are precisely the finest specimens in the menagerie. But that's always the way, so long as the commonness still lingers in your system, and you haven't worked your way up to spiritual distinction.

HOVSTAD. I make no pretence to any sort of distinction. I come of simple peasant folk, and I am proud that my root should lie deep down among the common people, who are here being insulted.

WORKMEN. Hurrah for Hovstad. Hurrah! hurrah!

DR. STOCKMANN. The sort of common people I am speaking of are not found among the lower classes alone; they crawl and swarm all around us—up to the very summits of society. Just look at your own smug, respectable Burgomaster! Why, my brother Peter belongs as clearly to the common people as any man that walks on two legs . . .

(Laughter and hisses.)

BURGOMASTER. I protest against such personalities.

DR. STOCKMANN *(imperturbably)*. . . . and that not because, like myself, he's descended from a good-for-nothing old pirate from Pomerania, or thereabouts—for that's our ancestry . . .

BURGOMASTER. An absurd tradition! Utterly groundless.

DR. STOCKMANN. . . . but he is so because he thinks the thoughts and holds the opinions of his official superiors. Men who do that, belong, intellectually-speaking, to the common people; and that is why my distinguished brother Peter is at bottom so undistinguished,—and consequently so illiberal.

BURGOMASTER. Mr. Chairman . . . !

HOVSTAD. So that the distinguished people in this country are the Liberals? That's quite a new light on the subject.

(Laughter.)

DR. STOCKMANN. Yes, that is part of my new discovery. And *this,* too, follows: that liberality of thought is almost precisely the same thing as morality. Therefore I say it's absolutely unpardonable of the *Messenger* to proclaim, day out, day in, the false doctrine that it's the masses, the multitude, the compact majority, that monopolise liberality and morality,—and that vice and corruption and all sorts of spiritual uncleanness ooze out of culture, as all that filth oozes down to the Baths from the Mill Dale tan-works!

(Noise and interruptions.)

DR. STOCKMANN *(goes on imperturbably, smiling in his eagerness).* And yet this same *Messenger* can preach about elevating the masses and the multitude to a higher level of well-being! Why, deuce take it, if the *Messenger's* own doctrine holds good, the elevation of the masses would simply mean hurling them straight to perdition! But, happily, the notion that culture demoralises is nothing but an old traditional lie. No, it's stupidity, poverty, the ugliness of life, that do the devil's work! In a house that isn't aired and swept every day —my wife maintains that the floors ought to be scrubbed too, but perhaps that is going too far;—well,—in such a house, I say, within two or three years, people lose the power of thinking or acting morally. Lack of oxygen enervates the conscience. And there seems to be precious little oxygen in many and many a house in this town, since the whole compact majority is unscrupulous enough to want to found its future upon a quagmire of lies and fraud.

ASLAKSEN. I cannot allow so gross an insult to be levelled against a whole community.

A GENTLEMAN. I move that the Chairman order the speaker to sit down.

EAGER VOICES. Yes, yes! That's right! Sit down! Sit down!

DR. STOCKMANN *(flaring up).* Then I shall proclaim the truth at every street corner! I shall write to newspapers in other towns! The whole country shall know how matters stand here!

HOVSTAD. It almost seems as if the Doctor's object were to ruin the town.

DR. STOCKMANN. Yes, so well do I love my native town that I would rather ruin it than see it flourishing upon a lie.

ASLAKSEN. That's plain speaking.

(Noise and whistling. Mrs. Stockmann coughs in vain; the Doctor no longer heeds her.)

HOVSTAD *(shouting amid the tumult)*. The man who would ruin a whole community must be an enemy to his fellow citizens!

DR. STOCKMANN *(with growing excitement)*. What does it matter if a lying community is ruined! Let it be levelled to the ground, say I! All men who live upon a lie ought to be exterminated like vermin! You'll end by poisoning the whole country; you'll bring it to such a pass that the whole country will deserve to perish. And if ever it comes to that, I shall say, from the bottom of my heart: Perish the country! Perish all its people!

A MAN *(in the crowd)*. Why, he talks like a regular enemy of the people!

BILLING. Strike me dead but there spoke the people's voice!

THE WHOLE ASSEMBLY *(shouting)*. Yes! yes! yes! He's an enemy of the people! He hates his country! He hates the whole people!

ASLAKSEN. Both as a citizen of this town and as a human being, I am deeply shocked at what it has been my lot to hear to-night. Dr. Stockmann has unmasked himself in a manner I should never have dreamt of. I must reluctantly subscribe to the opinion just expressed by some estimable citizens; and I think we ought to formulate this opinion in a resolution. I therefore beg to move, "That this meeting declares the medical officer of the Baths, Dr. Thomas Stockmann, to be an enemy of the people."

(Thunders of applause and cheers. Many form a circle round the Doctor and hoot at him. Mrs. Stockmann and Petra have risen. Morten and Eilif fight the other schoolboys, who have also been hooting. Some grown-up persons separate them.)

DR. STOCKMANN *(to the people hooting)*. Ah, fools that you are! I tell you that . . .

ASLAKSEN *(ringing)*. The Doctor is out of order in speaking. A formal vote must be taken; but out of consideration for personal feelings, it will be taken in writing and without names. Have you any blank paper, Mr. Billing?

BILLING. Here's both blue and white paper . . .

ASLAKSEN. Capital; that will save time. Cut it up into slips. That's it. *(To the meeting.)* Blue means no, white means aye. I myself will go round and collect the votes.

(The Burgomaster leaves the room. Aslaksen and a few others go round with pieces of paper in hats.)

A GENTLEMAN *(to Hovstad)*. What can be the matter with the Doctor? What does it all mean?

HOVSTAD. Why, you know what a hare-brained creature he is.

ANOTHER GENTLEMAN *(to Billing)*. I say, you're often at his house. Have you ever noticed if the fellow drinks?

BILLING. Strike me dead if I know what to say. The toddy's always on the table when any one looks in.

A THIRD GENTLEMAN. No, I should rather say he went off his head at times.

FIRST GENTLEMAN. I wonder if there's madness in the family?

BILLING. I shouldn't be surprised.

A FOURTH GENTLEMAN. No, it's pure malice. He wants to be revenged for something or other.

BILLING. He was certainly talking about a rise in his salary the other day; but he didn't get it.

ALL THE GENTLEMEN *(together)*. Aha! That explains everything.

THE DRUNKEN MAN *(in the crowd)*. I want a blue one, I do! And I'll have a white one too.

SEVERAL PEOPLE. There's the tipsy man again! Turn him out!

MORTEN KIIL *(approaching the Doctor)*. Well, Stockmann, you see now what such monkey-tricks lead to?

DR. STOCKMANN. I have done my duty.

MORTEN KIIL. What was that you said about the Mill Dale tanneries?

DR. STOCKMANN. You heard what I said—that all the filth comes from them.

MORTEN KIIL. From my tannery as well?

DR. STOCKMANN. I'm sorry to say yours is the worst of all.

MORTEN KIIL. Are you going to put *that* in the papers, too?

DR. STOCKMANN. I can't gloze anything over.

MORTEN KIIL. This may cost you dear, Stockmann!

(He goes out.)

A FAT GENTLEMAN *(goes up to Horster, without bowing to the ladies).* Well, Captain, so you lend your house to enemies of the people.

HORSTER. I suppose I can do as I please with my own property, Sir.

THE GENTLEMAN. Then of course you can have no objection if I follow your example?

HORSTER. What do you mean, Sir?

THE GENTLEMAN. You shall hear from me to-morrow.

(Turns away and goes out.)

PETRA. Wasn't that the owner of your ship, Captain Horster?

HORSTER. Yes, that was Mr. Vik.

ASLAKSEN *(with the voting papers in his hands, ascends the platform and rings).* Gentlemen! I have now to announce the result of the vote. All the votes, with one exception . . .

A YOUNG GENTLEMAN. That's the tipsy man!

ASLAKSEN. With the exception of one intoxicated person, this meeting of citizens unanimously declares the medical officer of the Baths, Dr. Thomas Stockmann, to be an enemy of the people. *(Cheers and applause.)* Three cheers for our fine old municipality! *(Cheers.)* Three cheers for our able and energetic Burgomaster, who has so loyally set family prejudice aside! *(Cheers.)* The meeting is dissolved. *(He descends.)*

BILLING. Three cheers for the Chairman!

ALL. Hurrah for Aslaksen!

DR. STOCKMANN. My hat and coat, Petra. Captain, have you room for passengers to the new world?

HORSTER. For you and yours, Doctor, we'll make room.

DR. STOCKMANN *(while Petra helps him to put on his coat)*. Good. Come Katrina, come boys!

(He gives his wife his arm.)

MRS. STOCKMANN *(in a low voice)*. Thomas, dear, let us go out by the back way.

DR. STOCKMANN. No back ways, Katrina! *(In a loud voice.)* You shall hear from the enemy of the people, before he shakes the dust from his feet! I am not so forbearing as a certain person; I don't say: I forgive you, for you know not what you do.

ASLAKSEN *(shouts)*. That is a blasphemous comparison, Dr. Stockmann.

BILLING. Strike me . . . ! This is more than a serious man can stand!

A COARSE VOICE. And he threatens us into the bargain!

ANGRY CRIES. Let's smash his windows! Duck him in the fiord!

A MAN *(in the crowd)*. Blow your horn, Evensen! Blow, man, blow!

(Horn-blowing, whistling, and wild shouting. The Doctor, with his family, goes towards the door. Horster clears the way for them.)

ALL *(yelling after them as they go out)*. Enemy of the people! Enemy of the people! Enemy of the people!

BILLING. Strike me dead if I'd care to drink toddy at Stockmann's to-night!

(The people throng towards the door; the shouting is taken up by others outside; from the street are heard cries of "Enemy of the people! Enemy of the people!")

ACT FIFTH

Dr. Stockmann's Study. Bookshelves and glass cases with various collections along the walls. In the back, a door leading to the hall; in front, on the left, a door to the sitting-room. In the wall to the right are two windows, all the panes of which are smashed. In the middle of the room is the Doctor's writing-table, covered with books and papers. The room is in disorder. It is forenoon. Dr. Stockmann, in dressing-gown, slippers, and skull-cap, is bending down and raking with an umbrella under one of the cabinets; at last he rakes out a stone.

DR. STOCKMANN *(speaking through the sitting-room doorway)*. Katrina, I've found another!

MRS. STOCKMANN *(in the sitting-room)*. Oh, I'm sure you'll find plenty more.

DR. STOCKMANN *(placing the stone on a pile of others on the table)*. I shall keep these stones as sacred relics. Eilif and Morten shall see them every day, and when I die they shall be heirlooms. *(Raking under the bookcase.)* Hasn't—what the devil is her name?—the girl—hasn't she been for the glazier yet?

MRS. STOCKMANN *(coming in)*. Yes, but he said he didn't know whether he would be able to come to-day.

DR. STOCKMANN. I believe, if the truth were told, he daren't come.

MRS. STOCKMANN. Well, Randina, too, had an idea he was afraid to come, because of the neighbours. *(Speaks through the sitting-room doorway.)* What is it, Randina?—Very well. *(Goes out, and returns immediately.)* Here is a letter for you, Thomas.

DR. STOCKMANN. Let me see. *(Opens the letter and reads.)* Aha!

MRS. STOCKMANN. Who is it from?

DR. STOCKMANN. From the landlord. He gives us notice.

MRS. STOCKMANN. Is it possible? He is such a nice man . . .

DR. STOCKMANN *(looking at the letter)*. He daren't do otherwise, he says. He is very unwilling to do it; but he daren't do otherwise— on account of his fellow citizens—out of respect for public opinion —is in a dependent position—doesn't dare to offend certain influential men . . .

MRS. STOCKMANN. There, you see, Thomas.

DR. STOCKMANN. Yes, yes, I see well enough; they are all cowards, every one of them, in this town; no one dares do anything for fear of all the rest. *(Throws the letter on the table.)* But it's all the same to us, Katrina. We will shape our course for the new world, and then . . .

MRS. STOCKMANN. But are you sure this idea of going abroad is altogether wise, Thomas?

DR. STOCKMANN. Would you have me stay here, where they have pilloried me as an enemy of the people, branded me, smashed my windows! And look here, Katrina, they've torn a hole in my black trousers, too.

MRS. STOCKMANN. Oh dear; and these are the best you have!

DR. STOCKMANN. A man should never put on his best trousers when he goes out to battle for freedom and truth. Well, I don't care so much about the trousers; them you can always patch up for me. But that the mob, the rabble, should dare to attack me as if they were my equals—*that* is what I can't, for the life of me, stomach!

MRS. STOCKMANN. Yes, they have behaved abominably to you here, Thomas; but is that any reason for leaving the country altogether?

DR. STOCKMANN. Do you think the plebeians aren't just as insolent in other towns? Oh yes, they are, my dear; it's six of one and half a dozen of the other. Well, never mind; let the curs yelp; *that's* not the worst; the worst is that every one, all over the country, is the slave of his party. Not that I suppose—very likely it's no better in the free West either; the compact majority, and enlightened public opinion, and all the other devil's trash is rampant there too. But you see the conditions are larger there than here; they may kill you, but they don't slow-torture you; they don't screw up a free soul in a vice, as they do at home here. And then, if need be, you can keep out of it all. *(Walks up and down.)* If I only knew of any primeval forest, or a little South Sea island to be sold cheap . . .

MRS. STOCKMANN. Yes, but the boys, Thomas.

DR. STOCKMANN *(comes to a standstill)*. What an extraordinary woman you are, Katrina! Would you rather have the boys grow up in such a society as ours? Why, you could see for yourself yesterday evening that one half of the population is stark mad, and if the other half hasn't lost its wits, that's only because they are brute beasts who haven't any wits to lose.

MRS. STOCKMANN. But really, my dear Thomas, you do say such imprudent things.

DR. STOCKMANN. What! Isn't it the truth that I tell them? Don't they turn all ideas upside down? Don't they stir up right and wrong into one hotch-potch? Don't they call lies everything that I know to be the truth? But the maddest thing of all is to see crowds of grown men, calling themselves Liberals, go about persuading themselves and others that they are friends of freedom! Did you ever hear anything like it, Katrina?

MRS. STOCKMANN. Yes, yes, no doubt. But . . .

(Petra enters from the sitting-room.)

MRS. STOCKMANN. Back from school already?

PETRA. Yes; I have been dismissed.

MRS. STOCKMANN. Dismissed?

DR. STOCKMANN. You too!

PETRA. Mrs. Busk gave me notice, and so I thought it best to leave there and then.

DR. STOCKMANN. You did perfectly right!

MRS. STOCKMANN. Who could have thought Mrs. Busk was such a bad woman!

PETRA. Oh mother, Mrs. Busk isn't bad at all; I saw clearly how sorry she was. But she dared not do otherwise, she said; and so I am dismissed.

DR. STOCKMANN (*laughing and rubbing his hands*). She dared not do otherwise—just like the rest! Oh, it's delicious.

MRS. STOCKMANN. Oh well, after that frightful scene last night...

PETRA. It wasn't only that. What do you think, father...?

DR. STOCKMANN. Well?

PETRA. Mrs. Busk showed me no fewer than three letters she had received this morning...

DR. STOCKMANN. Anonymous, of course?

PETRA. Yes.

DR. STOCKMANN. They never dare give their names, Katrina!

PETRA. And two of them stated that a gentleman who is often at our house said at the club last night that I held extremely advanced opinions upon various things...

DR. STOCKMANN. Of course you didn't deny it.

PETRA. Of course not. You know Mrs. Busk herself is pretty advanced in her opinions when we're alone together; but now that this has come out about me, she dared not keep me on.

MRS. STOCKMANN. Some one that is often at our house, too. There, you see, Thomas, what comes of all your hospitality.

DR. STOCKMANN. We won't live any longer in such a pig-sty! Pack up as quickly as you can, Katrina; let's get away—the sooner the better.

MRS. STOCKMANN. Hush! I think there is some one in the passage. See who it is, Petra.

PETRA (*opening the door*). Oh, is it you, Captain Horster? Please come in.

HORSTER *(from the hall)*. Good morning. I thought I might just look in and ask how you are.

DR. STOCKMANN *(shaking his hand)*. Thanks; that's very good of you.

MRS. STOCKMANN. And thank you for helping us through the crowd last night, Captain Horster.

PETRA. How did you ever get home again?

HORSTER. Oh, that was all right, I am tolerably able-bodied, you know; and those fellows' bark is worse than their bite.

DR. STOCKMANN. Yes, isn't it extraordinary, this piggish cowardice? Come here, and let me show you something! Look, here are all the stones they threw in at us. Only look at them? Upon my soul there aren't more than two decent-sized lumps in the whole heap; the rest are nothing but pebbles—mere gravel. They stood down there, and yelled, and swore they'd half kill me;—but as for really doing it— no, there's mighty little fear of *that* in this town!

HORSTER. You may thank your stars for that this time, Doctor.

DR. STOCKMANN. So I do, of course. But it's depressing all the same; for if ever it should come to a serious national struggle, you may be sure public opinion would be for taking to its heels, and the compact majority would scamper for their lives like a flock of sheep, Captain Horster. *That* is what's so melancholy to think of; it grieves me to the heart.—But deuce take it—it's foolish of me to feel anything of the sort! They have called me an enemy of the people; well then, let me *be* an enemy of the people!

MRS. STOCKMANN. That you'll never be, Thomas.

DR. STOCKMANN. You'd better not take your oath on it, Katrina. A bad name may act like a pin-scratch in the lung. And that confounded word—I can't get rid of it; it has sunk deep into my heart; and there it lies gnawing and sucking like an acid. And no magnesia can cure me.

PETRA. Pooh; you should only laugh at them, father.

HORSTER. People will think differently yet, Doctor.

MRS. STOCKMANN. Yes, Thomas, that's as certain as that you are standing here.

DR. STOCKMANN. Yes, perhaps, when it is too late. Well, as they make their bed so they must lie! Let them go on wallowing here in their pig-sty, and learn to repent having driven a patriot into exile. When do you sail, Captain Horster?

HORSTER. Well—that's really what I came to speak to you about . . .

DR. STOCKMANN. What? Anything wrong with the ship?

HORSTER. No; but the fact is, I shan't be sailing in her.

PETRA. Surely you have not been dismissed?

HORSTER *(smiling)*. Yes. I have.

PETRA. You too!

MRS. STOCKMANN. There, you see, Thomas.

DR. STOCKMANN. And for the truth's sake! Oh, if I could possibly have imagined such a thing . . .

HORSTER. You mustn't be troubled about this; I shall soon find a berth with some other company, elsewhere.

DR. STOCKMANN. And this is that man Vik! A wealthy man, independent of every one! Faugh!

HORSTER. Oh, for that matter, he's a very well-meaning man. He said himself he would gladly have kept me on if only he dared . . .

DR. STOCKMANN. But he didn't dare? Of course not!

HORSTER. It's not so easy, he said, when you belong to a party . . .

DR. STOCKMANN. My gentleman has hit it there! A party is like a sausage-machine; it grinds all the brains together in one mash; and that's why we see nothing but porridge-heads and pulp-heads all around!

MRS. STOCKMANN. Now really, Thomas!

PETRA *(to Horster)*. If only you hadn't seen us home, perhaps it would not have come to this.

HORSTER. I don't regret it.

PETRA *(gives him her hand)*. Thank you for that!

HORSTER *(to Dr. Stockmann)*. And then too, I wanted to tell you this: if you are really determined to go abroad, I've thought of another way.

DR. STOCKMANN. That's good—if only we can get off quickly . . .

MRS. STOCKMANN. Hush! Isn't that a knock?

PETRA. I believe it is uncle.

DR. STOCKMANN. Aha! *(Calls.)* Come in!

MRS. STOCKMANN. My dear Thomas, now do promise me . . .

(The Burgomaster enters from the hall.)

BURGOMASTER *(in the doorway)*. Oh, you are engaged. Then I'd better . . .

DR. STOCKMANN. No no; come in.

BURGOMASTER. But I wanted to speak to you alone.

MRS. STOCKMANN. We can go into the sitting-room.

HORSTER. And I shall look in again presently.

DR. STOCKMANN. No no; go with the ladies, Captain Horster; I must hear more about . . .

HORSTER. All right, then I'll wait.

(He follows Mrs. Stockmann and Petra into the sitting-room. The Burgomaster says nothing, but casts glances at the windows.)

DR. STOCKMANN. I daresay you find it rather draughty here to-day? Put on your cap.

BURGOMASTER. Thanks, if I may. *(Does so.)* I fancy I caught cold yesterday evening. I stood there shivering . . .

DR. STOCKMANN. Really. On my soul, now, I found it quite warm enough.

BURGOMASTER. I regret that it was not in my power to prevent these nocturnal excesses.

DR. STOCKMANN. Have you anything else in particular to say to me?

BURGOMASTER *(producing a large letter)*. I have this document for you from the Directors of the Baths.

DR. STOCKMANN. My dismissal?

BURGOMASTER. Yes; dated from to-day. *(Places the letter on the table.)* We are very sorry—but frankly, we dared not do otherwise, on account of public opinion.

DR. STOCKMANN *(smiling)*. Dared not? I've heard that phrase already to-day.

BURGOMASTER. I beg you to realise your position clearly. For the future, you cannot count upon any sort of practice in the town.

DR. STOCKMANN. Devil take the practice! But how can you be so sure
of that?

BURGOMASTER. The House-owners' Association is sending round a
circular from house to house, in which all well-disposed citizens
are called upon not to employ you; and I dare swear that not a
single head of a family will venture to refuse his signature; he
simply *dare* not.

DR. STOCKMANN. Well, well; I don't doubt that. But what then?

BURGOMASTER. If I might advise, I would suggest that you should
leave the town for a time . . .

DR. STOCKMANN. Yes, I've had some such idea in my mind already.

BURGOMASTER. Good. And when you have had six months or so for
mature deliberation, if you could make up your mind to acknowledge
your error, with a few words of regret . . .

DR. STOCKMANN. I might perhaps be reinstated, you think?

BURGOMASTER. Perhaps it's not quite out of the question.

DR. STOCKMANN. Yes, but how about public opinion? You daren't,
on account of public opinion.

BURGOMASTER. Opinion is extremely variable. And, to speak candidly,
it is of the greatest importance for us to have such an admission
under your own hand.

DR. STOCKMANN. Yes, I daresay it would be mightily convenient for
you! But you remember what I've said to you before about such
foxes' tricks!

BURGOMASTER. At that time your position was infinitely more favourable; at that time you thought you had the whole town at your
back . . .

DR. STOCKMANN. Yes, and now I have the whole town *on* my back . . .
(Flaring up.) But no—not if I had the devil and his dam on my
back—! Never—never, I tell you!

BURGOMASTER. The father of a family has no right to act as you are
doing. You have no right to do it, Thomas.

DR. STOCKMANN. I have no right! There's only one thing in the world
that a free man has no right to do; and do you know what that is?

BURGOMASTER. No.

DR. STOCKMANN. Of course not; but *I* will tell you. A free man has no right to wallow in filth like a cur; he has no right to act so that he ought to spit in his own face!

BURGOMASTER. That sounds extremely plausible; and if there were not another explanation of your obstinacy—but we all know there is . . .

DR. STOCKMANN. What do you mean by that?

BURGOMASTER. You understand well enough. But as your brother, and as a man who knows the world, I warn you not to build too confidently upon prospects and expectations that may very likely come to nothing.

DR. STOCKMANN. Why, what on earth are you driving at?

BURGOMASTER. Do you really want me to believe that you are ignorant of the terms of old Morten Kiil's will?

DR. STOCKMANN. I know that the little he has is to go to a home for old and needy artizans. But what has that got to do with me?

BURGOMASTER. To begin with, "the little he has" is no trifle. Morten Kiil is a tolerably wealthy man.

DR. STOCKMANN. I have never had the least notion of that!

BURGOMASTER. H'm—really? Then I suppose you have no notion that a not inconsiderable part of his fortune is to go to your children, you and your wife having a life-interest in it. Has he not told you that?

DR. STOCKMANN. No, I'll be hanged if he has! On the contrary, he has done nothing but grumble about being so preposterously over-taxed. But are you really sure of this, Peter?

BURGOMASTER. I have it from a thoroughly trustworthy source.

DR. STOCKMANN. Why, good heavens, then Katrina's provided for—and the children too! Oh, I must tell her . . . (*Calls.*) Katrina, Katrina!

BURGOMASTER (*holding him back*). Hush! don't say anything about it yet.

MRS. STOCKMANN (*opening the door*). What is it?

DR. STOCKMANN. Nothing, my dear; go in again.

(*Mrs. Stockmann closes the door.*)

DR. STOCKMANN (*pacing up and down*). Provided for! Only think—all of them provided for! And for life! After all, it's a grand thing to feel yourself secure!

BURGOMASTER. Yes, but that is just what you are not. Morten Kiil can revoke his will any day or hour he chooses.

DR. STOCKMANN. But he won't, my good Peter. The Badger is only too delighted to see me fall foul of you and your wiseacre friends.

BURGOMASTER (*starts and looks searchingly at him*). Aha! That throws a new light on a good many things.

DR. STOCKMANN. What things?

BURGOMASTER. So the whole affair has been a carefully-concocted intrigue. Your recklessly violent onslaught—in the name of truth —upon the leading men of the town . . .

DR. STOCKMANN. Well, what of it?

BURGOMASTER. It was nothing but a preconcerted requital for that vindictive old Morten Kiil's will.

DR. STOCKMANN (*almost speechless*). Peter—you are the most abominable plebeian I have ever known in all my born days.

BURGOMASTER. All is over between us. Your dismissal is irrevocable— for now we have a weapon against you.

(*He goes out.*)

DR. STOCKMANN. Shame! shame! shame! (*Calls.*) Katrina! The floor must be scrubbed after him! Tell her to come here with a pail— what's her name? confound it—the girl with the smudge on her nose . . .

MRS. STOCKMANN (*in the sitting-room doorway*). Hush, hush, Thomas!

PETRA (*also in the doorway*). Father, here's grandfather; he wants to know if he can speak to you alone.

DR. STOCKMANN. Yes, of course he can. (*By the door.*) Come in, father-in-law.

(*Morten Kiil enters. Dr. Stockmann closes the door behind him.*)

DR. STOCKMANN. Well, what is it? Sit down.

MORTEN KIIL. I won't sit down. *(Looking about him.)* It looks cheerful here to-day, Stockmann.

DR. STOCKMANN. Yes, don't you think so?

MORTEN KIIL. Sure enough. And you've plenty of fresh air too; you've got your fill of that oxygen you were talking about yesterday. You must have a rare good conscience to-day, I should think.

DR. STOCKMANN. Yes, I have.

MORTEN KIIL. So I should suppose. *(Tapping himself on the breast.)* But do you know what *I* have got here?

DR. STOCKMANN. A good conscience too, I hope.

MORTEN KIIL. Pooh! No; something far better than that. *(Takes out a large pocket-book, opens it, and shows Stockmann a bundle of papers.)*

DR. STOCKMANN *(looking at him in astonishment)*. Shares in the Baths!

MORTEN KIIL. They weren't difficult to get to-day.

DR. STOCKMANN. And you've gone and bought these up . . . ?

MORTEN KIIL. All I had the money to pay for.

DR. STOCKMANN. Why, my dear sir,—just when things are in such a desperate way at the Baths . . .

MORTEN KIIL. If you behave like a reasonable being, you can soon set the Baths all right again.

DR. STOCKMANN. Well, you can see for yourself I'm doing all I can. But the people of this town are mad!

MORTEN KIIL. You said yesterday that the worst filth came from my tannery. Now, if that's true, then my grandfather, and my father before me, and I myself, have for ever so many years been poisoning the town with filth, like three destroying angels. Do you think I'm going to sit quiet under such a reproach?

DR. STOCKMANN. Unfortunately, you can't help it.

MORTEN KIIL. No, thank you. I hold fast to my good name. I've heard that people call me "the Badger." A badger's a sort of a pig, I know; but I'm determined to give them the lie. I will live and die a clean man.

DR. STOCKMANN. And how will you manage *that?*

MORTEN KIIL. You shall make me clean, Stockmann.

DR. STOCKMANN. I!

MORTEN KIIL. Do you know what money I've used to buy these shares with? No, you can't know; but now I'll tell you. It's the money Katrina and Petra and the boys are to have after my death. For, you see, I've laid by something after all.

DR. STOCKMANN *(flaring up).* And you've taken Katrina's money and done *this* with it!

MORTEN KIIL. Yes; the whole of it is invested in the Baths now. And now I want to see if you're really so stark, staring mad, after all, Stockmann. If you go on making out that these beasts and other abominations dribble down from my tannery, it'll be just as if you were to flay broad stripes of Katrina's skin—and Petra's too, and the boys'. No decent father would ever do that—unless he were a madman.

DR. STOCKMANN *(walking up and down).* Yes, but I *am* a madman; I *am* a madman!

MORTEN KIIL. You surely can't be so raving, ramping mad where your wife and children are concerned.

DR. STOCKMANN *(stopping in front of him).* Why couldn't you have spoken to me before you went and bought all that rubbish?

MORTEN KIIL. What's done can't be undone.

DR. STOCKMANN *(walking restlessly about).* If only I weren't so certain about the affair . . . ! But I am absolutely convinced that I'm right.

MORTEN KIIL *(weighing the pocket-book in his hand).* If you stick to this lunacy, these aren't worth much. *(Puts the book into his pocket.)*

DR. STOCKMANN. But, deuce take it! surely science ought to be able to hit upon some antidote, some sort of prophylactic . . .

MORTEN KIIL. Do you mean something to kill the beasts?

DR. STOCKMANN. Yes, or at least to make them harmless.

MORTEN KIIL. Couldn't you try ratsbane?

DR. STOCKMANN. Oh, nonsense, nonsense!—But since every one declares it's nothing but fancy, why fancy let it be! Let them have it their own way! Haven't the ignorant, narrow-hearted curs reviled me as an enemy of the people?—and weren't they on the point of tearing the clothes off my back?

MORTEN KIIL. And they've smashed all your windows for you too!

DR. STOCKMANN. Yes, and then there's one's duty to one's family! I must talk that over with Katrina; such things are more in her line.

MORTEN KIIL. That's right! You just follow the advice of a sensible woman.

DR. STOCKMANN *(turning upon him angrily)*. How could you act so preposterously! Risking Katrina's money, and putting me to this horrible torture! When I look at you, I seem to see the devil himself . . . !

MORTEN KIIL. Then I'd better be off. But I must hear from you, yes or no, by two o'clock. If it's *no,* all the shares go to the Hospital— and that this very day.

DR. STOCKMANN. And what will Katrina get?

MORTEN KIIL. Not a rap.

(The door leading to the hall opens. Hovstad and Aslaksen are seen outside it.)

MORTEN KIIL. Hullo! look at these two!

DR. STOCKMANN *(staring at them)*. What! Do *you* actually venture to come here?

HOVSTAD. Why, to be sure we do.

ASLAKSEN. You see, we've something to discuss with you.

MORTEN KIIL *(whispers)*. Yes or no—by two o'clock.

ASLAKSEN *(with a glance at Hovstad)*. Aha!

(Morten Kiil goes out.)

DR. STOCKMANN. Well, what do you want with me? Be brief.

HOVSTAD. I can quite understand that you resent our attitude at the meeting yesterday . . .

DR. STOCKMANN. Your attitude, you say? Yes, it was a pretty attitude! I call it the attitude of cowards—of old women . . . Shame upon you!

HOVSTAD. Call it what you will; but we *could* not act otherwise.

DR. STOCKMANN. You *dared* not, I suppose? Isn't that so?

HOVSTAD. Yes, if you like to put it so.

ASLAKSEN. But why didn't you just say a word to us beforehand? The merest hint to Mr. Hovstad or to me ...

DR. STOCKMANN. A hint? What about?

ASLAKSEN. About what was really behind it all.

DR. STOCKMANN. I don't in the least understand you.

ASLAKSEN *(nods confidentially)*. Oh yes, you do, Dr. Stockmann.

HOVSTAD. It's no good making a mystery of it any longer.

DR. STOCKMANN *(looking from one to the other)*. Why, what in the devil's name ... !

ASLAKSEN. May I ask—isn't your father-in-law going about the town buying up all the Bath stock?

DR. STOCKMANN. Yes, he has been buying Bath stock to-day, but ...

ASLAKSEN. It would have been more prudent to let somebody else do that—some one not so closely connected with you.

HOVSTAD. And then you ought not to have appeared in the matter under your own name. No one need have known that the attack on the Baths came from you. You should have taken me into your counsels, Dr. Stockmann.

DR. STOCKMANN *(stares straight in front of him; a light seems to break in upon him, and he says as though thunderstruck):* Is this possible? Can such things be?

ASLAKSEN *(smiling)*. It's plain enough that they can. But they ought to be managed delicately, you understand.

HOVSTAD. And there ought to be more people in it; for the responsibility always falls more lightly when there are several to share it.

DR. STOCKMANN *(calmly)*. In one word, gentlemen—what is it you want?

ASLAKSEN. Mr. Hovstad can best ...

HOVSTAD. No, you explain, Aslaksen.

ASLAKSEN. Well, it's this: now that we know how the matter really stands, we believe we can venture to place the *People's Messenger* at your disposal.

DR. STOCKMANN. You can venture to *now*, eh? But how about public opinion? Aren't you afraid of bringing down a storm upon us?

HOVSTAD. We must manage to ride out the storm.

ASLAKSEN. And you must be ready to put about quickly, Doctor. As soon as your attack has done its work . . .

DR. STOCKMANN. As soon as my father-in-law and I have bought up the shares at a discount, you mean?

HOVSTAD. I presume it is mainly on scientific grounds that you want to take the management of the Baths into your own hands.

DR. STOCKMANN. Of course; it was on scientific grounds that I got the old Badger to stand in with me. And then we'll tinker up the water-works a little, and potter about a bit down at the beach, without its costing the town sixpence. That ought to do the business? Eh?

HOVSTAD. I think so—if you have the *Messenger* to back you up.

ASLAKSEN. In a free community the press is a power, Doctor.

DR. STOCKMANN. Yes, indeed; and so is public opinion. And you, Mr. Aslaksen—I suppose you will answer for the House-owners' Association?

ASLAKSEN. Both for the House-owners' Association and the Temperance Society. You may make your mind easy.

DR. STOCKMANN. But, gentlemen—really I'm quite ashamed to mention such a thing—but—what return . . . ?

HOVSTAD. Of course, we should prefer to give you our support for nothing. But the *Messenger* is not very firmly established; it's not getting on as it ought to; and I should be very sorry to have to stop the paper just now, when there's so much to be done in general politics.

DR. STOCKMANN. Naturally; that would be very hard for a friend of the people like you. *(Flaring up.)* But I—I am an enemy of the people! *(Striding about the room.)* Where's my stick? Where the devil is my stick?

HOVSTAD. What do you mean?

ASLAKSEN. Surely you wouldn't . . .

DR. STOCKMANN *(standing still)*. And suppose I don't give you a single farthing out of all my shares? You must remember we rich folk don't like parting with our money.

HOVSTAD. And you must remember that this business of the shares can be represented in two ways.

DR. STOCKMANN. Yes, you are the man for that; if I don't come to the rescue of the *Messenger,* you'll manage to put a vile complexion on the affair; you'll hunt me down, I suppose—bait me—try to throttle me as a dog throttles a hare!

HOVSTAD. That's a law of nature—every animal fights for its own subsistence.

ASLAKSEN. And must take its food where it can find it, you know.

DR. STOCKMANN. Then see if you can't find some out in the gutter; *(striding about the room)* for now, by heaven! we shall see which is the strongest animal of us three. *(Finds his umbrella and brandishes it.)* Now, look here . . . !

HOVSTAD. You surely don't mean to assault us?

ASLAKSEN. I say, be careful with that umbrella.

DR. STOCKMANN. Out at the window with you, Mr. Hovstad!

HOVSTAD *(by the hall door).* Are you utterly crazy?

DR. STOCKMANN. Out at the window, Mr. Aslaksen! Jump, I tell you! Be quick about it!

ASLAKSEN *(running round the writing-table).* Moderation, Doctor; I'm not at all strong; I can't stand much . . . *(Screams.)* Help! help!

(Mrs. Stockmann, Petra, and Horster enter from sitting-room.)

MRS. STOCKMANN. Good heavens, Thomas! what *can* be the matter?

DR. STOCKMANN *(brandishing the umbrella).* Jump, I tell you! Out into the gutter!

HOVSTAD. An unprovoked assault! I call you to witness, Captain Horster. *(Rushes off through the hall.)*

ASLAKSEN *(bewildered).* If one only *knew* the local situation . . . ! *(He slinks out by the sitting-room door.)*

MRS. STOCKMANN *(holding back the Doctor).* Now, *do* restrain yourself, Thomas!

DR. STOCKMANN *(throwing down the umbrella)*. I'll be hanged if they haven't got off after all.

MRS. STOCKMANN. Why, what can they have wanted with you?

DR. STOCKMANN. I'll tell you afterwards; I have other things to think of now. *(Goes to the table and writes on a visiting-card.)* Look here, Katrina: what's written here?

MRS. STOCKMANN. Three big *Noes;* what does that mean?

DR. STOCKMANN. That I'll tell you afterwards, too. *(Handing the card.)* There, Petra; let smudgy-face run to the Badger's with this as fast as she can. Be quick!

(Petra goes out through the hall with the card.)

DR. STOCKMANN. Well, if I haven't had visits to-day from all the emissaries of the devil! But now I'll sharpen my pen against them till it becomes a goad; I'll dip it in gall and venom; I'll hurl my inkstand straight at their skulls.

MRS. STOCKMANN. You forget we are going away, Thomas.

(Petra returns.)

DR. STOCKMANN. Well?

PETRA. She has gone.

DR. STOCKMANN. Good. Going away, do you say? No, I'll be damned
if we do; we stay where we are, Katrina!

PETRA. Stay!

MRS. STOCKMANN. Here in the town?

DR. STOCKMANN. Yes, here; the field of battle is here; here the fight
must be fought; here I will conquer! As soon as my trousers are
mended, I shall go out into the town and look for a house; we must
have a roof over our heads for the winter.

HORSTER. That you can have in my house.

DR. STOCKMANN. Can I?

HORSTER. Yes, there's no difficulty about that. I have room enough,
and I'm hardly ever at home myself.

MRS. STOCKMANN. Oh, how kind of you, Captain Horster.

PETRA. Thank you!

DR. STOCKMANN *(shaking his hand)*. Thanks, thanks! So that is off
my mind. And this very day I shall set to work in earnest. Oh,
there's no end of work to be done here, Katrina! It's a good thing
I shall have all my time at my disposal now; for you must know
I've had notice from the Baths . . .

MRS. STOCKMANN *(sighing)*. Oh yes, I was expecting that.

DR. STOCKMANN. . . . And now they want to take away my practice
as well. But let them! The poor I shall keep anyhow—those that
can't pay; and, good Lord! it's they that need me most. But by
heaven! I'll make them listen to me; I'll preach to them in season
and out of season, as the saying goes.

MRS. STOCKMANN. My dear Thomas, I should have thought you had
learnt what good preaching does.

DR. STOCKMANN. You really are absurd, Katrina. Am I to let myself
be beaten off the field by public opinion, and the compact majority,
and all that sort of devilry? No, thank you! Besides, my point is

so simple, so clear and straightforward. I only want to drive it into the heads of these curs that the Liberals are the craftiest foes free men have to face; that party-programmes wring the necks of all young and living truths; that considerations of expediency turn justice and morality upside down, until life here becomes simply unlivable. Come, Captain Horster, don't you think I shall be able to make the people understand that?

HORSTER. Maybe; I don't know much about these things myself.

DR. STOCKMANN. Well, you see—this is the way of it! It's the party-leaders that must be exterminated. For a party-leader is just like a wolf, you see—like a ravening wolf; he must devour a certain number of smaller animals a year, if he's to exist at all. Just look at Hovstad and Aslaksen! How many small animals they polish off —or at least mangle and maim, so that they're fit for nothing else but to be house-owners and subscribers to the *People's Messenger!* (*Sits on the edge of the table.*) Just come here, Katrina—see how bravely the sun shines to-day! And how the blessed fresh spring air blows in upon me!

MRS. STOCKMANN. Yes, if only we could live on sunshine and spring air, Thomas.

DR. STOCKMANN. Well, you'll have to pinch and save to eke them out —and then we shall get on all right. That's what troubles me least. No, what *does* trouble me is that I don't see any man free enough and high-minded enough to dare to take up my work after me.

PETRA. Oh, don't think about that, father; you have time enough before you.—-Why, see, there are the boys already.

(*Eilif and Morten enter from the sitting-room.*)

MRS. STOCKMANN. Have you a holiday to-day?

MORTEN. No; but we had a fight with the other fellows in play-time . . .

EILIF. That's not true; it was the other fellows that fought us.

MORTEN. Yes, and then Mr. Rörlund said we had better stop at home for a few days.

DR. STOCKMANN (*snapping his fingers and springing down from the table).* Now I have it! Now I have it, on my soul! You shall never set foot in school again!

THE BOYS. Never go to school!

MRS. STOCKMANN. Why, Thomas . . .

DR. STOCKMANN. Never, I say! I shall teach you myself—that's to say, I won't teach you any mortal thing . . .

MORTEN. Hurrah!

DR. STOCKMANN. . . . but I shall help you to grow into free, high-minded men.—Look here, you'll have to help me, Petra.

PETRA. Yes, father, you may be sure I will.

DR. STOCKMANN. And we'll have our school in the room where they reviled me as an enemy of the people. But we must have more pupils. I must have at least a dozen boys to begin with.

MRS. STOCKMANN. You'll never get them in this town.

DR. STOCKMANN. We shall see. *(To the boys.)* Don't you know any street urchins—any regular ragamuffins . . . ?

MORTEN. Yes, father, I know lots!

DR. STOCKMANN. That's all right; bring me a few of them. I shall experiment with the street-curs for once in a way; there are sometimes excellent heads amongst them.

MORTEN. But what are we to do when we've grown into free and high-minded men?

DR. STOCKMANN. Drive all the wolves out to the far west, boys!
(Eilif looks rather doubtful; and Morten jumps about shouting "Hurrah!")

MRS. STOCKMANN. If only the wolves don't drive you out, Thomas.

DR. STOCKMANN. Are you quite mad, Katrina! *Drive me out!* Now that I am the strongest man in the town?

MRS. STOCKMANN. The strongest—now?

DR. STOCKMANN. Yes, I venture to say this: that now I am one of the strongest men in the whole world.

MORTEN. I say, what fun!

DR. STOCKMANN *(in a subdued voice).* Hush; you mustn't speak about it yet; but I have made a great discovery.

MRS. STOCKMANN. What, another?

DR. STOCKMANN. Yes, of course! *(Gathers them about him, and speaks confidentially.)* This is what I have discovered, you see: the strongest man in the world is he who stands most alone.

MRS. STOCKMANN *(shakes her head, smiling).* Ah, Thomas dear ... !

PETRA *(grasping his hands cheerily).* Father!

THE END

THE WILD DUCK

TRANSLATED BY
FRANCES E. ARCHER

CHARACTERS

WERLE
A merchant, manufacturer, etc.

GREGERS WERLE
His son

OLD EKDAL

HIALMAR EKDAL
His son, a photographer

GINA EKDAL
Hialmar's wife

HEDVIG
Their daughter, a girl of fourteen

MRS. SØRBY
Werle's housekeeper

RELLING
A doctor

MOLVIK
Ex-student of theology

GRÅBERG
Werle's bookkeeper

PETTERSEN
Werle's servant

JENSEN
A hired waiter

A FLABBY GENTLEMAN

A THIN-HAIRED GENTLEMAN

A SHORT-SIGHTED GENTLEMAN

*Six other gentlemen, guests at Werle's dinner-party
Several hired waiters*

*The first act passes in Werle's house, the remaining acts
at Hialmar Ekdal's*

Pronunciation of names: Gregers Werle = *Grayghers Verlë;*
Hialmar Ekdal = *Yalmar Aykdal;* Gina = *Gheena;*
Sørby = *Surby;* Gråberg = *Grawberg;* Jensen = *Yensen.*

ACT FIRST

*At Werle's house. A richly and comfortably furnished study; book-
cases and upholstered furniture; a writing-table, with papers and documents, in the centre of the room; lighted lamps with green shades,
giving a subdued light. At the back, open folding-doors with curtains
drawn back. Within is seen a large and handsome room, brilliantly
lighted with lamps and branching candlesticks. In front, on the right
(in the study), a small baize door leads into Werle's office. On the left,
in front, a fireplace with a glowing coal fire, and farther back a double
door leading into the dining-room.*

*Werle's servant, Pettersen, in livery, and Jensen, the hired waiter,
in black, are putting the study in order. In the large room, two or
three other hired waiters are moving about, arranging things and
lighting more candles. From the dining-room, the hum of conversation
and laughter of many voices are heard; a glass is tapped with a knife;
silence follows, and a toast is proposed; shouts of "Bravo!" and then
again a buzz of conversation.*

PETTERSEN *(lights a lamp on the chimney-place and places a shade over
it).* Hark to them, Jensen! now the old man's on his legs holding
a long palaver about Mrs. Sørby.

JENSEN (*pushing forward an arm-chair*). Is it true, what folks say, that they're—very good friends, eh?

PETTERSEN. Lord knows.

JENSEN. I've heard tell as he's been a lively customer in his day.

PETTERSEN. May be.

JENSEN. And he's giving this spread in honour of his son, they say.

PETTERSEN. Yes. His son came home yesterday.

JENSEN. This is the first time I ever heard as Mr. Werle *had* a son.

PETTERSEN. Oh yes, he has a son, right enough. But he's a fixture, as you might say, up at the Høidal works. He's never once come to town all the years I've been in service here.

A WAITER (*in the doorway of the other room*). Pettersen, here's an old fellow wanting . . .

PETTERSEN (*mutters*). The devil—who's this now?

(*Old Ekdal appears from the right, in the inner room. He is dressed in a threadbare overcoat with a high collar; he wears woollen mittens, and carries in his hand a stick and a fur cap. Under his arm, a brown paper parcel. Dirty red-brown wig and small grey moustache.*)

PETTERSEN (*goes towards him*). Good Lord—what do *you* want here?

EKDAL (*in the doorway*). Must get into the office, Pettersen.

PETTERSEN. The office was closed an hour ago, and . . .

EKDAL. So they told me at the front door. But Gråberg's in there still. Let me slip in this way, Pettersen; there's a good fellow. (*Points towards the baize door.*) It's not the first time I've come this way.

PETTERSEN. Well, you may pass. (*Opens the door.*) But mind you go out again the proper way, for we've got company.

EKDAL. I know, I know—h'm! Thanks, Pettersen, good old friend! Thanks! (*Mutters softly.*) Ass! (*He goes into the office; Pettersen shuts the door after him.*)

JENSEN. Is he one of the office people?

PETTERSEN. No, he's only an outside hand that does odd jobs of copying. But he's been a tip-topper in his day, has old Ekdal.

JENSEN. You can see he's been through a lot.

PETTERSEN. Yes; he was an army officer, you know.

JENSEN. You don't say so?

PETTERSEN. No mistake about it. But then he went into the timber trade or something of the sort. They say he once played Mr. Werle a very nasty trick. They were partners in the Høidal works at the time. Oh, I know old Ekdal well, I do. Many a nip of bitters and bottle of ale we two have drunk at Madam Eriksen's.

JENSEN. He don't look as if he'd much to stand treat with.

PETTERSEN. Why, bless you, Jensen, it's *me* that stands treat. I always think there's no harm in being a bit civil to folks that have seen better days.

JENSEN. Did he go bankrupt then?

PETTERSEN. Worse than that. He went to prison.

JENSEN. To prison!

PETTERSEN. Or perhaps it was the Penitentiary. *(Listens.)* Sh! They're leaving the table.

(The dining-room door is thrown open from within, by a couple of

waiters. Mrs. Sørby comes out conversing with two gentlemen. Gradually the whole company follows, amongst them Werle. Last come Hialmar Ekdal and Gregers Werle.)

MRS. SØRBY *(in passing, to the servant)*. Tell them to serve the coffee in the music-room, Pettersen.

PETTERSEN. Very well, Madam.

(She goes with the two Gentlemen into the inner room, and thence out to the right. Pettersen and Jensen go out the same way.)

A FLABBY GENTLEMAN *(to a thin-haired Gentleman)*. Whew! What a dinner!—It was no joke to do it justice!

THE THIN-HAIRED GENTLEMAN. Oh, with a little good-will one can get through a lot in three hours.

THE FLABBY GENTLEMAN. Yes, but afterwards, afterwards, my dear Chamberlain!

A THIRD GENTLEMAN. I hear the coffee and maraschino are to be served in the music-room.

THE FLABBY GENTLEMAN. Bravo! Then perhaps Mrs. Sørby will play us something.

THE THIN-HAIRED GENTLEMAN *(in a low voice)*. I hope Mrs. Sørby mayn't play us a tune we don't like, one of these days!

THE FLABBY GENTLEMAN. Oh no, not she! Bertha will never turn against her old friends.

(They laugh and pass into the inner room.)

WERLE *(in a low voice, dejectedly)*. I don't think anybody noticed it, Gregers.

GREGERS *(looks at him)*. Noticed what?

WERLE. Did you not notice it either?

GREGERS. What do you mean?

WERLE. We were thirteen at table.

GREGERS. Indeed? Were there thirteen of us?

WERLE *(glances towards Hialmar Ekdal)*. Our usual party is twelve. *(To the others.)* This way, gentlemen!

(Werle and the others, all except Hialmar and Gregers, go out by the back, to the right.)

HIALMAR (*who has overheard the conversation*). You ought not to have invited me, Gregers.

GREGERS. What? Not ask my best and only friend to a party supposed to be in my honour . . . ?

HIALMAR. But I don't think your father likes it. You see I am quite outside his circle.

GREGERS. So I hear. But I wanted to see you and have a talk with you, and I certainly shan't be staying long.—Ah, we two old school-fellows have drifted far apart from each other. It must be sixteen or seventeen years since we met.

HIALMAR. Is it so long?

GREGERS. It is indeed. Well, how goes it with you? You look well. You have put on flesh, and grown almost stout.

HIALMAR. Well, "stout" is scarcely the word; but I daresay I look a little more of a man than I used to.

GREGERS. Yes, you do; your outer man is in first-rate condition.

HIALMAR (*in a tone of gloom*). Ah, but the inner man! That is a very different matter, I can tell you! Of course you know of the terrible catastrophe that has befallen me and mine since last we met.

GREGERS (*more softly*). How are things going with your father now?

HIALMAR. Don't let us talk of it, old fellow. Of course my poor unhappy father lives with me. He hasn't another soul in the world to care for him. But you can understand that this is a miserable subject for me.—Tell me, rather, how you have been getting on up at the works.

GREGERS. I have had a delightfully lonely time of it—plenty of leisure to think and think about things. Come over here; we may as well make ourselves comfortable.

(*He seats himself in an arm-chair by the fire and draws Hialmar down into another alongside of it.*)

HIALMAR (*sentimentally*). After all, Gregers, I thank you for inviting me to your father's table; for I take it as a sign that you have got over your feeling against me.

GREGERS *(surprised)*. How could you imagine I had any feeling against you?

HIALMAR. You had at first, you know.

GREGERS. How at first?

HIALMAR. After the great misfortune. It was natural enough that you should. Your father was within an ace of being drawn into that—well, that terrible business.

GREGERS. Why should that give me any feeling against you? Who can have put that into your head?

HIALMAR. I know it did, Gregers; your father told me so himself.

GREGERS *(starts)*. My father! Oh indeed. H'm.—Was that why you never let me hear from you?—not a single word.

HIALMAR. Yes.

GREGERS. Not even when you made up your mind to become a photographer?

HIALMAR. Your father said I had better not write to you at all, about anything.

GREGERS *(looking straight before him)*. Well well, perhaps he was right.—But tell me now, Hialmar: are you pretty well satisfied with your present position?

HIALMAR *(with a little sigh)*. Oh yes, I am; I have really no cause to complain. At first, as you may guess, I felt it a little strange. It was such a totally new state of things for me. But of course my whole circumstances were totally changed. Father's utter, irretrievable ruin,—the shame and disgrace of it, Gregers . . .

GREGERS *(affected)*. Yes, yes; I understand.

HIALMAR. I couldn't think of remaining at college; there wasn't a shilling to spare; on the contrary, there were debts—mainly to your father I believe . . .

GREGERS. H'm . . .

HIALMAR. In short, I thought it best to break, once for all, with my old surroundings and associations. It was your father that specially urged me to it; and since he interested himself so much in me . . .

GREGERS. My father did?

HIALMAR. Yes, you surely knew that, didn't you? Where do you suppose I found the money to learn photography, and to furnish a studio and make a start? All that costs a pretty penny, I can tell you.

GREGERS. And *my father* provided the money?

HIALMAR. Yes, my dear fellow, didn't you know? I understood him to say he had written to you about it.

GREGERS. Not a word about *his* part in the business. He must have forgotten it. Our correspondence has always been purely a business one. So it was my father that . . . !

HIALMAR. Yes, certainly. He didn't wish it to be generally known; but he it was. And of course it was he, too, that put me in a position to marry. Don't you—don't you know about that either?

GREGERS. No, I haven't heard a word of it. *(Shakes him by the arm.)* But, my dear Hialmar, I can't tell you what pleasure all this gives me—pleasure, and self-reproach. I have perhaps done my father injustice after all—in some things. This proves that he has a heart. It shows a sort of compunction . . .

HIALMAR. Compunction . . . ?

GREGERS. Yes, yes—whatever you like to call it. Oh, I can't tell you how glad I am to hear this of father.—So you are a married man, Hialmar! That is further than I shall ever get. Well, I hope you are happy in your married life?

HIALMAR. Yes, thoroughly happy. She is as good and capable a wife as any man could wish for. And she is by no means without culture.

GREGERS *(rather surprised)*. No, of course not.

HIALMAR. You see, life is itself an education. Her daily intercourse with me . . . And then we know one or two rather remarkable men, who come a good deal about us. I assure you, you would hardly know Gina again.

GREGERS. Gina?

HIALMAR. Yes; had you forgotten that her name was Gina?

GREGERS. Whose name? I haven't the slightest idea . . .

HIALMAR. Don't you remember that she used to be in service here?

GREGERS *(looks at him)*. Is it Gina Hansen . . . ?

HIALMAR. Yes, of course it is Gina Hansen.

GREGERS. . . . who kept house for us during the last year of my mother's illness?

HIALMAR. Yes, exactly. But my dear friend, I'm quite sure your father told you that I was married.

GREGERS *(who has risen)*. Oh yes, he mentioned it; but not that . . . *(Walking about the room.)* Stay—perhaps he did—now that I think of it. My father always writes such short letters. *(Half seats himself on the arm of the chair.)* Now, tell me, Hialmar—this is interesting—how did you come to know Gina—your wife?

HIALMAR. The simplest thing in the world. You know Gina did not stay here long; everything was so much upset at that time, owing to your mother's illness and so forth, that Gina was not equal to it all; so she gave notice and left. That was the year before your mother died—or it may have been the same year.

GREGERS. It was the same year. I was up at the works then. But afterwards . . . ?

HIALMAR. Well, Gina lived at home with her mother, Madam Hansen, an excellent hard-working woman, who kept a little eating-house. She had a room to let too; a very nice comfortable room.

GREGERS. And I suppose you were lucky enough to secure it?

HIALMAR. Yes; in fact, it was your father that recommended it to me. So it was there, you see, that I really came to know Gina.

GREGERS. And then you got engaged?

HIALMAR. Yes. It doesn't take young people long to fall in love . . . ; h'm . . .

GREGERS *(rises and moves about a little)*. Tell me: was it after your engagement—was it then that my father—I mean was it then that you began to take up photography?

HIALMAR. Yes, precisely. I wanted to make a start, and to set up house as soon as possible; and your father and I agreed that this photography business was the readiest way. Gina thought so too. Oh, and there was another thing in its favour, by-the-bye: it happened, luckily, that Gina had learnt to retouch.

GREGERS. That chimed in marvellously.

HIALMAR *(pleased, rises)*. Yes, didn't it? Don't you think it was a marvellous piece of luck?

GREGERS. Oh, unquestionably. My father seems to have been almost a kind of providence for you.

HIALMAR *(with emotion)*. He did not forsake his old friend's son in the hour of his need. For he *has* a heart, you see.

MRS. SØRBY *(enters, arm-in-arm with Werle)*. Nonsense, my dear Mr. Werle; you mustn't stop there any longer staring at all the lights. It's very bad for you.

WERLE *(lets go her arm and passes his hand over his eyes)*. I daresay you are right.

(Pettersen and Jensen carry round refreshment trays.)

MRS. SØRBY *(to the Guests in the other room)*. This way, if you please, gentlemen. Whoever wants a glass of punch must be so good as to come in here.

THE FLABBY GENTLEMAN *(comes up to Mrs. Sørby)*. Surely, it isn't possible that you have suspended our cherished right to smoke?

MRS. SØRBY. Yes. No smoking here, in Mr. Werle's sanctum, Chamberlain.

THE THIN-HAIRED GENTLEMAN. When did you enact these stringent amendments on the cigar law, Mrs. Sørby?

MRS. SØRBY. After the last dinner, Chamberlain, when certain persons permitted themselves to overstep the mark.

THE THIN-HAIRED GENTLEMAN. And may one never overstep the mark a little bit, Madame Bertha? Not the least little bit?

MRS. SØRBY. Not in any respect whatsoever, Mr. Balle.

(Most of the Guests have assembled in the study; servants hand round glasses of punch.)

WERLE *(to Hialmar, who is standing beside a table)*. What are you studying so intently, Ekdal?

HIALMAR. Only an album, Mr. Werle.

THE THIN-HAIRED GENTLEMAN *(who is wandering about)*. Ah, photographs! They are quite in your line of course.

THE FLABBY GENTLEMAN *(in an arm-chair)*. Haven't you brought any of your own with you?

HIALMAR. No, I haven't.

THE FLABBY GENTLEMAN. You ought to have; it's very good for the digestion to sit and look at pictures.

THE THIN-HAIRED GENTLEMAN. And it contributes to the entertainment, you know.

THE SHORT-SIGHTED GENTLEMAN. And all contributions are thankfully received.

MRS. SØRBY. The Chamberlains think that when one is invited out to dinner, one ought to exert oneself a little in return, Mr. Ekdal.

THE FLABBY GENTLEMAN. Where one dines so well, that duty becomes a pleasure.

THE THIN-HAIRED GENTLEMAN. And when it's a case of the struggle for existence, you know . . .

MRS. SØRBY. I quite agree with you!

(They continue the conversation, with laughter and joking.)

GREGERS *(softly)*. You must join in, Hialmar.

HIALMAR *(writhing)*. What am I to talk about?

THE FLABBY GENTLEMAN. Don't you think, Mr. Werle, that Tokay may be considered one of the more wholesome sorts of wine?

WERLE *(by the fire)*. I can answer for the Tokay you had to-day, at any rate; it's of one of the very finest seasons. Of course you would notice that.

THE FLABBY GENTLEMAN. Yes, it had a remarkably delicate flavour.

HIALMAR *(shyly)*. Is there any difference between the seasons?

THE FLABBY GENTLEMAN *(laughs)*. Come! That's good!

WERLE *(smiles)*. It really doesn't pay to set fine wine before you.

THE THIN-HAIRED GENTLEMAN. Tokay is like photographs, Mr. Ekdal: they both need sunshine. Am I not right?

HIALMAR. Yes, light is important no doubt.

MRS. SØRBY. And it's exactly the same with Chamberlains—they, too, depend very much on sunshine,[1] as the saying is.

[1] The "sunshine" of Court favour.

THE THIN-HAIRED GENTLEMAN. Oh fie! That's a very threadbare sarcasm!

THE SHORT-SIGHTED GENTLEMAN. Mrs. Sørby is coming out . . .

THE FLABBY GENTLEMAN. . . . and at our expense, too. *(Holds up his finger reprovingly.)* Oh, Madame Bertha, Madame Bertha!

MRS. SØRBY. Yes, and there's not the least doubt that the seasons differ greatly. The old vintages are the finest.

THE SHORT-SIGHTED GENTLEMAN. Do you reckon me among the old vintages?

MRS. SØRBY. Oh, far from it.

THE THIN-HAIRED GENTLEMAN. There now! But *me,* dear Mrs. Sørby . . . ?

THE FLABBY GENTLEMAN. Yes, and me? What vintage should you say that we belong to?

MRS. SØRBY. Why, to the sweet vintages, gentlemen. *(She sips a glass of punch. The Gentlemen laugh and flirt with her.)*

WERLE. Mrs. Sørby can always find a loop-hole—when she wants to. Fill your glasses, gentlemen! Pettersen, will you see to it . . . ! Gregers, suppose we have a glass together. *(Gregers does not move.)* Won't you join us, Ekdal? I found no opportunity of drinking with you at table.

(Gråberg, the Bookkeeper, looks in at the baize door.)

GRÅBERG. Excuse me, sir, but I can't get out.

WERLE. Have you been locked in again?

GRÅBERG. Yes, and Flakstad has carried off the keys.

WERLE. Well, you can pass out this way.

GRÅBERG. But there's some one else . . .

WERLE. All right; come through, both of you. Don't be afraid.

(Gråberg and Old Ekdal come out of the office.)

WERLE *(involuntarily).* Ugh!

(The laughter and talk among the Guests cease. Hialmar starts at the sight of his father, puts down his glass, and turns towards the fireplace.)

EKDAL *(does not look up, but makes little bows to both sides as he*

passes, murmuring). Beg pardon, come the wrong way. Door locked
—door locked. Beg pardon.

(He and Gråberg go out by the back, to the right.)

WERLE *(between his teeth).* That idiot Gråberg!

GREGERS *(open-mouthed and staring, to Hialmar).* Why surely that
wasn't . . . !

THE FLABBY GENTLEMAN. What's the matter? Who was it?

GREGERS. Oh, nobody, only the bookkeeper and some one with him.

THE SHORT-SIGHTED GENTLEMAN *(to Hialmar).* Did *you* know that
man?

HIALMAR. I don't know—I didn't notice . . .

THE FLABBY GENTLEMAN. What the deuce has come over every one?

(He joins another group who are talking softly.)

MRS. SØRBY *(whispers to the Servant).* Give him something to take
with him;—something good, mind.

PETTERSEN *(nods).* I'll see to it. *(Goes out.)*

GREGERS *(softly and with emotion, to Hialmar).* So that was really he!

HIALMAR. Yes.

GREGERS. And you could stand there and deny that you knew him!

HIALMAR *(whispers vehemently).* But how *could* I . . . !

GREGERS. . . . acknowledge your own father?

HIALMAR *(with pain).* Oh, if you were in my place . . .

*(The conversation among the Guests, which has been carried on in
a low tone, now swells into constrained joviality.)*

THE THIN-HAIRED GENTLEMAN *(approaching Hialmar and Gregers in
a friendly manner).* Aha! Reviving old college memories, eh? Don't
you smoke, Mr. Ekdal? May I give you a light? Oh, by-the-bye, we
mustn't . . .

HIALMAR. No, thank you, I won't . . .

THE FLABBY GENTLEMAN. Haven't you a nice little poem you could
recite to us, Mr. Ekdal? You used to recite so charmingly.

HIALMAR. I am sorry I can't remember anything.

THE FLABBY GENTLEMAN. Oh, that's a pity. Well, what shall we do,
Balle? *(Both Gentlemen move away and pass into the other room.)*

HIALMAR *(gloomily)*. Gregers—I am going! When a man has felt the crushing hand of Fate, you see ... Say good-bye to your father for me.

GREGERS. Yes, yes. Are you going straight home?

HIALMAR. Yes. Why?

GREGERS. Oh, because I may perhaps look in on you later.

HIALMAR. No, you mustn't do that. You must not come to my home. Mine is a melancholy abode, Gregers; especially after a splendid banquet like this. We can always arrange to meet somewhere in the town.

MRS. SØRBY *(who has quietly approached)*. Are you going, Ekdal?

HIALMAR. Yes.

MRS. SØRBY. Remember me to Gina.

HIALMAR. Thanks.

MRS. SØRBY. And say I am coming up to see her one of these days.

HIALMAR. Yes, thank you. *(To Gregers.)* Stay here; I will slip out unobserved. *(He saunters away, then into the other room, and so out to the right.)*

MRS. SØRBY *(softly to the Servant, who has come back)*. Well, did you give the old man something?

PETTERSEN. Yes; I sent him off with a bottle of cognac.

MRS. SØRBY. Oh, you might have thought of something better than that.

PETTERSEN. Oh no, Mrs. Sørby; cognac is what he likes best in the world.

THE FLABBY GENTLEMAN *(in the doorway with a sheet of music in his hand)*. Shall we play a duet, Mrs. Sørby?

MRS. SØRBY. Yes, suppose we do.

THE GUESTS. Bravo, bravo!

(She goes with all the Guests through the back room, out to the right. Gregers remains standing by the fire. Werle is looking for something on the writing-table, and appears to wish that Gregers would go; as Gregers does not move, Werle goes towards the door.)

GREGERS. Father, won't you stay a moment?

WERLE *(stops)*. What is it?

GREGERS. I must have a word with you.

WERLE. Can it not wait till we are alone?

GREGERS. No, it cannot; for perhaps we shall never be alone together.

WERLE *(drawing nearer)*. What do you mean by that?

(During what follows, the pianoforte is faintly heard from the distant music-room.)

GREGERS. How has that family been allowed to go so miserably to the wall?

WERLE. You mean the Ekdals, I suppose.

GREGERS. Yes, I mean the Ekdals. Lieutenant Ekdal was once so closely associated with you.

WERLE. Much too closely; I have felt that to my cost for many a year. It is thanks to him that I—yes *I*—have had a kind of slur cast upon my reputation.

GREGERS *(softly)*. Are you sure that *he* alone was to blame?

WERLE. Who else do you suppose . . . ?

GREGERS. You and he acted together in that affair of the forests . . .

WERLE. But was it not Ekdal that drew the map of the tracts we had bought—that fraudulent map! It was he who felled all that timber illegally on Government ground. In fact, the whole management was in his hands. I was quite in the dark as to what Lieutenant Ekdal was doing.

GREGERS. Lieutenant Ekdal himself seems to have been very much in the dark as to what he was doing.

WERLE. That may be. But the fact remains that he was found guilty and I acquitted.

GREGERS. Yes, I know that nothing was proved against you.

WERLE. Acquittal is acquittal. Why do you rake up these old miseries that turned my hair grey before its time? Is that the sort of thing you have been brooding over up there, all these years? I can assure you, Gregers, here in the town the whole story has been forgotten long ago—so far as *I* am concerned.

GREGERS. But that unhappy Ekdal family . . .

WERLE. What would you have had me do for the people? When Ekdal came out of prison he was a broken-down being, past all help. There are people in the world who dive to the bottom the moment they get a couple of slugs in their body, and never come to the surface again. You may take my word for it, Gregers, I have done all I could without positively laying myself open to all sorts of suspicion and gossip . . .

GREGERS. Suspicion . . . ? Oh, I see.

WERLE. I have given Ekdal copying to do for the office, and I pay him far, far more for it than his work is worth . . .

GREGERS *(without looking at him)*. H'm; *that* I don't doubt.

WERLE. You laugh? Do you think I am not telling you the truth? Well, I certainly can't refer you to my books, for I never enter payments of that sort.

GREGERS *(smiles coldly)*. No, there are certain payments it is best to keep no account of.

WERLE *(taken aback)*. What do you mean by *that?*

GREGERS *(mustering up courage)*. Have you entered what it cost you to have Hialmar Ekdal taught photography?

WERLE. I? How "entered" it?

GREGERS. I have learnt that it was you who paid for his training. And I have learnt, too, that it was you who enabled him to set up house so comfortably.

WERLE. Well, and yet you can talk as though I had done nothing for the Ekdals! I can assure you these people have cost me enough in all conscience.

GREGERS. Have you entered any of these expenses in your books?

WERLE. Why do you ask?

GREGERS. Oh, I have my reasons. Now tell me: when you interested yourself so warmly in your old friend's son—it was just before his marriage, was it not?

WERLE. Why, deuce take it—after all these years, how can I . . . ?

GREGERS. You wrote me a letter about that time—a business letter, of

course; and in a postscript you mentioned—quite briefly—that Hialmar Ekdal had married a Miss Hansen.

WERLE. Yes, that was quite right. That was her name.

GREGERS. But you did not mention that this Miss Hansen was Gina
Hansen—our former housekeeper.

WERLE *(with a forced laugh of derision)*. No; to tell the truth, it
didn't occur to me that you were so particularly interested in our
former housekeeper.

GREGERS. No more I was. But *(lowers his voice)* there were others in
this house who *were* particularly interested in her.

WERLE. What do you mean by that? *(Flaring up.)* You are not alluding to me, I hope?

GREGERS *(softly but firmly)*. Yes, I am alluding to you.

WERLE. And you dare . . . ! You presume to . . . ! How can that un-
grateful hound—that photographer fellow—how dare he go making
such insinuations!

GREGERS. Hialmar has never breathed a word about this. I don't
believe he has the faintest suspicion of such a thing.

WERLE. Then where have you got it from? Who can have put such
notions in your head?

GREGERS. My poor unhappy mother told me; and that the very last
time I saw her.

WERLE. Your mother! I might have known as much! You and she—
you always held together. It was she who turned you against me,
from the first.

GREGERS. No, it was all that she had to suffer and submit to, until she
broke down and came to such a pitiful end.

WERLE. Oh, she had nothing to suffer or submit to; not more than
most people, at all events. But there's no getting on with morbid,
overstrained creatures—that I have learnt to my cost.—And you
could go on nursing such a suspicion—burrowing into all sorts of
old rumours and slanders against your own father! I must say,
Gregers, I really think that at your age you might find something
more useful to do.

GREGERS. Yes, it is high time.

WERLE. Then perhaps your mind would be easier than it seems to be now. What can be your object in remaining up at the works, year out and year in, drudging away like a common clerk, and not drawing a farthing more than the ordinary monthly wage? It is downright folly.

GREGERS. Ah, if I were only sure of *that.*

WERLE. I understand you well enough. You want to be independent; you won't be beholden to me for anything. Well, now there happens to be an opportunity for you to become independent, your own master in everything.

GREGERS. Indeed? In what way . . . ?

WERLE. When I wrote you insisting on your coming to town at once —h'm . . .

GREGERS. Yes, what is it you really want of me? I have been waiting all day to know.

WERLE. I want to propose that you should enter the firm, as partner.

GREGERS. I? Join your firm? As partner?

WERLE. Yes. It would not involve our being constantly together. You could take over the business here in town, and I should move up to the works.

GREGERS. *You* would?

WERLE. The fact is, I am not so fit for work as I once was. I am obliged to spare my eyes, Gregers; they have begun to trouble me.

GREGERS. They have always been weak.

WERLE. Not as they are now. And besides, circumstances might possibly make it desirable for me to live up there—for a time, at any rate.

GREGERS. That is certainly quite a new idea to me.

WERLE. Listen, Gregers: there are many things that stand between us; but we are father and son after all. We ought surely to be able to come to some sort of understanding with each other.

GREGERS. Outwardly, you mean, of course?

WERLE. Well, even that would be something. Think it over, Gregers. Don't you think it ought to be possible? Eh?

GREGERS *(looking at him coldly)*. There is something behind all this.

WERLE. How so?

GREGERS. You want to make use of me in some way.

WERLE. In such a close relationship as ours, the one can always be useful to the other.

GREGERS. Yes, so people say.

WERLE. I want very much to have you at home with me for a time. I am a lonely man, Gregers; I have always felt lonely, all my life through; but most of all now that I am getting up in years. I feel the need of some one about me ...

GREGERS. You have Mrs. Sørby.

WERLE. Yes, I have her; and she has become, I may say, almost indispensable to me. She is lively and even-tempered; she brightens up the house; and that is a very great thing for me.

GREGERS. Well then, you have everything just as you wish it.

WERLE. Yes, but I am afraid it can't last. A woman so situated may easily find herself in a false position, in the eyes of the world. For that matter it does a man no good, either.

GREGERS. Oh, when a man gives such dinners as you give, he can risk a great deal.

WERLE. Yes, but how about the woman, Gregers? I fear she won't accept the situation much longer; and even if she did—even if, out of attachment to me, she were to take her chance of gossip and scandal and all that ... ? Do you think, Gregers—you with your strong sense of justice ...

GREGERS *(interrupts him)*. Tell me in one word: are you thinking of marrying her?

WERLE. Suppose I were thinking of it? What then?

GREGERS. That's what I say: what then?

WERLE. Should you be inflexibly opposed to it?

GREGERS. Not at all. Not by any means.

WERLE. I just was not sure whether your devotion to your mother's memory ...

GREGERS. I am not overstrained.

WERLE. Well, whatever you may or may not be, at all events you have lifted a great weight from my mind. I am extremely pleased that I can reckon on your concurrence in this matter.

GREGERS *(looking intently at him)*. Now I see the use you want to put me to.

WERLE. Use to put you to? What an expression!

GREGERS. Oh, don't let us be nice in our choice of words—not when we are alone together, at any rate. *(With a short laugh.)* Well well! So this is what made it absolutely essential that I should come to town in person. For the sake of Mrs. Sørby, we are to get up a pretence at family life in the house—a tableau of filial affection! That will be something new indeed.

WERLE. How dare you speak in that tone!

GREGERS. Was there ever any family life here? Never since I can remember. But now, forsooth, your plans demand something of the sort. No doubt it will have an excellent effect when it is reported that the son has hastened home, on the wings of filial piety, to the grey-haired father's wedding-feast. What will then remain of all the rumours as to the wrongs the poor dead mother had to submit to? Not a vestige. Her son annihilates them at one stroke.

WERLE. Gregers—I believe there is no one in the world you detest as you do me.

GREGERS *(softly)*. I have seen you at too close quarters.

WERLE. You have seen me with your mother's eyes. *(Lowers his voice a little.)* But you should remember that her eyes were—clouded now and then.

GREGERS *(quivering)*. I see what you are hinting at. But who was to blame for mother's unfortunate weakness? Why you, and all those . . . ! The last of them was this woman that you palmed off upon Hialmar Ekdal, when you were . . . Ugh!

WERLE *(shrugs his shoulders)*. Word for word as if it were your mother speaking!

GREGERS *(without heeding)*. And there he is now, with his great, confiding, childlike mind, compassed about with all this treachery—

living under the same roof with such a creature, and never dreaming that what he calls his home is built upon a lie! *(Comes a step nearer.)* When I look back upon your past, I seem to see a battle-field with shattered lives on every hand.

WERLE. I begin to think the chasm that divides us is too wide.

GREGERS *(bowing, with self-command).* So I have observed; and there-fore I take my hat and go.

WERLE. You are going! Out of the house?

GREGERS. Yes. For at last I see my mission in life.

WERLE. What mission?

GREGERS. You would only laugh if I told you.

WERLE. A lonely man doesn't laugh so easily, Gregers.

GREGERS *(pointing towards the background).* Look, father,—the Cham-berlains are playing blind-man's-buff with Mrs. Sørby.—Good-night and good-bye.

(He goes out by the back to the right. Sounds of laughter and merri-ment from the Company, who are now visible in the other room.)

WERLE *(muttering contemptuously after Gregers).* Ha . . . ! Poor wretch —and he says he is not overstrained!

ACT SECOND

Hialmar Ekdal's studio, a good-sized room, evidently in the top storey of the building. On the right, a sloping roof of large panes of glass, half-covered by a blue curtain. In the right-hand corner, at the back, the entrance door; farther forward, on the same side, a door leading to the sitting-room. Two doors on the opposite side, and between them an iron stove. At the back, a wide double sliding-door. The studio is plainly but comfortably fitted up and furnished. Between the doors on the right, standing out a little from the wall, a sofa with a table and some chairs; on the table a lighted lamp with a shade; beside the stove an old arm-chair. Photographic instruments and apparatus of different kinds lying about the room. Against the back wall, to the left of the double door, stands a bookcase containing a few books, boxes, and bottles of chemicals, instruments, tools, and other objects. Photographs and small articles, such as camel's-hair pencils, paper, and so forth, lie on the table. Gina Ekdal sits on a chair by the table, sewing. Hedvig is sitting on the sofa, with her hands shading her eyes and her thumbs in her ears, reading a book.

GINA *(glances once or twice at Hedvig, as if with secret anxiety; then says):* Hedvig!

(Hedvig does not hear.)

GINA (*repeats more loudly*). Hedvig!

HEDVIG (*takes away her hands and looks up*). Yes, mother?

GINA. Hedvig dear, you mustn't sit reading any longer now.

HEDVIG. Oh mother, mayn't I read a little more? Just a little bit?

GINA. No no, you must put away your book now. Father doesn't like it; he never reads hisself in the evening.

HEDVIG (*shuts the book*). No, father doesn't care much about reading.

GINA (*puts aside her sewing and takes up a lead pencil and a little account-book from the table*). Can you remember how much we paid for the butter to-day?

HEDVIG. It was one crown sixty-five.

GINA. That's right. (*Puts it down.*) It's terrible what a lot of butter we get through in this house. Then there was the smoked sausage, and the cheese—let me see—(*writes*)—and the ham—(*adds up*). Yes, that makes just . . .

HEDVIG. And then the beer.

GINA. Yes, to be sure. (*Writes.*) How it do mount up! But we can't manage with no less.

HEDVIG. And then you and I didn't need anything hot for dinner, as father was out.

GINA. No; that was so much to the good. And then I took eight crowns fifty for the photographs.

HEDVIG. Really! So much as that?

GINA. Exactly eight crowns fifty.

(*Silence. Gina takes up her sewing again, Hedvig takes paper and pencil and begins to draw, shading her eyes with her left hand.*)

HEDVIG. Isn't it jolly to think that father is at Mr. Werle's big dinner-party?

GINA. You know he's not really Mr. Werle's guest. It was the son invited him. (*After a pause.*) We have nothing to do with that Mr. Werle.

HEDVIG. I'm longing for father to come home. He promised to ask Mrs. Sørby for something nice for me.

GINA. Yes, there's plenty of good things in *that* house, I can tell you.

HEDVIG *(goes on drawing)*. And I believe I'm a little hungry too.

(Old Ekdal, with the paper parcel under his arm and another parcel in his coat pocket, comes in by the entrance door.)

GINA. How late you are to-day, grandfather!

EKDAL. They had locked the office door. Had to wait in Gråberg's room. And then they let me through—h'm.

HEDVIG. Did you get some more copying to do, grandfather?

EKDAL. This whole packet. Just look.

GINA. That's capital.

HEDVIG. And you have another parcel in your pocket.

EKDAL. Eh? Oh never mind, that's nothing. *(Puts his stick away in a corner.)* This work will keep me going a long time, Gina. *(Opens one of the sliding-doors in the back wall a little.)* Hush! *(Peeps into the room for a moment, then pushes the door carefully to again.)* Hee-hee! They're fast asleep, all the lot of them. And she's gone into the basket herself. Hee-hee!

HEDVIG. Are you sure she isn't cold in that basket, grandfather?

EKDAL. Not a bit of it! Cold? With all that straw? *(Goes towards the farther door on the left.)* There are matches in here, I suppose.

GINA. The matches is on the drawers.

(Ekdal goes into his room.)

HEDVIG. It's nice that grandfather has got all that copying.

GINA. Yes, poor old father; it means a bit of pocket-money for him.

HEDVIG. And he won't be able to sit the whole forenoon down at that horrid Madam Eriksen's.

GINA. No more he won't.

(Short silence.)

HEDVIG. Do you suppose they are still at the dinner-table?

GINA. Goodness knows; as like as not.

HEDVIG. Think of all the delicious things father is having to eat! I'm certain he'll be in splendid spirits when he comes. Don't you think so, mother?

GINA. Yes; and if only we could tell him that we'd got the room let . . .

HEDVIG. But we don't need that this evening.

GINA. Oh, we'd be none the worse of it, I can tell you. It's no use to us as it is.

HEDVIG. I mean we don't need it this evening, for father will be in a good humour at any rate. It is best to keep the letting of the room for another time.

GINA *(looks across at her)*. You like having some good news to tell father when he comes home in the evening?

HEDVIG. Yes; for then things are pleasanter somehow.

GINA *(thinking to herself)*. Yes, yes, there's something in that.

(Old Ekdal comes in again and is going out by the foremost door to the left.)

GINA *(half turning in her chair)*. Do you want something out of the kitchen, grandfather?

EKDAL. Yes, yes, I do. Don't you trouble. *(Goes out.)*

GINA. He's not poking away at the fire, is he? *(Waits a moment.)* Hedvig, go and see what he's about.

(Ekdal comes in again with a small jug of steaming hot water.)

HEDVIG. Have you been getting some hot water, grandfather?

EKDAL. Yes, hot water. Want it for something. Want to write, and the ink has got as thick as porridge—h'm.

GINA. But you'd best have your supper, first, grandfather. It's laid in there.

EKDAL. Can't be bothered with supper, Gina. Very busy, I tell you. No one's to come to my room. No one—h'm.

(He goes into his room; Gina and Hedvig look at each other.)

GINA *(softly)*. Can you imagine where he's got money from?

HEDVIG. From Gråberg, perhaps.

GINA. Not a bit of it. Gråberg always sends the money to me.

HEDVIG. Then he must have got a bottle on credit somewhere.

GINA. Poor grandfather, who'd give him credit?

(Hialmar Ekdal, in an overcoat and grey felt hat, comes in from the right.)

GINA *(throws down her sewing and rises)*. Why, Ekdal. Is that you already?

HEDVIG *(at the same time jumping up)*. Fancy your coming so soon, father!

HIALMAR *(taking off his hat)*. Yes, most of the people were coming away.

HEDVIG. So early?

HIALMAR. Yes, it was a dinner-party, you know. *(Is taking off his over-coat.)*

GINA. Let me help you.

HEDVIG. Me too.

(They draw off his coat; Gina hangs it up on the back wall.)

HEDVIG. Were there many people there, father?

HIALMAR. Oh no, not many. We were about twelve or fourteen at table.

GINA. And you had some talk with them all?

HIALMAR. Oh yes, a little; but Gregers took me up most of the time.

GINA. Is Gregers as ugly as ever?

HIALMAR. Well, he's not very much to look at. Hasn't that old man come home?

HEDVIG. Yes, grandfather is in his room, writing.

HIALMAR. Did he say anything?

GINA. No, what should he say?

HIALMAR. Didn't he say anything about . . . ? I heard something about his having been with Gråberg. I'll go in and see him for a moment.

GINA. No, no, better not.

HIALMAR. Why not? Did he say he didn't want me to go in?

GINA. I don't think he wants to see *nobody* this evening . . .

HEDVIG *(making signs)*. H'm—h'm!

GINA *(not noticing)*. . . . he has been in to fetch hot water . . .

HIALMAR. Aha! Then he's . . .

GINA. Yes, I suppose so.

HIALMAR. Oh God! my poor old white-haired father!—Well, well; there let him sit and get all the enjoyment he can.

(Old Ekdal, in an indoor coat and with a lighted pipe, comes from his room.)

EKDAL. Got home? Thought it was you I heard talking.

HIALMAR. Yes, I have just come.

EKDAL. You didn't see me, did you?

HIALMAR. No; but they told me you had passed through—so I thought I would follow you.

EKDAL. H'm, good of you, Hialmar.—Who were they, all those fellows?

HIALMAR. Oh, all sorts of people. There was Chamberlain Flor, and Chamberlain Balle, and Chamberlain Kaspersen, and Chamberlain —this, that, and the other—I don't know who all . . .

EKDAL *(nodding)*. Hear that, Gina! Chamberlains every one of them!

GINA. Yes, I hear as they're terrible genteel in that house nowadays.

HEDVIG. Did the Chamberlains sing, father? Or did they read aloud?

HIALMAR. No, they only talked nonsense. They wanted *me* to recite something for them; but I knew better than that.

EKDAL. You weren't to be persuaded, eh?

GINA. Oh, you might have done it.

HIALMAR. No; one mustn't be at everybody's beck and call. *(Walks about the room.)* That's not *my* way, at any rate.

EKDAL. No no; Hialmar's not to be had for the asking, he isn't.

HIALMAR. I don't see why *I* should bother myself to entertain people on the rare occasions when I go into society. Let the others exert themselves. These fellows go from one great dinner-table to the next and gorge and guzzle day out and day in. It's for them to bestir themselves and do something in return for all the good feeding they get.

GINA. But you didn't say that?

HIALMAR *(humming)*. Ho-ho-ho . . . ; faith, I gave them a bit of my mind.

EKDAL. Not the Chamberlains?

HIALMAR. Oh, why not? *(Lightly.)* After that, we had a little discussion about Tokay.

EKDAL. Tokay! There's a fine wine for you!

HIALMAR *(comes to a standstill)*. It *may* be a fine wine. But of course you know the vintages differ; it all depends on how much sunshine the grapes have had.

GINA. Why, you know everything, Ekdal.

EKDAL. And did they dispute that?

HIALMAR. They tried to; but they were requested to observe that it was just the same with Chamberlains—that with them, too, different batches were of different qualities.

GINA. What things you do think of!

EKDAL. Hee-hee! So they got that in their pipes too?

HIALMAR. Right in their teeth.

EKDAL. Do you hear that, Gina? He said it right in the very teeth of all the Chamberlains.

GINA. Fancy . . . ! Right in their teeth!

HIALMAR. Yes, but I don't want it talked about. One doesn't speak of such things. The whole affair passed off quite amicably of course.

They were nice, genial fellows; I didn't want to wound *them* — not I!

EKDAL. Right in their teeth, though . . . !

HEDVIG *(caressingly)*. How nice it is to see you in a dress-coat! It suits you so well, father.

HIALMAR. Yes, don't you think so? And this one really sits to perfection. It fits almost as if it had been made for me;—a little tight in the arm-holes perhaps;—help me, Hedvig. *(Takes off the coat.)* I think I'll put on my jacket. Where is my jacket, Gina?

GINA. Here it is. *(Brings the jacket and helps him.)*

HIALMAR. That's it! Don't forget to send the coat back to Molvik first thing to-morrow morning.

GINA *(laying it away)*. I'll be sure and see to it.

HIALMAR *(stretching himself)*. After all, there's a more homely feeling about this. A free-and-easy indoor costume suits my whole personality better. Don't you think so, Hedvig?

HEDVIG. Yes, father.

HIALMAR. When I loosen my necktie into a pair of flowing ends—like this—eh?

HEDVIG. Yes, that goes so well with your moustache and the sweep of your curls.

HIALMAR. I should not call them curls exactly; I should rather say locks.

HEDVIG. Yes, they are too big for curls.

HIALMAR. Locks describes them better.

HEDVIG *(after a pause, twitching his jacket)*. Father.

HIALMAR. Well, what is it?

HEDVIG. Oh, you know very well.

HIALMAR. No, really I don't . . .

HEDVIG *(half laughing, half whispering)*. Oh yes, father; now don't tease me any longer!

HIALMAR. Why, what *do* you mean?

HEDVIG *(shaking him)*. Oh what nonsense; come, where are they, father? All the good things you promised me, you know?

HIALMAR. Oh—if I haven't forgotten all about them!

HEDVIG. Now you're only teasing me, father! Oh, it's too bad of you! Where have you put them?

HIALMAR. No, I positively forgot to get anything. But wait a little! I have something else for you, Hedvig. *(Goes and searches in the pocket of the coat.)*

HEDVIG *(skipping and clapping her hands)*. Oh mother, mother!

GINA. There, you see; if you only give him time . . .

HIALMAR *(with a paper)*. Look, here it is.

HEDVIG. That? Why, that's only a paper.

HIALMAR. That is the bill of fare, my dear; the whole bill of fare. Here you see: "Menu"—that means bill of fare.

HEDVIG. Haven't you anything else?

HIALMAR. I forgot the other things, I tell you. But you may take my word for it, these dainties are very unsatisfying. Sit down at the table and read the bill of fare, and then I'll describe to you how the dishes taste. Here you are, Hedvig.

HEDVIG *(gulping down her tears)*. Thank you.

(She seats herself, but does not read; Gina makes signs to her; Hialmar notices it.)

HIALMAR *(pacing up and down the room)*. It's monstrous what absurd things the father of a family is expected to think of; and if he forgets the smallest trifle, he is treated to sour faces at once. Well, well, one gets used to that too. *(Stops near the stove, by the old man's chair.)* Have you peeped in there this evening, father?

EKDAL. Yes, to be sure I have. She's gone into the basket.

HIALMAR. Ah, she *has* gone into the basket. Then she's beginning to get used to it.

EKDAL. Yes; just as I prophesied. But you know there are still a few little things . . .

HIALMAR. A few improvements, yes.

EKDAL. They've *got* to be made, you know.

HIALMAR. Yes, let us have a talk about the improvements, father. Come, let us sit on the sofa.

EKDAL. All right. H'm—think I'll just fill my pipe first. Must clean it out, too. H'm. *(He goes into his room.)*

GINA *(smiling to Hialmar).* His pipe!

HIALMAR. Oh yes yes, Gina; let him alone—the poor shipwrecked old man.—Yes, these improvements—we had better get them out of hand to-morrow.

GINA. You'll hardly have time to-morrow, Ekdal.

HEDVIG *(interposing).* Oh yes he will, mother!

GINA. . . . for remember them prints that has to be retouched; they've sent for them time after time.

HIALMAR. There now! those prints again! I shall get them finished all right! Have any new orders come in?

GINA. No, worse luck; to-morrow I have nothing but those two sittings, you know.

HIALMAR. Nothing else? Oh no, if people won't set about things with a will . . .

GINA. But what more can I do? Don't I advertise in the papers as much as we can afford?

HIALMAR. Yes, the papers, the papers; you see how much good *they* do. And I suppose no one has been to look at the room either?

GINA. No, not yet.

HIALMAR. That was only to be expected. If people won't keep their eyes open . . . Nothing can be done without a real effort, Gina!

HEDVIG *(going towards him).* Shall I fetch you the flute, father?

HIALMAR. No; no flute for me; *I* want no pleasures in this world. *(Pacing about.)* Yes, indeed I will work to-morrow; you shall see if I don't. You may be sure I shall work as long as my strength holds out.

GINA. But my dear good Ekdal, I didn't mean it in *that* way.

HEDVIG. Father, mayn't I bring in a bottle of beer?

HIALMAR. No, certainly not. I require nothing, nothing . . . *(Comes to a standstill.)* Beer? Was it beer you were talking about?

HEDVIG *(cheerfully).* Yes, father; beautiful fresh beer.

HIALMAR. Well—since you insist upon it, you may bring in a bottle.

GINA. Yes, do; and we'll be nice and cosy.

(*Hedvig runs towards the kitchen door.*)

HIALMAR (*by the stove, stops her, looks at her, puts his arm round her neck and presses her to him*). Hedvig, Hedvig!

HEDVIG (*with tears of joy*). My dear, kind father!

HIALMAR. No, don't call me that. Here have I been feasting at the rich man's table,—battening at the groaning board . . . ! And I couldn't even . . . !

GINA (*sitting at the table*). Oh nonsense, nonsense, Ekdal.

HIALMAR. It's not nonsense! And yet you mustn't be too hard upon me. You know that I love you for all that.

HEDVIG (*throwing her arms round him*). And we love you, oh so dearly, father!

HIALMAR. And if I am unreasonable once in a while,—why then—you must remember that I am a man beset by a host of cares. There, there! (*Dries his eyes.*) No beer at such a moment as this. Give me the flute.

(*Hedvig runs to the bookcase and fetches it.*)

HIALMAR. Thanks! That's right. With my flute in my hand and you two at my side—ah . . . !

(*Hedvig seats herself at the table near Gina; Hialmar paces backwards and forwards, pipes up vigorously, and plays a Bohemian peasant dance, but in a slow plaintive tempo, and with sentimental expression.*)

HIALMAR (*breaking off the melody, holds out his left hand to Gina, and says with emotion*): Our roof may be poor and humble, Gina; but it is home. And with all my heart I say: here dwells my happiness. (*He begins to play again; almost immediately after, a knocking is heard at the entrance door.*)

GINA (*rising*). Hush, Ekdal,—I think there's some one at the door.

HIALMAR (*laying the flute on the bookcase*). There! Again!

(*Gina goes and opens the door.*)

GREGERS WERLE (*in the passage*). Excuse me . . .

GINA (*starting back slightly*). Oh!

GREGERS. . . . does not Mr. Ekdal, the photographer, live here?

GINA. Yes, he does.

HIALMAR *(going towards the door)*. Gregers! You here after all? Well, come in then.

GREGERS *(coming in)*. I told you I would come and look you up.

HIALMAR. But this evening . . . ? Have you left the party?

GREGERS. I have left both the party and my father's house.—Good evening, Mrs. Ekdal. I don't know whether you recognise me?

GINA. Oh yes; it's not difficult to know young Mr. Werle again.

GREGERS. No, I am like my mother; and no doubt you remember her.

HIALMAR. Left your father's house, did you say?

GREGERS. Yes, I have gone to a hotel.

HIALMAR. Indeed. Well, since you're here, take off your coat and sit down.

GREGERS. Thanks.

(He takes off his overcoat. He is now dressed in a plain grey suit of a countrified cut.)

HIALMAR. Here, on the sofa. Make yourself comfortable.

(Gregers seats himself on the sofa; Hialmar takes a chair at the table.)

GREGERS *(looking around him)*. So these are your quarters, Hialmar—this is your home.

HIALMAR. This is the studio, as you see . . .

GINA. But it's the largest of our rooms, so we generally sit here.

HIALMAR. We used to live in a better place; but this flat has one great advantage: there are such capital outer rooms . . .

GINA. And we have a room on the other side of the passage that we can let.

GREGERS *(to Hialmar)*. Ah—so you have lodgers too?

HIALMAR. No, not yet. They're not so easy to find, you see; you have to keep your eyes open. *(To Hedvig.)* What about that beer, eh?

(Hedvig nods and goes out into the kitchen.)

GREGERS. So that is your daughter?

HIALMAR. Yes, that is Hedvig.

GREGERS. And she is your only child?

HIALMAR. Yes, the only one. She is the joy of our lives, and—*(lowering his voice)*—at the same time our deepest sorrow, Gregers.

GREGERS. What do you mean?

HIALMAR. She is in serious danger of losing her eyesight.

GREGERS. Becoming blind?

HIALMAR. Yes. Only the first symptoms have appeared as yet, and she may not feel it much for some time. But the doctor has warned us. It is coming, inexorably.

GREGERS. What a terrible misfortune! How do you account for it?

HIALMAR *(sighs)*. Hereditary, no doubt.

GREGERS *(starting)*. Hereditary?

GINA. Ekdal's mother had weak eyes.

HIALMAR. Yes, so my father says; I can't remember her.

GREGERS. Poor child! And how does she take it?

HIALMAR. Oh, you can imagine we haven't the heart to tell her of it. She dreams of no danger. Gay and careless and chirping like a little bird, she flutters onward into a life of endless night. *(Overcome.)* Oh, it is cruelly hard on me, Gregers.

(Hedvig brings a tray with beer and glasses, which she sets upon the table.)

HIALMAR *(stroking her hair)*. Thanks, thanks, Hedvig.

(Hedvig puts her arm round his neck and whispers in his ear.)

HIALMAR. No, no bread and butter just now. *(Looks up.)* But perhaps you would like some, Gregers.

GREGERS *(with a gesture of refusal)*. No, no thank you.

HIALMAR *(still melancholy)*. Well, you can bring in a little all the same. If you have a crust, that is all I want. And plenty of butter on it, mind.

(Hedvig nods gaily and goes out into the kitchen again.)

GREGERS *(who has been following her with his eyes)*. She seems quite strong and healthy otherwise.

GINA. Yes. In other ways there's nothing amiss with her, thank goodness.

GREGERS. She promises to be very like you, Mrs. Ekdal. How old is she now?

GINA. Hedvig is close on fourteen; her birthday is the day after to-morrow.

GREGERS. She is pretty tall for her age, then.

GINA. Yes, she's shot up wonderful this last year.

GREGERS. It makes one realise one's own age to see these young people growing up.—How long is it now since you were married?

GINA. We've been married—let me see—just on fifteen years.

GREGERS. Is it so long as that?

GINA *(becomes attentive; looks at him)*. Yes, it is indeed.

HIALMAR. Yes, so it is. Fifteen years all but a few months. *(Changing his tone.)* They must have been long years for you, up at the works, Gregers.

GREGERS. They seemed long while I was living them; now they are over, I hardly know how the time has gone.

(Old Ekdal comes from his room without his pipe, but with his old-fashioned uniform cap on his head; his gait is somewhat unsteady.)

EKDAL. Come now, Hialmar, let's sit down and have a good talk about this—h'm—what was it again?

HIALMAR *(going towards him)*. Father, we have a visitor here—Gregers Werle.—I don't know if you remember him.

EKDAL *(looking at Gregers, who has risen)*. Werle? Is that the son? What does he want with me?

HIALMAR. Nothing; it's me he has come to see.

EKDAL. Oh! Then there's nothing wrong?

HIALMAR. No, no, of course not.

EKDAL *(with a large gesture)*. Not that I'm afraid, you know; but . . .

GREGERS *(goes over to him)*. I bring you a greeting from your old hunting-grounds, Lieutenant Ekdal.

EKDAL. Hunting-grounds?

GREGERS. Yes, up in Høidal, about the works, you know.

EKDAL. Oh, up there. Yes, I knew all those places well in the old days.

GREGERS. You were a great sportsman then.

EKDAL. So I was, I don't deny it. You're looking at my uniform cap. I don't ask anybody's leave to wear it in the house. So long as I don't go out in the street with it . . .

(Hedvig brings a plate of bread and butter, which she puts upon the table.)

HIALMAR. Sit down, father, and have a glass of beer. Help yourself, Gregers.

(Ekdal mutters and stumbles over to the sofa. Gregers seats himself on the chair nearest to him, Hialmar on the other side of Gregers. Gina sits a little way from the table, sewing; Hedvig stands beside her father.)

GREGERS. Can you remember, Lieutenant Ekdal, how Hialmar and I used to come up and visit you in the summer and at Christmas?

EKDAL. Did you? No, no, no; I don't remember it. But sure enough I've been a tidy bit of a sportsman in my day. I've shot bears too. I've shot nine of 'em, no less.

GREGERS *(looking sympathetically at him)*. And now you never get any shooting?

EKDAL. Can't just say that, sir. Get a shot now and then perhaps. Of course not in the old way. For the woods you see—the woods, the woods . . . ! *(Drinks.)* Are the woods fine up there now?

GREGERS. Not so fine as in your time. They have been thinned a good deal.

EKDAL. Thinned? *(More softly, and as if afraid.)* It's dangerous work that. Bad things come of it. The woods revenge themselves.

HIALMAR *(filling up his glass)*. Come—a little more, father.

GREGERS. How can a man like you—such a man for the open air—live in the midst of a stuffy town, boxed within four walls?

EKDAL *(laughs quietly and glances at Hialmar)*. Oh, it's not so bad here. Not at all so bad.

GREGERS. But don't you miss all the things that used to be a part of your very being—the cool sweeping breezes, the free life in the woods and on the uplands, among beasts and birds . . . ?

EKDAL *(smiling)*. Hialmar, shall we let him see it?

HIALMAR *(hastily and a little embarrassed)*. Oh no no, father; not this evening.

GREGERS. What does he want to show me?

HIALMAR. Oh, it's only something—you can see it another time.

GREGERS *(continues, to the old man)*. You see I have been thinking, Lieutenant Ekdal, that you should come up with me to the works; I am sure to be going back soon. No doubt you could get some copying there too. And here, you have nothing on earth to interest you—nothing to liven you up.

EKDAL *(stares in astonishment at him)*. Have *I* nothing on earth to . . . !

GREGERS. Of course you have Hialmar; but then he has his own family. And a man like you, who has always had such a passion for what is free and wild . . .

EKDAL *(thumps the table)*. Hialmar, he *shall* see it!

HIALMAR. Oh, do you think it's worth while, father? It's all dark.

EKDAL. Nonsense; it's moonlight. *(Rises.)* He *shall* see it, I tell you. Let me pass! Come and help me, Hialmar.

HEDVIG. Oh yes, do, father!

HIALMAR *(rising)*. Very well then.

GREGERS *(to Gina)*. What is it?

GINA. Oh, nothing so very wonderful, after all.

(Ekdal and Hialmar have gone to the back wall and are each pushing back a side of the sliding door; Hedvig helps the old man; Gregers remains standing by the sofa; Gina sits still and sews. Through the open doorway a large, deep irregular garret is seen with odd nooks and corners; a couple of stove-pipes running through it, from rooms below. There are skylights through which clear moonbeams shine in on some parts of the great room; others lie in deep shadow.)

EKDAL *(to Gregers)*. You may come close up if you like.

GREGERS *(going over to them)*. Why, what is it?

EKDAL. Look for yourself. H'm.

HIALMAR *(somewhat embarrassed)*. This belongs to father, you understand.

GREGERS *(at the door, looks into the garret)*. Why, you keep poultry, Lieutenant Ekdal.

EKDAL. Should think we *did* keep poultry. They've gone to roost now. But you should just see our fowls by daylight, sir!

HEDVIG. And there's a . . .

EKDAL. Sh—sh! don't say anything about it yet.

GREGERS. And you have pigeons too, I see.

EKDAL. Oh yes, haven't we just got pigeons! They have their nest-boxes up there under the roof-tree; for pigeons like to roost high, you see.

HIALMAR. They aren't all common pigeons.

EKDAL. Common! Should think not indeed! We have tumblers, and a pair of pouters, too. But come here! Can you see that hutch down there by the wall?

GREGERS. Yes; what do you use it for?

EKDAL. That's where the rabbits sleep, sir.

GREGERS. Dear me; so you have rabbits too?

EKDAL. Yes, you may take my word for it, we have rabbits! He wants to know if we have rabbits, Hialmar! H'm! But now comes the thing, let me tell you! Here we have it! Move away, Hedvig. Stand here; that's right,—and now look down there.—Don't you see a basket with straw in it?

GREGERS. Yes. And I can see a fowl lying in the basket.

EKDAL. H'm—"a fowl" . . .

GREGERS. Isn't it a duck?

EKDAL *(hurt)*. Why, of course it's a duck.

HIALMAR. But what kind of duck, do you think?

HEDVIG. It's not just a common duck . . .

EKDAL. Sh!

GREGERS. And it's not a Muscovy duck either.

EKDAL. No, Mr.—Werle; it's not a Muscovy duck; for it's a wild duck!

GREGERS. Is it really? A wild duck?

EKDAL. Yes, that's what it is. That "fowl" as you call it—is the wild duck. It's our wild duck, sir.

HEDVIG. My wild duck. It belongs to me.

GREGERS. And can it live up here in the garret? Does it thrive?

EKDAL. Of course it has a trough of water to splash about in, you know.

HIALMAR. Fresh water every other day.

GINA *(turning towards Hialmar)*. But my dear Ekdal, it's getting icy cold here.

EKDAL. H'm, we had better shut up then. It's as well not to disturb their night's rest, too. Close up, Hedvig.

(Hialmar and Hedvig push the garret doors together.)

EKDAL. Another time you shall see her properly. *(Seats himself in the arm-chair by the stove.)* Oh, they're curious things, these wild ducks, I can tell you.

GREGERS. How did you manage to catch it, Lieutenant Ekdal?

EKDAL. *I* didn't catch it. There's a certain man in this town whom we have to thank for it.

GREGERS *(starts slightly)*. That man was not my father, was he?

EKDAL. You've hit it. Your father and no one else. H'm.

HIALMAR. Strange that you should guess that, Gregers.

GREGERS. You were telling me that you owed so many things to my father; and so I thought perhaps . . .

GINA. But we didn't get the duck from Mr. Werle himself . . .

EKDAL. It's Håkon Werle we have to thank for her, all the same, Gina. *(To Gregers.)* He was shooting from a boat, you see, and he brought her down. But your father's sight is not very good now. H'm; she was only wounded.

GREGERS. Ah! She got a couple of slugs in her body, I suppose.

HIALMAR. Yes, two or three.

HEDVIG. She was hit under the wing, so that she couldn't fly.

GREGERS. And I suppose she dived to the bottom, eh?

EKDAL *(sleepily, in a thick voice)*. Of course. Always do that, wild ducks do. They shoot to the bottom as deep as they can get, sir— and bite themselves fast in the tangle and seaweed—and all the devil's own mess that grows down there. And they never come up again.

GREGERS. But *your* wild duck came up again, Lieutenant Ekdal.

EKDAL. He had such an amazingly clever dog, your father had. And that dog—he dived in after the duck and fetched her up again.

GREGERS *(who has turned to Hialmar)*. And then she was sent to you here?

HIALMAR. Not at once; at first your father took her home. But she wouldn't thrive there; so Pettersen was told to put an end to her ...

EKDAL *(half asleep)*. H'm—yes—Pettersen—that ass ...

HIALMAR *(speaking more softly)*. That was how we got her, you see; for father knows Pettersen a little; and when he heard about the wild duck he got him to hand her over to us.

GREGERS. And now she thrives as well as possible in the garret there?

HIALMAR. Yes, wonderfully well. She has got fat. You see, she has lived in there so long now that she has forgotten her natural wild life; and it all depends on *that*.

GREGERS. You are right there, Hialmar. Be sure you never let her get a glimpse of the sky and the sea ... But I mustn't stay any longer; I think your father is asleep.

HIALMAR. Oh, as for that ...

GREGERS. But, by-the-bye—you said you had a room to let—a spare room?

HIALMAR. Yes; what then? Do you know of anybody ... ?

GREGERS. Can *I* have that room?

HIALMAR. You?

GINA. Oh no, Mr. Werle, *you* ...

GREGERS. May I have the room? If so, I'll take possession first thing to-morrow morning.

HIALMAR. Yes, with the greatest pleasure ...

GINA. But, Mr. Werle, I'm sure it's not at all the sort of room for *you*.

HIALMAR. Why, Gina! how can you say that?

GINA. Why, because the room's neither large enough nor light enough, and ...

GREGERS. That really doesn't matter, Mrs. Ekdal.

HIALMAR. I call it quite a nice room, and not at all badly furnished either.

GINA. But remember the pair of them underneath.

GREGERS. What pair?

GINA. Well, there's one as has been a tutor . . .

HIALMAR. That's Molvik—Mr. Molvik, B.A.

GINA. And then there's a doctor, by the name of Relling.

GREGERS. Relling? I know him a little; he practised for a time up in Høidal.

GINA. They're a regular rackety pair, they are. As often as not, they're out on the loose in the evenings; and then they come home at all hours, and they're not always just . . .

GREGERS. One soon gets used to that sort of thing. I daresay I shall be like the wild duck . . .

GINA. H'm; I think you ought to sleep upon it first, anyway.

GREGERS. You seem very unwilling to have me in the house, Mrs. Ekdal.

GINA. Oh no! What makes you think *that?*

HIALMAR. Well, you really behave strangely about it, Gina. *(To Gregers.)* Then I suppose you intend to remain in the town for the present?

GREGERS *(putting on his overcoat).* Yes, now I intend to remain here.

HIALMAR. And yet not at your father's? What do you propose to do, then?

GREGERS. Ah, if I only knew *that,* Hialmar, I shouldn't be so badly off! But when one has the misfortune to be called Gregers—! "Gregers"—and then "Werle" after it; did you ever hear anything so hideous?

HIALMAR. Oh, I don't think so at all.

GREGERS. Ugh! Bah! I feel I should like to spit upon the fellow that answers to such a name. But when a man is once for all doomed to be Gregers—Werle in this world, as I am . . .

HIALMAR *(laughs).* Ha ha! If you weren't Gregers Werle, what would you like to be?

GREGERS. If I could choose, I should like best to be a clever dog.

GINA. A dog!

HEDVIG *(involuntarily)*. Oh no!

GREGERS. Yes, an amazingly clever dog; one that goes to the bottom after wild ducks when they dive and bite themselves fast in tangle and sea-weed, down among the ooze.

HIALMAR. Upon my word now, Gregers—I don't in the least know what you're driving at.

GREGERS. Oh well, you might not be much the wiser if you did. It's understood, then, that I move in early to-morrow morning. *(To Gina.)* I won't give you any trouble; I do everything for myself. *(To Hialmar.)* We can talk about the rest to-morrow.—Good-night, Mrs. Ekdal. *(Nods to Hedvig.)* Good-night.

GINA. Good-night, Mr. Werle.

HEDVIG. Good-night.

HIALMAR *(who has lighted a candle)*. Wait a moment; I must show you a light; the stairs are sure to be dark.

(Gregers and Hialmar go out by the passage door.)

GINA *(looking straight before her, with her sewing in her lap)*. Wasn't that queer-like talk about wanting to be a dog?

HEDVIG. Do you know, mother—I believe he meant something quite different by that.

GINA. Why, what *should* he mean?

HEDVIG. Oh, I don't know; but it seemed to me he meant something different from what he said—all the time.

GINA. Do you think so? Yes, it was sort of queer.

HIALMAR *(comes back)*. The lamp was still burning. *(Puts out the candle and sets it down.)* Ah, now one can get a mouthful of food at last. *(Begins to eat the bread and butter.)* Well, you see, Gina— if only you keep your eyes open . . .

GINA. How, keep your eyes open . . . ?

HIALMAR. Why, haven't we at last had the luck to get the room let? And just think—to a person like Gregers—a good old friend.

GINA. Well, I don't know what to say about it.

HEDVIG. Oh mother, you'll see; it'll be such fun!

HIALMAR. You're very strange. You were so bent upon getting the room let before; and now you don't like it.

GINA. Yes I do, Ekdal; if it had only been to some one else . . . But what do you suppose Mr. Werle will say?

HIALMAR. Old Werle? It doesn't concern him.

GINA. But surely you can see that there's something amiss between them again, or the young man wouldn't be leaving home. You know very well those two can't get on with each other.

HIALMAR. Very likely not, but . . .

GINA. And now Mr. Werle may fancy it's you that has egged him on . . .

HIALMAR. Let him fancy so, then! Mr. Werle has done a great deal for me; far be it from me to deny it. But that doesn't make me everlastingly dependent upon him.

GINA. But my dear Ekdal, maybe grandfather 'll suffer for it. He may lose the little bit of work he gets from Gråberg.

HIALMAR. I could almost say: so much the better! Is it not humiliating for a man like me to see his grey-haired father treated as a pariah? But now I believe the fulness of time is at hand. *(Takes a fresh piece of bread and butter.)* As sure as I have a mission in life, I mean to fulfil it now!

HEDVIG. Oh yes, father, do!

GINA. Hush! Don't wake him!

HIALMAR *(more softly)*. I *will* fulfil, I say. The day shall come when . . . And that is why I say it's a good thing we have let the room; for that makes me more independent. The man who has a mission in life must be independent. *(By the arm-chair, with emotion.)* Poor old white-haired father! Rely on your Hialmar. He has broad shoulders—strong shoulders, at any rate. You shall yet wake up some fine day and . . . *(To Gina.)* Do you not believe it?

GINA *(rising)*. Yes, of course I do; but in the meantime suppose we see about getting him to bed.

HIALMAR. Yes, come.

(They take hold of the old man carefully.)

ACT THIRD

Hialmar Ekdal's studio. It is morning: the daylight shines through the large window in the slanting roof; the curtain is drawn back.

Hialmar is sitting at the table, busy retouching a photograph; several others lie before him. Presently Gina, wearing her hat and cloak, enters by the passage door; she has a covered basket on her arm.

HIALMAR. Back already, Gina?

GINA. Oh yes, one can't let the grass grow under one's feet.

(Sets her basket on a chair, and takes off her things.)

HIALMAR. Did you look in at Gregers' room?

GINA. Yes, that I did. It's a rare sight, I can tell you; he's made a pretty mess to start off with.

HIALMAR. How so?

GINA. He was determined to do everything for himself, he said; so he sets to work to light the stove, and what must he do but screw down the damper till the whole room is full of smoke. Ugh! There was a smell fit to . . .

HIALMAR. Well, really!

GINA. But that's not the worst of it; for then he thinks he'll put out the fire, and goes and empties his water-jug into the stove, and so makes the whole floor one filthy puddle.

HIALMAR. How annoying!

GINA. I've got the porter's wife to clean up after him, pig that he is! But the room won't be fit to live in till the afternoon.

HIALMAR. What's he doing with himself in the meantime?

GINA. He said he was going out for a little while.

HIALMAR. I looked in upon him too, for a moment—after you had gone.

GINA. So I heard. You've asked him to lunch.

HIALMAR. Just to a little bit of early lunch, you know. It's his first day —we can hardly do less. You've got something in the house, I suppose?

GINA. I shall have to find something or other.

HIALMAR. And don't cut it too fine, for I fancy Relling and Molvik are coming up too. I just happened to meet Relling on the stairs, you see; so I had to . . .

GINA. Oh, are we to have those two as well?

HIALMAR. Good Lord—a couple more or less can't make any difference.

OLD EKDAL *(opens his door and looks in).* I say, Hialmar . . . *(Sees Gina.)* Oh!

GINA. Do you want anything, grandfather?

EKDAL. Oh no, it doesn't matter. H'm!

(Retires again.)

GINA *(takes up the basket).* Be sure you see that he doesn't go out.

HIALMAR. All right, all right. And, Gina, a little herring-salad wouldn't be a bad idea; Relling and Molvik were out on the loose again last night.

GINA. If only they don't come before I'm ready for them . . .

HIALMAR. No, of course they won't; take your own time.

GINA. Very well; and meanwhile you can be working a bit.

HIALMAR. Well, I *am* working! I am working as hard as I can!

GINA. Then you'll have that job off your hands, you see.

(She goes out to the kitchen with her basket. Hialmar sits for a time pencilling away at the photograph, in an indolent and listless manner.)

EKDAL *(peeps in, looks round the studio, and says softly):* Are you busy?

HIALMAR. Yes, I'm toiling at these wretched pictures . . .

EKDAL. Well well, never mind,—since you're so busy—h'm!

(He goes out again; the door stands open.)

HIALMAR *(continues for some time in silence; then he lays down his brush and goes over to the door).* Are *you* busy, father?

EKDAL *(in a grumbling tone, within).* If you're busy, I'm busy too. H'm!

HIALMAR. Oh, very well, then.

(Goes to his work again.)

EKDAL *(presently, coming to the door again).* H'm; I say, Hialmar, I'm not so *very* busy, you know.

HIALMAR. I thought you were writing.

EKDAL. Oh, devil take it! can't Gråberg wait a day or two? After all, it's not a matter of life or death.

HIALMAR. No; and you're not his slave either.

EKDAL. And about that other business in there . . .

HIALMAR. Just what I was thinking of. Do you want to go in? Shall I open the door for you?

EKDAL. Well, it wouldn't be a bad notion.

HIALMAR *(rises).* Then we'd have *that* off our hands.

EKDAL. Yes, exactly. It's got to be ready first thing to-morrow. It is to-morrow, isn't it? H'm?

HIALMAR. Yes, of course it's to-morrow.

(Hialmar and Ekdal push aside each his half of the sliding door. The morning sun is shining in through the skylights; some doves are flying about; others sit cooing, upon the perches; the hens are heard clucking now and then, further back in the garret.)

HIALMAR. There; now you can get to work, father.

EKDAL *(goes in).* Aren't you coming too?

HIALMAR. Well really, do you know . . . ; I almost think . . . *(Sees Gina at the kitchen door.)* I? No; I haven't time; I must work.— But now for our new contrivance . . .

(He pulls a cord, a curtain slips down inside, the lower part consisting of a piece of old sailcloth, the upper part of a stretched fishing net. The floor of the garret is thus no longer visible.)

HIALMAR *(goes to the table).* So! Now, perhaps I can sit in peace for a little while.

GINA. Is he rampaging in there again?

HIALMAR. Would you rather have had him slip down to Madam Eriksen's? *(Seats himself.)* Do you want anything? You know you said . . .

GINA. I only wanted to ask if you think we can lay the table for lunch here?

HIALMAR. Yes; we have no early appointment, I suppose?

GINA. No, I expect no one to-day except those two sweethearts that are to be taken together.

HIALMAR. Why the deuce couldn't they be taken together another day!

GINA. Don't you know, I told them to come in the afternoon, when you are having your nap.

HIALMAR. Oh, that's capital. Very well, let us have lunch here then.

GINA. All right; but there's no hurry about laying the cloth; you can have the table for a good while yet.

HIALMAR. Do you think I am not sticking at my work? I'm at it as hard as I can!

GINA. Then you'll be free later on, you know.

(Goes out into the kitchen again. Short pause.)

EKDAL *(in the garret doorway, behind the net).* Hialmar!

HIALMAR. Well?

EKDAL. Afraid we shall have to move the water-trough, after all.

HIALMAR. What else have I been saying all along?

EKDAL. H'm—h'm—h'm.

(Goes away from the door again.
Hialmar goes on working a little; glances towards the garret and half rises. Hedvig comes in from the kitchen.)

HIALMAR *(sits down again hurriedly).* What do you want?

HEDVIG. I only wanted to come in beside you, father.

HIALMAR *(after a pause)*. What makes you go prying around like that? Perhaps you are told off to watch me?

HEDVIG. No, no.

HIALMAR. What is your mother doing out there?

HEDVIG. Oh, mother's in the middle of making herring-salad. *(Goes to the table.)* Isn't there any little thing I could help you with, father?

HIALMAR. Oh no. It is right that I should bear the whole burden—so long as my strength holds out. Set your mind at rest, Hedvig; if only your father keeps his health . . .

HEDVIG. Oh no, father! You mustn't talk in that horrid way.

(She wanders about a little, stops by the doorway and looks into the garret.)

HIALMAR. Tell me, what is he doing?

HEDVIG. I think he's making a new path to the water-trough.

HIALMAR. He can never manage *that* by himself! And here am I doomed to sit . . . !

HEDVIG *(goes to him)*. Let *me* take the brush, father; I *can* do it, quite well.

HIALMAR. Oh nonsense; you will only hurt your eyes.

HEDVIG. Not a bit. Give me the brush.

HIALMAR *(rising)*. Well, it won't take more than a minute or two.

HEDVIG. Pooh, what harm can it do then? *(Takes the brush.)* There! *(Seats herself.)* I can begin upon this one.

HIALMAR. But mind you don't hurt your eyes! Do you hear? *I* won't be answerable; you do it on your own responsibility—understand that.

HEDVIG *(retouching)*. Yes, yes, I understand.

HIALMAR. You are quite clever at it, Hedvig. Only a minute or two.

(He slips through by the edge of the curtain into the garret. Hedvig sits at her work. Hialmar and Ekdal are heard disputing inside.)

HIALMAR *(appears behind the net)*. I say, Hedvig—give me those pincers that are laying on the shelf. And the chisel. *(Turns away inside.)* Now you shall see, father. Just let me show you first what I mean!

(Hedvig has fetched the required tools from the shelf, and hands them to him through the net.)

HIALMAR. Ah, thanks. I didn't come a moment too soon.

(Goes back from the curtain again; they are heard carpentering and talking inside. Hedvig stands looking in at them. A moment later there is a knock at the passage door; she does not notice it.)

GREGERS WERLE *(bareheaded, in indoor dress, enters and stops near the door)*. H'm . . . !

HEDVIG *(turns and goes towards him)*. Good morning. Please come in.

GREGERS. Thank you. *(Looking towards the garret.)* You seem to have workpeople in the house.

HEDVIG. No, it is only father and grandfather. I'll tell them you are here.

GREGERS. No no, don't do that; I would rather wait a little. *(Seats himself on the sofa.)*

HEDVIG. It looks so untidy here . . . *(Begins to clear away the photographs.)*

GREGERS. Oh, don't take them away. Are those prints that have to be finished off?

HEDVIG. Yes, they are a few I was helping father with.

GREGERS. Please don't let me disturb you.

HEDVIG. Oh no.

(She gathers the things to her and sits down to work; Gregers looks at her, meanwhile, in silence.)

GREGERS. Did the wild duck sleep well last night?

HEDVIG. Yes, I think so, thanks.

GREGERS *(turning towards the garret)*. It looks quite different by day from what it did last night in the moonlight.

HEDVIG. Yes, it changes ever so much. It looks different in the morning and in the afternoon; and it's different on rainy days from what it is in fine weather.

GREGERS. Have you noticed that?

HEDVIG. Yes, how could I help it?

GREGERS. Are you, too, fond of being in there with the wild duck?

HEDVIG. Yes, when I can manage it . . .

GREGERS. But I suppose you haven't much spare time; you go to school, no doubt.

HEDVIG. No, not now; father is afraid of my hurting my eyes.

GREGERS. Oh; then he reads with you himself?

HEDVIG. Father has promised to read with me; but he has never had time yet.

GREGERS. Then is there nobody else to give you a little help?

HEDVIG. Yes, there is Mr. Molvik; but he is not always exactly— quite—

GREGERS. Sober?

HEDVIG. Yes, I suppose that's it!

GREGERS. Why, then you must have any amount of time on your hands. And in there I suppose it is a sort of world by itself?

HEDVIG. Oh yes, quite. And there are such lots of wonderful things.

GREGERS. Indeed?

HEDVIG. Yes, there are big cupboards full of books; and a great many of the books have pictures in them.

GREGERS. Aha!

HEDVIG. And there's an old bureau with drawers and flaps, and a big clock with figures that go out and in. But the clock isn't going now.

GREGERS. So time has come to a standstill in there—in the wild duck's domain.

HEDVIG. Yes. And then there's an old paint-box and things of that sort; and all the books.

GREGERS. And you read the books, I suppose?

HEDVIG. Oh yes, when I get the chance. Most of them are English though, and I don't understand English. But then I look at the pic- tures.—There is one great big book called "Harrison's History of London." It must be a hundred years old; and there are such heaps of pictures in it. At the beginning there is Death with an hour-glass and a woman. I think that is horrid. But then there are all the other pictures of churches, and castles, and streets, and great ships sailing on the sea.

GREGERS. But tell me, where did all those wonderful things come from?

HEDVIG. Oh, an old sea captain once lived here, and he brought them home with him. They used to call him "The Flying Dutchman." That was curious, because he wasn't a Dutchman at all.

GREGERS. Was he not?

HEDVIG. No. But at last he was drowned at sea; and so he left all those things behind him.

GREGERS. Tell me now—when you are sitting in there looking at the pictures, don't you wish you could travel and see the real world for yourself?

HEDVIG. Oh no! I mean always to stay at home and help father and mother.

GREGERS. To retouch photographs?

HEDVIG. No, not only that. I should love above everything to learn to engrave pictures like those in the English books.

GREGERS. H'm. What does your father say to that?

HEDVIG. I don't think father likes it; father is strange about such things. Only think, he talks of my learning basket-making, and straw-plaiting! But I don't think *that* would be much good.

GREGERS. Oh no, I don't think so either.

HEDVIG. But father was right in saying that if I had learnt basket-making I could have made the new basket for the wild duck.

GREGERS. So you could; and it was you that ought to have done it, wasn't it?

HEDVIG. Yes, for it's *my* wild duck.

GREGERS. Of course it is.

HEDVIG. Yes, it belongs to *me*. But I lend it to father and grandfather as often as they please.

GREGERS. Indeed? What do they do with it?

HEDVIG. Oh, they look after it, and build places for it, and so on.

GREGERS. I see; for no doubt the wild duck is by far the most distinguished inhabitant of the garret?

HEDVIG. Yes, indeed she is; for she is a *real* wild fowl, you know.

And then she is so much to be pitied; she has no one to care for, poor thing.

GREGERS. She has no family, as the rabbits have . . .

HEDVIG. No. The hens too, many of them, were chickens together; but she has been taken right away from all her friends. And then there is so much that is strange about the wild duck. Nobody knows her, and nobody knows where she came from either.

GREGERS. And she has been down in the depths of the sea.

HEDVIG *(with a quick glance at him, represses a smile and asks):* Why do you say "the depths of the sea"?

GREGERS. What else should I say?

HEDVIG. You could say "the bottom of the sea."[1]

GREGERS. Oh, mayn't I just as well say the depths of the sea?

HEDVIG. Yes; but it sounds so strange to me when other people speak of the depths of the sea.

GREGERS. Why so? Tell me why?

HEDVIG. No, I won't; it's so stupid.

GREGERS. Oh no, I am sure it's not. Do tell me why you smiled.

HEDVIG. Well, this is the reason: whenever I come to realise suddenly —in a flash—what is in there, it always seems to me that the whole room and everything in it should be called "the depths of the sea." —But that is so stupid.

GREGERS. You mustn't say that.

HEDVIG. Oh yes, for you know it is only a garret.

GREGERS *(looks fixedly at her).* Are you so sure of that?

HEDVIG *(astonished).* That it's a garret?

GREGERS. Are you quite certain of it?

(Hedvig is silent, and looks at him open-mouthed. Gina comes in from the kitchen with the table things.)

GREGERS *(rising).* I have come in upon you too early.

GINA. Oh, you must be somewhere; and we're nearly ready, any way. Clear the table, Hedvig.

---

[1] Gregers here uses the old-fashioned expression "havsens bund," while Hedvig would have him use the more commonplace "havets bund" or "havbunden."

(Hedvig clears away her things; she and Gina lay the cloth during what follows. Gregers seats himself in the arm-chair, and turns over an album.)

GREGERS. I hear you can retouch, Mrs. Ekdal.

GINA *(with a side glance)*. Yes, I can.

GREGERS. That was exceedingly lucky.

GINA. How—lucky?

GREGERS. Since Ekdal took to photography, I mean.

HEDVIG. Mother can take photographs too.

GINA. Oh, yes; I was bound to learn *that.*

GREGERS. So it is really you that carry on the business, I suppose?

GINA. Yes, when Ekdal hasn't time himself . . .

GREGERS. He is a great deal taken up with his old father, I daresay.

GINA. Yes; and then you can't expect a man like Ekdal to do nothing but take car-de-visits of Dick, Tom and Harry.

GREGERS. I quite agree with you; but having once gone in for the thing . . .

GINA. You can surely understand, Mr. Werle, that Ekdal's not like one of your common photographers.

GREGERS. Of course not; but still . . .

(A shot is fired within the garret.)

GREGERS *(starting up)*. What's that?

GINA. Ugh! now they're firing again!

GREGERS. Have they firearms there?

HEDVIG. They are out shooting.

GREGERS. What! *(At the door of the garret.)* Are you shooting, Hialmar?

HIALMAR *(inside the net)*. Are you there? I didn't know; I was so taken up . . . *(To Hedvig.)* Why did you not let us know?

(Comes into the studio.)

GREGERS. Do you go shooting in the garret?

HIALMAR *(showing a double-barrelled pistol)*. Oh, only with this thing.

GINA. Yes, you and grandfather will do yourselves a mischief some day with that there pigstol.

HIALMAR *(with irritation)*. I believe I have told you that this kind of firearm is called a *pistol*.

GINA. Oh, that doesn't make it much better, that I can see.

GREGERS. So you have become a sportsman too, Hialmar.

HIALMAR. Only a little rabbit-shooting now and then. Mostly to please father, you understand.

GINA. Men are strange beings; they must always have something to pervert theirselves with.

HIALMAR *(snappishly)*. Just so; we must always have something to *divert* ourselves with.

GINA. Yes, that's just what I say.

HIALMAR. H'm. *(To Gregers.)* You see the garret is fortunately so situated that no one can hear us shooting. *(Lays the pistol on the top shelf of the bookcase.)* Don't touch the pistol, Hedvig! One of the barrels is loaded; remember that.

GREGERS *(looking through the net)*. You have a fowling-piece too, I see.

HIALMAR. That is father's old gun. It's of no use now; something has gone wrong with the lock. But it's fun to have it all the same; for we can take it to pieces now and then, and clean and grease it, and screw it together again.—Of course, it's mostly father that fiddle-faddles with all that sort of thing.

HEDVIG *(beside Gregers)*. Now you can see the wild duck properly.

GREGERS. I was just looking at her. One of her wings seems to me to droop a bit.

HEDVIG. Well, no wonder; her wing was broken, you know.

GREGERS. And she trails one foot a little. Isn't that so?

HIALMAR. Perhaps a very little bit.

HEDVIG. Yes, it was by that foot the dog took hold of her.

HIALMAR. But otherwise she hasn't the least thing the matter with her; and that is simply marvellous for a creature that has a charge of shot in her body, and has been between a dog's teeth . . .

GREGERS *(with a glance at Hedvig)*. . . . and that has lain in the depths of the sea—so long.

HEDVIG *(smiling)*. Yes.

GINA *(laying the table)*. That blessed wild duck! What a lot of fuss you do make over her.

HIALMAR. H'm;—will lunch soon be ready?

GINA. Yes, directly. Hedvig, you must come and help me now.

(Gina and Hedvig go out in the kitchen.)

HIALMAR *(in a low voice)*. I think you had better not stand there looking in at father; he doesn't like it. *(Gregers moves away from the garret door.)* Besides I may as well shut up before the others come. *(Claps his hands to drive the fowls back.)* Shh—shh, in with you! *(Draws up the curtain and pulls the doors together.)* All the contrivances are my own invention. It's really quite amusing to have things of this sort to potter with, and to put to rights when they get out of order. And it's absolutely necessary, too; for Gina objects to having rabbits and fowls in the studio.

GREGERS. To be sure; and I suppose the studio is your wife's special department?

HIALMAR. As a rule, I leave the everyday details of business to her; for then I can take refuge in the parlour and give my mind to more important things.

GREGERS. What things may *they* be, Hialmar?

HIALMAR. I wonder you have not asked *that* question sooner. But perhaps you haven't heard of the invention?

GREGERS. The invention? No.

HIALMAR. Really? Have you not? Oh no, out there in the wilds . . .

GREGERS. So you have invented something, have you?

HIALMAR. It is not quite completed yet; but I am working at it. You can easily imagine that when I resolved to devote myself to photography, it wasn't simply with the idea of taking likenesses of all sorts of commonplace people.

GREGERS. No; your wife was saying the same thing just now.

HIALMAR. I swore that if I consecrated my powers to this handicraft, I would so exalt it that it should become both an art and a science. And to that end I determined to make this great invention.

GREGERS. And what is the nature of the invention? What purpose does it serve?

HIALMAR. Oh, my dear fellow, you mustn't ask for details yet. It takes time, you see. And you must not think that my motive is vanity. It is not for my own sake that I am working. Oh no; it is my life's mission that stands before me night and day.

GREGERS. What is your life's mission?

HIALMAR. Do you forget the old man with the silver hair?

GREGERS. Your poor father? Well, but what can you do for him?

HIALMAR. I can raise up his self-respect from the dead, by restoring the name of Ekdal to honour and dignity.

GREGERS. Then that is your life's mission?

HIALMAR. Yes. I will rescue the shipwrecked man. For shipwrecked he was, by the very first blast of the storm. Even while those terrible investigations were going on, he was no longer himself. That pistol there—the one we use to shoot rabbits with—has played its part in the tragedy of the house of Ekdal.

GREGERS. The pistol? Indeed?

HIALMAR. When the sentence of imprisonment was passed—he had the pistol in his hand . . .

GREGERS. Had he . . . ?

HIALMAR. Yes; but he dared not use it. His courage failed him. So broken, so demoralised was he even then! Oh, can you understand it? He, a soldier; he, who had shot nine bears, and who was descended from two lieutenant-colonels—one after the other of course. Can you understand it, Gregers?

GREGERS. Yes, I understand it well enough.

HIALMAR. I cannot. And once more the pistol played a part in the history of our house. When he had put on the grey clothes and was under lock and key—oh, that was a terrible time for me, I can tell you. I kept the blinds drawn down over both my windows. When I peeped out, I saw the sun shining as if nothing had happened. I could not understand it. I saw people going along the street, laughing and talking about indifferent things. I could not understand it.

It seemed to me that the whole of existence must be at a standstill
—as if under an eclipse.

GREGERS. I felt like that too, when my mother died.

HIALMAR. It was in such an hour that Hialmar Ekdal pointed the pistol
at his own breast.

GREGERS. You too thought of . . . !

HIALMAR. Yes.

GREGERS. But you did not fire?

HIALMAR. No. At the decisive moment I won the victory over myself.
I remained in life. But I can assure you it takes some courage to
choose life under circumstances like those.

GREGERS. Well, that depends on how you look at it.

HIALMAR. Yes, indeed, it takes courage. But I am glad I was firm: for
now I shall soon perfect my invention; and Dr. Relling thinks, as I
do myself, that father may be allowed to wear his uniform again.
I will demand that as my sole reward.

GREGERS. So *that* is what he meant about his uniform . . . ?

HIALMAR. Yes, that is what he most yearns for. You can't think how
my heart bleeds for him. Every time we celebrate any little family
festival—Gina's and my wedding-day, or whatever it may be—in
comes the old man in the lieutenant's uniform of happier days. But
if he only hears a knock at the door—for he daren't show himself
to strangers, you know—he hurries back to his room again as fast as
his old legs can carry him. Oh, it's heart-rending for a son to see
such things!

GREGERS. How long do you think it will take you to finish your invention?

HIALMAR. Come now, you mustn't expect me to enter into particulars
like that. An invention is not a thing completely under one's own
control. It depends largely on inspiration—on intuition—and it is
almost impossible to predict when the inspiration may come.

GREGERS. But it's advancing?

HIALMAR. Yes, certainly, it is advancing. I turn it over in my mind
every day; I am full of it. Every afternoon, when I have had my

dinner, I shut myself up in the parlour, where I can ponder undisturbed. But I can't be goaded to it; it's not a bit of good; Relling
says so too.

GREGERS. And you don't think that all that business in the garret draws
you off and distracts you too much?

HIALMAR. No no no; quite the contrary. You mustn't say that. I cannot
be everlastingly absorbed in the same laborious train of thought. I
must have something alongside of it to fill up the time of waiting.
The inspiration, the intuition, you see—when it comes, it comes, and
there's an end of it.

GREGERS. My dear Hialmar, I almost think you have something of the
wild duck in you.

HIALMAR. Something of the wild duck? How do you mean?

GREGERS. You have dived down and bitten yourself fast in the under-
growth.

HIALMAR. Are you alluding to the well-nigh fatal shot that has broken
my father's wing—and mine too?

GREGERS. Not exactly to *that*. I don't say that your wing has been
broken; but you have strayed into a poisonous marsh, Hialmar; an
insidious disease has taken hold of you, and you have sunk down
to die in the dark.

HIALMAR. I? To die in the dark? Look here, Gregers, you must really
leave off talking such nonsense.

GREGERS. Don't be afraid; I shall find a way to help you up again.
I too have a mission in life now; I found it yesterday.

HIALMAR. That's all very well; but you will please leave *me* out of it.
I can assure you that—apart from my very natural melancholy, of
course—I am as contented as any one can wish to be.

GREGERS. Your contentment is an effect of the marsh poison.

HIALMAR. Now, my dear Gregers, pray do not go on about disease
and poison; I am not used to that sort of talk. In *my* house nobody
ever speaks to me about unpleasant things.

GREGERS. Ah, *that* I can easily believe.

HIALMAR. It's not good for me, you see. And there *are* no marsh poisons

here, as you express it. The poor photographer's roof is lowly, I
know—and my circumstances are narrow. But I am an inventor, and
I am the breadwinner of a family. That exalts me above my mean
surroundings.—Ah, here comes lunch!

(*Gina and Hedvig bring bottles of ale, a decanter of brandy, glasses,
etc. At the same time, Relling and Molvik enter from the passage;
they are both without hat or overcoat. Molvik is dressed in black.*)

GINA (*placing the things upon the table*). Ah, you two have come in
the nick of time.

RELLING. Molvik got it into his head that he could smell herring-
salad, and then there was no holding him.—Good morning again,
Ekdal.

HIALMAR. Gregers, let me introduce you to Mr. Molvik. Doctor . . .
Oh, you know Relling, don't you?

GREGERS. Yes, slightly.

RELLING. Oh, Mr. Werle, junior! Yes, we two have had one or two
little skirmishes up at the Høidal works. You've just moved in?

GREGERS. I moved in this morning.

RELLING. Molvik and I live right under you; so you haven't far to go
for the doctor and the clergyman, if you should need anything in
that line.

GREGERS. Thanks, it's not quite unlikely; for yesterday we were thirteen at table.

HIALMAR. Oh, come now, don't let us get upon unpleasant subjects
again!

RELLING. You may make your mind easy, Ekdal; I'll be hanged if the
finger of fate points to *you.*

HIALMAR. I should hope not, for the sake of my family. But let us sit
down now, and eat and drink and be merry.

GREGERS. Shall we not wait for your father?

HIALMAR. No, his lunch will be taken in to him later. Come along!

(*The men seat themselves at table, and eat and drink. Gina and
Hedvig go in and out and wait upon them.*)

RELLING. Molvik was frightfully screwed yesterday, Mrs. Ekdal.

GINA. Really? Yesterday again?

RELLING. Didn't you hear him when I brought him home last night?

GINA. No, I can't say I did.

RELLING. That was a good thing, for Molvik was disgusting last night.

GINA. Is that true, Molvik?

MOLVIK. Let us draw a veil over last night's proceedings. That sort of thing is totally foreign to my better self.

RELLING *(to Gregers)*. It comes over him like a sort of possession, and then I have to go out on the loose with him. Mr. Molvik is dæmonic, you see.

GREGERS. Dæmonic?

RELLING. Molvik is dæmonic, yes.

GREGERS. H'm.

RELLING. And dæmonic natures are not made to walk straight through the world; they must meander a little now and then.—Well, so you still stick up there at those horrible grimy works?

GREGERS. I have stuck there until now.

RELLING. And did you ever manage to collect that claim you went about presenting?

GREGERS. Claim? *(Understands him.)* Ah, I see.

HIALMAR. Have you been presenting claims, Gregers?

GREGERS. Oh, nonsense.

RELLING. Faith, but he has, though! He went round to all the cotters' cabins presenting something he called "the claim of the ideal."

GREGERS. I was young then.

RELLING. You're right; you were very young. And as for the claim of the ideal—you never got it honoured while *I* was up there.

GREGERS. Nor since either.

RELLING. Ah, then you've learnt to knock a little discount off, I expect.

GREGERS. Never, when I have a true man to deal with.

HIALMAR. No, I should think not, indeed. A little butter, Gina.

RELLING. And a slice of bacon for Molvik.

MOLVIK. Ugh! not bacon!

(A knock at the garret door.)

HIALMAR. Open the door, Hedvig; father wants to come out.

(Hedvig goes over and opens the door a little way; Ekdal enters with a fresh rabbit-skin; she closes the door after him.)

EKDAL. Good morning, gentlemen! Good sport to-day. Shot a big one.

HIALMAR. And you've gone and skinned it without waiting for *me* . . . !

EKDAL. Salted it too. It's good tender meat, is rabbit; it's sweet; it tastes like sugar. Good appetite to you, gentlemen! *(Goes into his room.)*

MOLVIK *(rising).* Excuse me . . . ; I can't . . . ; I must get downstairs immediately . . .

RELLING. Drink some soda water, man!

MOLVIK *(hurrying away).* Ugh—ugh! *(Goes out by the passage door.)*

RELLING *(to Hialmar).* Let us drain a glass to the old hunter.

HIALMAR *(clinks glasses with him).* To the undaunted sportsman who has looked death in the face!

RELLING. To the grey-haired . . . *(Drinks.)* By-the-bye, is his hair grey or white?

HIALMAR. Something between the two, I fancy; for that matter, he has very few hairs left of any colour.

RELLING. Well well, one can get through the world with a wig. After all, you are a happy man, Ekdal; you have your noble mission to labour for . . .

HIALMAR. And I do labour, I can tell you.

RELLING. And then you have your excellent wife, shuffling quietly in and out in her felt slippers, with that see-saw walk of hers, and making everything cosy and comfortable about you.

HIALMAR. Yes, Gina—*(nods to her)*—you are a good helpmate on the path of life.

GINA. Oh, don't sit there cricketizing me.

RELLING. And your Hedvig too, Ekdal!

HIALMAR *(affected).* The child, yes! The child before everything! Hedvig, come here to me. *(Strokes her hair.)* What day is it to-morrow, eh?

HEDVIG *(shaking him).* Oh no, you're not to say anything, father.

HIALMAR. It cuts me to the heart when I think what a poor affair it will be; only a little festivity in the garret . . .

HEDVIG. Oh, but that's just what I like!

RELLING. Just you wait till the wonderful invention sees the light, Hedvig!

HIALMAR. Yes indeed—then you shall see . . . ! Hedvig, I have resolved to make your future secure. You shall live in comfort all your days.

I will demand—something or other—on your behalf. *That* shall be the poor inventor's sole reward.

HEDVIG *(whispering, with her arms round his neck)*. Oh you dear, kind father!

RELLING *(to Gregers)*. Come now, don't you find it pleasant, for once in a way, to sit at a well-spread table in a happy family circle?

HIALMAR. Ah yes, I really prize these social hours.

GREGERS. For my part, I don't thrive in marsh vapours.

RELLING. Marsh vapours?

HIALMAR. Oh, don't begin with that stuff again!

GINA. Goodness knows there's no vapours in *this* house, Mr. Werle; I give the place a good airing every blessed day.

GREGERS *(leaves the table)*. No airing *you* can give will drive out the taint I mean.

HIALMAR. Taint!

GINA. Yes, what do you say to that, Ekdal!

RELLING. Excuse me—may it not be you yourself that have brought the taint from those mines up there?

GREGERS. It is like you to call what I bring into this house a taint.

RELLING *(goes up to him)*. Look here, Mr. Werle, junior: I have a strong suspicion that you are still carrying about that "claim of the ideal" large as life, in your coat-tail pocket.

GREGERS. I carry it in my breast.

RELLING. Well, wherever you carry it, I advise you not to come dunning us with it here, so long as *I* am on the premises.

GREGERS. And if I do so none the less?

RELLING. Then you'll go head-foremost down the stairs; now I've warned you.

HIALMAR *(rising)*. Oh, but Relling . . . !

GREGERS. Yes, you may turn me out . . .

GINA *(interposing between them)*. We can't have that, Relling. But I must say, Mr. Werle, it ill becomes you to talk about vapours and taints, after all the mess you made with your stove.

(A knock at the passage door.)

HEDVIG. Mother, there's somebody knocking.

HIALMAR. There now, we're going to have a whole lot of people!

GINA. I'll go . . . *(Goes over and opens the door, starts, and draws back.)* Oh—oh dear!

(Werle, in a fur coat, advances one step into the room.)

WERLE. Excuse me; but I think my son is staying here.

GINA *(with a gulp)*. Yes.

HIALMAR *(approaching him)*. Won't you do us the honour to . . . ?

WERLE. Thank you, I merely wish to speak to my son.

GREGERS. What is it? Here I am.

WERLE. I want a few words with you, in your room.

GREGERS. In my room? Very well . . . *(About to go.)*

GINA. No, no, your room's not in a fit state . . .

WERLE. Well then, out in the passage here; I want to have a few words with you alone.

HIALMAR. You can have them here, sir. Come into the parlour, Relling. *(Hialmar and Relling go off to the right. Gina takes Hedvig with her into the kitchen.)*

GREGERS *(after a short pause)*. Well, now we are alone.

WERLE. From something you let fall last evening, and from your coming to lodge with the Ekdals, I can't help inferring that you intend to make yourself unpleasant to me, in one way or another.

GREGERS. I intend to open Hialmar Ekdal's eyes. He shall see his position as it really is—that is all.

WERLE. Is *that* the mission in life you spoke of yesterday?

GREGERS. Yes. You have left me no other.

WERLE. Is it I, then, that have crippled your mind, Gregers?

GREGERS. You have crippled my whole life. I am not thinking of all that about mother . . . But it's thanks to you that I am continually haunted and harassed by a guilty conscience.

WERLE. Indeed! It is your conscience that troubles you, is it?

GREGERS. I ought to have taken a stand against you when the trap was set for Lieutenant Ekdal. I ought to have cautioned him; for I had a misgiving as to what was in the wind.

WERLE. Yes, that was the time to have spoken.

GREGERS. I did not dare to, I was so cowed and spiritless. I was mortally afraid of you—not only then, but long afterwards.

WERLE. You have got over that fear now, it appears.

GREGERS. Yes, fortunately. The wrong done to old Ekdal, both by me and by—others, can never be undone; but Hialmar I can rescue from all the falsehood and deception that are bringing him to ruin.

WERLE. Do you think *that* will be doing him a kindness?

GREGERS. I have not the least doubt of it.

WERLE. You think our worthy photographer is the sort of man to appreciate such friendly offices?

GREGERS. Yes, I do.

WERLE. H'm—we shall see.

GREGERS. Besides, if I am to go on living, I must try to find some cure for my sick conscience.

WERLE. It will never be sound. Your conscience has been sickly from childhood. That is a legacy from your mother, Gregers—the only one she left you.

GREGERS *(with a scornful half-smile)*. Have you not yet forgiven her for the mistake you made in supposing she would bring you a fortune?

WERLE. Don't let us wander from the point.—Then you hold to your purpose of setting young Ekdal upon what you imagine to be the right scent?

GREGERS. Yes, that is my fixed resolve.

WERLE. Well, in that case I might have spared myself this visit; for of course it is useless to ask whether you will return home with me?

GREGERS. Quite useless.

WERLE. And I suppose you won't enter the firm either?

GREGERS. No.

WERLE. Very good. But as I am thinking of marrying again, your share in the property will fall to you at once.[1]

GREGERS *(quickly)*. No, I do not want that.

WERLE. You don't want it?

GREGERS. No, I dare not take it, for conscience' sake.

WERLE *(after a pause)*. Are you going up to the works again?

GREGERS. No; I consider myself released from your service.

WERLE. But what are you going to do?

GREGERS. Only to fulfil my mission; nothing more.

WERLE. Well, but afterwards? What are you going to live upon?

GREGERS. I have laid by a little out of my salary.

---

[1] By Norwegian law, before a widower can marry again, a certain proportion of his property must be settled on his children by his former marriage.

WERLE. How long will *that* last?

GREGERS. I think it will last *my* time.

WERLE. What do you mean?

GREGERS. I shall answer no more questions.

WERLE. Good-bye then, Gregers.

GREGERS. Good-bye.

(*Werle goes.*)

HIALMAR (*peeping in*). He's gone, isn't he?

GREGERS. Yes.

(*Hialmar and Relling enter; also Gina and Hedvig from the kitchen.*)

RELLING. That luncheon-party was a failure.

GREGERS. Put on your coat, Hialmar; I want you to come for a long walk with me.

HIALMAR. With pleasure. What was it your father wanted? Had it anything to do with me?

GREGERS. Come along. We must have a talk. I'll go and put on my overcoat. (*Goes out by the passage door.*)

GINA. You shouldn't go out with him, Ekdal.

RELLING. No, don't you do it. Stay where you are.

HIALMAR (*gets his hat and overcoat*). Oh, nonsense! When a friend of my youth feels impelled to open his mind to me in private...

RELLING. But devil take it—don't you see that the fellow's mad, cracked, demented!

GINA. There, what did I tell you! His mother before him had crazy fits like that sometimes.

HIALMAR. The more need for a friend's watchful eye. (*To Gina.*) Be sure you have dinner ready in good time. Good-bye for the present. (*Goes out by the passage door.*)

RELLING. It's a thousand pities the fellow didn't go to hell through one of the Høidal mines.

GINA. Good Lord! what makes you say that?

RELLING (*muttering*). Oh, I have my own reasons.

GINA. Do you think young Werle is really mad?

RELLING. No, worse luck; he's no madder than most other people. But one disease he has certainly got in his system.

GINA. What is it that's the matter with him?

RELLING. Well, I'll tell you, Mrs. Ekdal. He is suffering from an acute attack of integrity.

GINA. Integrity?

HEDVIG. Is that a kind of disease?

RELLING. Yes, it's a national disease; but it only appears sporadically. *(Nods to Gina.)* Thanks for your hospitality. *(He goes out by the passage door.)*

GINA *(moving restlessly to and fro)*. Ugh, that Gregers Werle—he was always a wretched creature.

HEDVIG *(standing by the table, and looking searchingly at her)*. I think all this is very strange.

ACT FOURTH

Hialmar Ekdal's studio. A photograph has just been taken; a camera with the cloth over it, a pedestal, two chairs, a folding table, etc., are standing out in the room. Afternoon light; the sun is going down; a little later it begins to grow dusk.

Gina stands in the passage doorway, with a little box and a wet glass plate in her hand, and is speaking to somebody outside.

GINA. Yes, certainly. When I make a promise I keep it. The first dozen shall be ready on Monday. Good afternoon.

(Some one is heard going downstairs. Gina shuts the door, slips the plate into the box, and puts it into the covered camera.)

HEDVIG *(comes in from the kitchen).* Are they gone?

GINA *(tidying up).* Yes, thank goodness, I've got rid of them at last.

HEDVIG. But can you imagine why father hasn't come home yet?

GINA. Are you sure he's not down in Relling's room?

HEDVIG. No, he's not; I ran down the kitchen stair just now and asked.

GINA. And his dinner standing and getting cold, too.

HEDVIG. Yes, I can't understand it. Father's always so careful to be home to dinner!

GINA. Oh, he'll be here directly, you'll see.

HEDVIG. I wish he would come; everything seems so queer to-day.

GINA *(calls out)*. There he is!

(Hialmar Ekdal comes in at the passage door.)

HEDVIG *(going to him)*. Father! Oh what a time we've been waiting for you!

GINA *(glancing sidelong at him)*. You've been out a long time, Ekdal.

HIALMAR *(without looking at her)*. Rather long, yes.

(He takes off his overcoat; Gina and Hedvig go to help him; he motions them away.)

GINA. Perhaps you've had dinner with Werle?

HIALMAR *(hanging up his coat)*. No.

GINA *(going towards the kitchen door)*. Then I'll bring some in for you.

HIALMAR. No; let the dinner alone. I want nothing to eat.

HEDVIG *(going nearer to him)*. Are you not well, father?

HIALMAR. Well? Oh yes, well enough. We have had a tiring walk, Gregers and I.

GINA. You didn't ought to have gone so far, Ekdal, you're not used to it.

HIALMAR. H'm; there's many a thing a man must get used to in this world. *(Wanders about the room.)* Has any one been here whilst I was out?

GINA. Nobody but the two sweethearts.

HIALMAR. No new orders?

GINA. No, not to-day.

HEDVIG. There will be some to-morrow, father, you'll see.

HIALMAR. I hope there will; for to-morrow I am going to set to work in real earnest.

HEDVIG. To-morrow! Don't you remember what day it is to-morrow?

HIALMAR. Oh yes, by-the-bye . . . Well, the day after, then. Henceforth I mean to do everything myself; I shall take all the work into my own hands.

GINA. Why, what can be the good of that, Ekdal? It'll only make your life a burden to you. I can manage the photography all right; and you can go on working at your invention.

HEDVIG. And think of the wild duck, father,—and all the hens and rabbits and . . . !

HIALMAR. Don't talk to me of all that trash! From to-morrow I will never set foot in the garret again.

HEDVIG. Oh but, father, you promised that we should have a little party . . .

HIALMAR. H'm, true. Well then, from the day after to-morrow. I should almost like to wring that cursed wild duck's neck!

HEDVIG *(shrieks)*. The wild duck!

GINA. Well I never!

HEDVIG *(shaking him)*. Oh no, father; you know it's *my* wild duck!

HIALMAR. That is why I don't do it. I haven't the heart to—for your sake, Hedvig. But in my inmost soul I feel that I ought to do it. I ought not to tolerate under my roof a creature that has been through *those* hands.

GINA. Why, good gracious, even if grandfather did *get* it from that poor creature, Pettersen . . .

HIALMAR *(wandering about)*. There are certain claims—what shall I call them?—let me say claims of the ideal—certain obligations, which a man cannot disregard without injury to his soul.

HEDVIG *(going after him)*. But think of the wild duck,—the poor wild duck!

HIALMAR *(stops)*. I tell you I will spare it—for your sake. Not a hair of its head shall be—I mean, it shall be spared. There are greater problems than that to be dealt with. But you should go out a little now, Hedvig, as usual; it is getting dusk enough for you now.

HEDVIG. No, I don't care about going out now.

HIALMAR. Yes do; it seems to me your eyes are blinking a great deal; all these vapours in here are bad for you. The air is heavy under this roof.

HEVDIG. Very well then, I'll run down the kitchen stair and go for a little walk. My cloak and hat?—oh, they're in my own room.

Father—be sure you don't do the wild duck any harm whilst I'm out.

HIALMAR. Not a feather of its head shall be touched. (*Draws her to him.*) You and I, Hedvig—we two . . . ! Well, go along.

(*Hedvig nods to her parents and goes out through the kitchen.*)

HIALMAR (*walks about without looking up*). Gina.

GINA. Yes?

HIALMAR. From to-morrow—or, say, from the day after to-morrow—I should like to keep the household account-book myself.

GINA. Do you want to keep the accounts too, now?

HIALMAR. Yes; or to check the receipts at any rate.

GINA. Lord help us! *that's* soon done.

HIALMAR. One would hardly think so; at any rate you seem to make the money go a very long way. (*Stops and looks at her.*) How do you manage it?

GINA. It's because me and Hedvig, we need so little.

HIALMAR. Is it the case that father is very liberally paid for the copying he does for Mr. Werle?

GINA. I don't know as he gets anything out of the way. I don't know the rates for that sort of work.

HIALMAR. Well, what does he get, about? Let me hear!

GINA. Oh, it varies; I daresay it'll come to about as much as he costs us, with a little pocket-money over.

HIALMAR. As much as he costs us! And you have never told me this before!

GINA. No, how could I tell you? It pleased you so much to think he got everything from you.

HIALMAR. And he gets it from Mr. Werle.

GINA. Oh well, he has plenty and to spare, he has.

HIALMAR. Light the lamp for me, please!

GINA (*lighting the lamp*). And of course we don't know as it's Mr. Werle himself; it may be Gråberg . . .

HIALMAR. Why attempt such an evasion?

GINA. I don't know; I only thought . . .

HIALMAR. H'm!

GINA. It wasn't me that got grandfather that copying. It was Bertha, when she used to come about us.

HIALMAR. It seems to me your voice is trembling.

GINA *(putting the lamp-shade on)*. Is it?

HIALMAR. And your hands are shaking, are they not?

GINA *(firmly)*. Come right out with it, Ekdal. What has he been saying about me?

HIALMAR. Is it true—*can* it be true that—that there was an—an understanding between you and Mr. Werle, while you were in service there?

GINA. That's not true. Not at that time. Mr. Werle did come after me, that's a fact. And his wife thought there was something in it, and then she made such a hocus-pocus and hurly-burly, and she hustled me and bustled me about so, that I left her service.

HIALMAR. But afterwards, then?

GINA. Well, then I went home. And mother—well, she wasn't the woman you took her for, Ekdal; she kept on worrying and worrying at me about one thing and another—for Mr. Werle was a widower by that time.

HIALMAR. Well, and then?

GINA. I suppose you've got to know it. He gave me no peace until he'd had his way.

HIALMAR (*striking his hands together*). And this is the mother of my child! How could you hide this from me?

GINA. Yes, it was wrong of me; I ought certainly to have told you long ago.

HIALMAR. You should have told me at the very first;—then I should have known the sort of woman you were.

GINA. But would you have married me all the same?

HIALMAR. How can you dream that I would?

GINA. That's just why I didn't dare tell you anything, then. For I'd come to care for you so much, you see; and I couldn't go and make myself utterly miserable . . .

HIALMAR (*walks about*). And this is my Hedvig's mother. And to know that all I see before me—(*kicks at a chair*)—all that I call my home—I owe to a favoured predecessor! Oh that scoundrel Werle!

GINA. Do you repent of the fourteen—the fifteen years as we've lived together?

HIALMAR (*placing himself in front of her*). Have *you* not every day, every hour, repented of the spider's-web of deceit you have spun around me? Answer me that! How could you help writhing with penitence and remorse?

GINA. Oh, my dear Ekdal, I've had all I could do to look after the house and get through the day's work . . .

HIALMAR. Then you never think of reviewing your past?

GINA. No; Heaven knows I'd almost forgotten those old stories.

HIALMAR. Oh, this dull, callous contentment! To me there is something revolting about it. Think of it—never so much as a twinge of remorse!

GINA. But tell me, Ekdal—what would have become of you if you hadn't had a wife like me?

HIALMAR. Like you . . . !

GINA. Yes; for you know I've always been a bit more practical and wide-awake than you. Of course I'm a year or two older.

HIALMAR. What would have become of me!

GINA. You'd got into all sorts of bad ways when first you met me; that you can't deny.

HIALMAR. "Bad ways" do you call them? Little do you know what a man goes through when he is in grief and despair—especially a man of my fiery temperament.

GINA. Well, well, that may be so. And I've no reason to crow over you, neither; for you turned a moral of a husband, that you did, as soon as ever you had a house and home of your own.—And now we'd got everything so nice and cosy about us; and me and Hedvig was just thinking we'd soon be able to let ourselves go a bit, in the way of both food and clothes.

HIALMAR. In the swamp of deceit, yes.

GINA. I wish to goodness that detestable being had never set his foot inside our doors!

HIALMAR. And I, too, thought my home such a pleasant one. That was a delusion. Where shall I now find the elasticity of spirit to bring my invention into the world of reality? Perhaps it will die with me; and then it will be your past, Gina, that will have killed it.

GINA (nearly crying). You mustn't say such things, Ekdal. Me, that has only wanted to do the best I could for you, all my days!

HIALMAR. I ask you, what becomes of the breadwinner's dream? When I used to lie in there on the sofa and brood over my invention, I had a clear enough presentiment that it would sap my vitality to the last drop. I felt even then that the day when I held the patent in my hand—that day—would bring my—release. And then it was my dream that you should live on after me, the dead inventor's well-to-do widow!

GINA *(drying her tears)*. No, you mustn't talk like that, Ekdal. May the Lord never let me see the day I am left a widow!

HIALMAR. Oh, the whole dream has vanished. It is all over now. All over!

(Gregers Werle opens the passage door cautiously and looks in.)

GREGERS. May I come in?

HIALMAR. Yes, come in.

GREGERS *(comes forward, his face beaming with satisfaction, and holds out both his hands to them)*. Well, dear friends ... ! *(Looks from one to the other, and whispers to Hialmar.)* Have you not done it yet?

HIALMAR *(aloud)*. It is done.

GREGERS. It is?

HIALMAR. I have passed through the bitterest moments of my life.

GREGERS. But also, I trust, the most ennobling.

HIALMAR. Well, at any rate, we have got through it for the present.

GINA. God forgive you, Mr. Werle.

GREGERS *(in great surprise)*. But I don't understand this.

HIALMAR. What don't you understand?

GREGERS. After so great a crisis—a crisis that is to be the starting-point of an entirely new life—of a communion founded on truth, and free from all taint of deception ...

HIALMAR. Yes yes, I know; I know that quite well.

GREGERS. I confidently expected, when I entered the room, to find the light of transfiguration shining upon me from both husband and wife. And now I see nothing but dulness, oppression, gloom ...

GINA. Oh, is that it? *(Takes off the lamp-shade.)*

GREGERS. You will not understand me, Mrs. Ekdal. Ah well, *you,* I suppose need time to ... But you, Hialmar? Surely you feel a new consecration after the great crisis.

HIALMAR. Yes, of course I do. That is—in a sort of way.

GREGERS. For surely nothing in the world can compare with the joy of forgiving one who has erred, and raising her up to oneself in love.

HIALMAR. Do you think a man can so easily throw off the effects of the bitter cup I have drained?

GREGERS. No, not a *common* man, perhaps. But a man like *you* . . . !

HIALMAR. Good God! I know that well enough. But you must keep me up to it, Gregers. It takes time, you know.

GREGERS. You have *much* of the wild duck in you, Hialmar.

(Relling has come in at the passage door.)

RELLING. Oho! is the wild duck to the fore again?

HIALMAR. Yes; Mr. Werle's wing-broken victim.

RELLING. Mr. Werle's . . . ? So it's *him* you are talking about?

HIALMAR. Him and—ourselves.

RELLING *(in an undertone to Gregers)*. May the devil fly away with you!

HIALMAR. What is that you are saying?

RELLING. Only uttering a heartfelt wish that this quacksalver would take himself off. If he stays here, he is quite equal to making an utter mess of life, for both of you.

GREGERS. These two will not make a mess of life, Mr. Relling. Of course I won't speak of Hialmar—him we know. But she, too, in her innermost heart, has certainly something loyal and sincere . . .

GINA *(almost crying)*. You might have let me alone for what I was, then.

RELLING *(to Gregers)*. Is it rude to ask what you really want in this house?

GREGERS. To lay the foundations of a true marriage.

RELLING. So you don't think Ekdal's marriage is good enough as it is?

GREGERS. No doubt it is as good a marriage as most others, worse luck. But a *true* marriage it has yet to become.

HIALMAR. You have never had eyes for the claims of the ideal, Relling.

RELLING. Rubbish, my boy!—But excuse me, Mr. Werle: how many —in round numbers—how many true marriages have you seen in the course of your life?

GREGERS. Scarcely a single one.

RELLING. Nor I either.

GREGERS. But I have seen innumerable marriages of the opposite kind. And it has been my fate to see at close quarters what ruin such a marriage can work in two human souls.

HIALMAR. A man's whole moral basis may give away beneath his feet; *that* is the terrible part of it.

RELLING. Well, I can't say I've ever been exactly married, so I don't pretend to speak with authority. But this I know, that the *child* enters into the marriage problem. And you must leave the child in peace.

HIALMAR. Oh—Hedvig! my poor Hedvig!

RELLING. Yes, you must be good enough to keep Hedvig outside of all this. You two are grown-up people; you are free, in God's name, to make what mess and muddle you please of your life. But you must deal cautiously with Hedvig, I tell you; else you may do her a great injury.

HIALMAR. An injury!

RELLING. Yes, or she may do herself an injury—and perhaps others too.

GINA. How can you know that, Relling?

HIALMAR. Her sight is in no immediate danger, is it?

RELLING. I am not talking about her sight. Hedvig is at a critical age. She may be getting all sorts of mischief into her head.

GINA. That's true—I've noticed it already! She's taken to carrying on with the fire, out in the kitchen. She calls it playing at house-on-fire. I'm often scared for fear she really sets fire to the house.

RELLING. You see; I thought as much.

GREGERS *(to Relling)*. But how do you account for that?

RELLING *(sullenly)*. Her constitution's changing, sir.

HIALMAR. So long as the child has *me* . . . ! So long as *I* am above ground . . . !

(A knock at the door.)

GINA. Hush, Ekdal; there's some one in the passage. *(Calls out.)* Come in!

(Mrs. Sørby, in walking dress, comes in.)

MRS. SØRBY. Good evening.

GINA (*going towards her*). Is it really you, Bertha?

MRS. SØRBY. Yes, of course it is. But I'm disturbing you, I'm afraid?

HIALMAR. No, not at all; an emissary from *that* house . . .

MRS. SØRBY (*to Gina*). To tell the truth, I hoped your men-folk would be out at this time. I just ran up to have a little chat with you, and to say good-bye.

GINA. Good-bye? Are you going away, then?

MRS. SØRBY. Yes, to-morrow morning,—up to Høidal. Mr. Werle started this afternoon. (*Lightly to Gregers.*) He asked me to say good-bye for him.

GINA. Only fancy . . . !

HIALMAR. So Mr. Werle has gone? And now you are going after him?

MRS. SØRBY. Yes, what do you say to *that*, Ekdal?

HIALMAR. I say: beware!

GREGERS. I must explain the situation. My father and Mrs. Sørby are going to be married.

HIALMAR. Going to be married!

GINA. Oh Bertha! So it's come to that at last!

RELLING (*his voice quivering a little*). This is surely not true?

MRS. SØRBY. Yes, my dear Relling, it's true enough.

RELLING. You are going to marry again?

MRS. SØRBY. Yes, it looks like it. Werle has got a special licence, and we are going to be married quite quietly, up at the works.

GREGERS. Then I must wish you all happiness, like a dutiful stepson.

MRS. SØRBY. Thank you very much—if you mean what you say. I certainly hope it will lead to happiness, both for Werle and for me.

RELLING. You have every reason to hope that. Mr. Werle never gets drunk—so far as I know; and I don't suppose he's in the habit of thrashing his wives, like the late lamented horse-doctor.

MRS. SØRBY. Come now, let Sørby rest in peace. He had his good points too.

RELLING. Mr. Werle has better ones, I have no doubt.

MRS. SØRBY. He hasn't frittered away all that was good in him, at any rate. The man who does that must take the consequences.

RELLING. I shall go out with Molvik this evening.

MRS. SØRBY. You mustn't do that, Relling. Don't do it—for my sake.

RELLING. There's nothing else for it. *(To Hialmar.)* If you're going with us, come along.

GINA. No, thank you. Ekdal doesn't go in for *that* sort of dissertation.

HIALMAR *(half aloud, in vexation).* Oh, do hold your tongue!

RELLING. Good-bye, Mrs.—Werle. *(Goes out through the passage door.)*

GREGERS *(to Mrs. Sørby).* You seem to know Dr. Relling pretty intimately.

MRS. SØRBY. Yes, we have known each other for many years. At one time it seemed as if things might have gone further between us.

GREGERS. It was surely lucky for you that they did not.

MRS. SØRBY. You may well say that. But I have always been wary of acting on impulse. A woman can't afford absolutely to throw herself away.

GREGERS. Are you not in the least afraid that I may let my father know about this old friendship?

MRS. SØRBY. Why, of course I have told him all about it myself.

GREGERS. Indeed?

MRS. SØRBY. Your father knows every single thing that can, with any truth, be said about me. I have told him all; it was the first thing I did when I saw what was in his mind.

GREGERS. Then you have been franker than most people, I think.

MRS. SØRBY. I have always been frank. We women find that the best policy.

HIALMAR. What do you say to that, Gina?

GINA. Oh, we're not all alike, us women aren't. Some are made one way, some another.

MRS. SØRBY. Well, for my part, Gina, I believe it's wisest to do as I've done. And Werle has no secrets either, on his side. That's really the great bond between us, you see. Now he can talk to me as openly as a child. He has never had the chance to do that before. Fancy a man like him, full of health and vigour, passing his whole youth and the best years of his life in listening to nothing but penitential sermons! And very often the sermons had for their text the most imaginary offences—at least so I understand.

GINA. That's true enough.

GREGERS. If you ladies are going to follow up this topic, I had better withdraw.

MRS. SØRBY. You can stay so far as that's concerned. I shan't say a word more. But I wanted you to know that I had done nothing secretly or in an underhand way. I may seem to have come in for a great piece of luck; and so I have, in a sense. But after all, I don't think I am getting any more than I am giving. I shall stand by him always, and I can tend and care for him as no one else can, now that he is getting helpless.

HIALMAR. Getting helpless?

GREGERS *(to Mrs. Sørby)*. Hush, don't speak of that here.

MRS. SØRBY. There is no disguising it any longer, however much he would like to. He is going blind.

HIALMAR *(starts)*. Going blind? That's strange. He too going blind!

GINA. Lots of people do.

MRS. SØRBY. And you can imagine what *that* means to a business man. Well, I shall try as well as I can to make my eyes take the place of his. But I mustn't stay any longer; I have such heaps of things to do.—Oh, by-the-bye, Ekdal, I was to tell you that if there is anything Werle can do for you, you must just apply to Gråberg.

GREGERS. That offer I am sure Hialmar Ekdal will decline with thanks.

MRS. SØRBY. Indeed? I don't think he used to be so . . .

GINA. No, Bertha, Ekdal doesn't need anything from Mr. Werle now.

HIALMAR *(slowly, and with emphasis)*. Will you present my compliments to your future husband, and say that I intend very shortly to call upon Mr. Gråberg . . .

GREGERS. What! You don't really mean that?

HIALMAR. To call upon Mr. Gråberg, I say, and obtain an account of the sum I owe his principal. I will pay that debt of honour—ha ha ha! a debt of honour, let us call it! In any case, I will pay the whole, with five per cent interest.

GINA. But my dear Ekdal, God knows we haven't got the money to do it.

HIALMAR. Be good enough to tell your future husband that I am working assiduously at my invention. Please tell him that what sustains me in this laborious task is the wish to free myself from a torturing burden of debt. That is my reason for proceeding with the invention. The entire profits shall be devoted to releasing me from my pecuniary obligations to your future husband.

MRS. SØRBY. Something has happened here.

HIALMAR. Yes, you are right.

MRS. SØRBY. Well, good-bye. I had something else to speak to you about, Gina; but it must keep till another time. Good-bye.

(Hialmar and Gregers bow silently. Gina follows Mrs. Sørby to the door.)

HIALMAR. Not beyond the threshold, Gina!

(Mrs. Sørby goes; Gina shuts the door after her.)

HIALMAR. There now, Gregers; I have got that burden of debt off my mind.

GREGERS. You soon will, at all events.

HIALMAR. I think my attitude may be called correct.

GREGERS. You are the man I have always taken you for.

HIALMAR. In certain cases, it is impossible to disregard the claim of the ideal. Yet, as the breadwinner of a family, I cannot but writhe and groan under it. I can tell you it is no joke for a man without capital to attempt the repayment of a long-standing obligation, over which, so to speak, the dust of oblivion had gathered. But it cannot be helped: the Man in me demands his rights.

GREGERS *(laying his hand on Hialmar's shoulder)*. My dear Hialmar —was it not a good thing I came?

HIALMAR. Yes.

GREGERS. Are you not glad to have had your true position made clear to you?

HIALMAR (*somewhat impatiently*). Yes, of course I am. But there is one thing that is revolting to my sense of justice.

GREGERS. And what is that?

HIALMAR. It is that—but I don't know whether I ought to express myself so unreservedly about your father.

GREGERS. Say what you please, so far as I am concerned.

HIALMAR. Well then, is it not exasperating to think that it is not I, but he, who will realise the true marriage?

GREGERS. How can you say such a thing?

HIALMAR. Because it is clearly the case. Isn't the marriage between your father and Mrs. Sørby founded upon complete confidence, upon entire and unreserved candour on both sides? They hide nothing from each other, they keep no secrets in the background; their relation is based, if I may put it so, on mutual confession and absolution.

GREGERS. Well, what then?

HIALMAR. Well, is not that the whole thing? Did you not yourself say that this was precisely the difficulty that had to be overcome in order to found a true marriage?

GREGERS. But this is a totally different matter, Hialmar. You surely don't compare either yourself or your wife with those two . . . ? Oh, you understand me well enough.

HIALMAR. Say what you like, there is something in all this that hurts and offends my sense of justice. It really looks as if there were no just providence to rule the world.

GINA. Oh no, Ekdal; for God's sake don't say such things.

GREGERS. H'm; don't let us get upon those questions.

HIALMAR. And yet, after all, I cannot but recognise the guiding finger of fate. He is going blind.

GINA. Oh, you can't be sure of that.

HIALMAR. There is no doubt about it. At all events there ought not to be; for in that very fact lies the righteous retribution. He has hoodwinked a confiding fellow creature in days gone by . . .

GREGERS. I fear he has hoodwinked many.

HIALMAR. And now comes inexorable, mysterious Fate, and demands Werle's own eyes.

GINA. Oh, how dare you say such dreadful things! You make me quite scared.

HIALMAR. It is profitable, now and then, to plunge deep into the night side of existence.

(Hedvig, in her hat and cloak, comes in by the passage door. She is pleasurably excited, and out of breath.)

GINA. Are you back already?

HEDVIG. Yes, I didn't care to go any farther. It was a good thing, too; for I've just met some one at the door.

HIALMAR. It must have been that Mrs. Sørby.

HEDVIG. Yes.

HIALMAR *(walks up and down)*. I hope you have seen her for the last time.

(Silence. Hedvig, discouraged, looks first at one and then at the other, trying to divine their frame of mind.)

HEDVIG *(approaching, coaxingly)*. Father.

HIALMAR. Well—what is it, Hedvig?

HEDVIG. Mrs. Sørby had something with her for me.

HIALMAR *(stops)*. For you?

HEDVIG. Yes. Something for to-morrow.

GINA. Bertha has always given you some little thing on your birthday.

HIALMAR. What is it?

HEDVIG. Oh, you mustn't see it now. Mother is to give it to me to-morrow morning before I'm up.

HIALMAR. What is all this hocus-pocus that I am to be kept in the dark about!

HEDVIG *(quickly)*. Oh no, you may see it if you like. It's a big letter. *(Takes the letter out of her cloak pocket.)*

HIALMAR. A letter too?

HEDVIG. Yes, it is only a letter. The rest will come afterwards, I suppose. But fancy—a letter! I've never had a letter before. And there's

"Miss" written upon it. *(Reads.)* "Miss Hedvig Ekdal." Only fancy
—that's me!

HIALMAR. Let me see that letter.

HEDVIG *(hands it to him)*. There it is.

HIALMAR. That is Mr. Werle's hand.

GINA. Are you sure of that, Ekdal?

HIALMAR. Look for yourself.

GINA. Oh, what do *I* know about such-like things?

HIALMAR. Hedvig, may I open the letter—and read it?

HEDVIG. Yes, of course you may, if you want to.

GINA. No, not to-night, Ekdal; it's to be kept till to-morrow.

HEDVIG *(softly)*. Oh, can't you let him read it! It's sure to be something good; and then father will be glad, and everything will be
nice again.

HIALMAR. I may open it then?

HEDVIG. Yes do, father. I'm so anxious to know what it is.

HIALMAR. Well and good. *(Opens the letter, takes out a paper, reads
it through, and appears bewildered.)* What is this . . . !

GINA. What does it say?

HEDVIG. Oh yes, father—tell us!

HIALMAR. Be quiet. *(Reads it through again; he has turned pale, but
says with self-control.)* It is a deed of gift, Hedvig.

HEDVIG. It is? What sort of gift am I to have?

HIALMAR. Read for yourself.

(Hedvig goes over and reads for a time by the lamp.)

HIALMAR *(half-aloud, clenching his hands)*. The eyes! The eyes—and
then that letter!

HEDVIG *(leaves off reading)*. Yes, but it seems to me that it's grandfather that's to have it.

HIALMAR *(takes the letter from her)*. Gina—can you understand this?

GINA. I know nothing whatever about it; tell me what's the matter.

HIALMAR. Mr. Werle writes to Hedvig that her old grandfather need
not trouble himself any longer with the copying, but that he can
henceforth draw on the office for a hundred crowns a month . . .

GREGERS. Aha!

HEDVIG. A hundred crowns, mother! I read that.

GINA. What a good thing for grandfather!

HIALMAR. . . . a hundred crowns a month so long as he needs it—that means, of course, so long as he lives.

GINA. Well, so he's provided for, poor dear.

HIALMAR. But there is more to come. You didn't read that, Hedvig. Afterwards this gift is to pass on to you.

HEDVIG. To me! The whole of it?

HIALMAR. He says that the same amount is assured to you for the whole of your life. Do you hear that, Gina?

GINA. Yes, I hear.

HEDVIG. Fancy—all that money for me! *(Shakes him.)* Father, father, aren't you glad . . . ?

HIALMAR *(eluding her).* Glad! *(Walks about.)* Oh what vistas—what perspectives open up before me! It is Hedvig, Hedvig that he showers these benefactions upon!

GINA. Yes, because it's Hedvig's birthday . . .

HEDVIG. And you'll get it all the same, father! You know quite well I shall give all the money to you and mother.

HIALMAR. To mother, yes! There we have it.

GREGERS. Hialmar, this is a trap he is setting for you.

HIALMAR. Do you think it's another trap?

GREGERS. When he was here this morning he said: Hialmar Ekdal is not the man you imagine him to be.

HIALMAR. Not the man . . . !

GREGERS. That you shall see, he said.

HIALMAR. He meant you should see that I would let myself be bought off . . . !

HEDVIG. Oh mother, what does all this mean?

GINA. Go and take off your things.

(Hedvig goes out by the kitchen door, half-crying.)

GREGERS. Yes, Hialmar—now is the time to show who was right, he or I.

HIALMAR (*slowly tears the paper across, lays both pieces on the table, and says*): Here is my answer.

GREGERS. Just what I expected.

HIALMAR (*goes over to Gina, who stands by the stove, and says in a low voice*): Now please make a clean breast of it. If the connection between you and him was quite over when you—came to care for me, as you call it—why did he place us in a position to marry?

GINA. I suppose he thought as he could come and go in our house.

HIALMAR. Only *that?* Was not he afraid of a possible contingency?

GINA. I don't know what you mean.

HIALMAR. I want to know whether—your child has the right to live under my roof.

GINA (*draws herself up; her eyes flash*). *You* ask that!

HIALMAR. You shall answer me this one question: Does Hedvig belong to me—or . . . ? Well!

GINA (*looking at him with cold defiance*). I don't know.

HIALMAR (*quivering a little*). You don't know!

GINA. How should *I* know? A creature like *me* . . .

HIALMAR (*quietly turning away from her*). Then I have nothing more to do in this house.

GREGERS. Take care, Hialmar! Think what you are doing!

HIALMAR (*puts on his overcoat*). In this case, there is nothing for a man like me to think twice about.

GREGERS. Yes indeed, there are endless things to be considered. You three must be together if you are to attain the true frame of mind for self-sacrifice and forgiveness.

HIALMAR. I don't want to attain it. Never, never! My hat! (*Takes his hat.*) My home has fallen in ruins about me. (*Bursts into tears.*) Gregers, I have no child!

HEDVIG (*who has opened the kitchen door*). What is that you're saying? (*Coming to him.*) Father, father!

GINA. There, you see!

HIALMAR. Don't come near me, Hedvig! Keep far away. I cannot bear to see you. Oh! those eyes . . . ! Good-bye. (*Makes for the door.*)

HEDVIG *(clinging close to him and screaming loudly).* No! no! Don't leave me!

GINA *(cries out).* Look at the child, Ekdal! Look at the child!

HIALMAR. I will not! I cannot! I must get out—away from all this! *(He tears himself away from Hedvig, and goes out by the passage door.)*

HEDVIG *(with despairing eyes).* He is going away from us, mother! He is going away from us! He will never come back again!

GINA. Don't cry, Hedvig. Father's sure to come back again.

HEDVIG *(throws herself sobbing on the sofa).* No, no, he'll never come home to us any more.

GREGERS. Do you believe I meant all for the best, Mrs. Ekdal?

GINA. Yes, I daresay you did; but God forgive you, all the same.

HEDVIG *(lying on the sofa).* Oh, this will kill me! What have I done to him? Mother, you must fetch him home again!

GINA. Yes yes yes; only be quiet, and I'll go out and look for him. *(Puts on her outdoor things.)* Perhaps he's gone in to Relling's. But you mustn't lie there and cry. Promise me!

HEDVIG *(weeping convulsively).* Yes, I'll stop, I'll stop; if only father comes back!

GREGERS *(to Gina, who is going).* After all, had you not better leave him to fight out his bitter fight to the end?

GINA. Oh, he can do that afterwards. First of all, we must get the child quieted. *(Goes out by the passage door.)*

HEDVIG *(sits up and dries her tears).* Now you must tell me what all this means. Why doesn't father want me any more?

GREGERS. You mustn't ask that till you are a big girl—quite grown-up.

HEDVIG *(sobs).* But I can't go on being as miserable as this till I'm grown-up.—I think I know what it is.—Perhaps I'm not really father's child.

GREGERS *(uneasily).* How could *that* be?

HEDVIG. Mother might have found me. And perhaps father has just got to know it; I've read of such things.

GREGERS. Well, but if it were so . . .

HEDVIG. I think he might be just as fond of me for all that. Yes, fonder almost. We got the wild duck in a present, you know, and I love it so dearly all the same.

GREGERS *(turning the conversation)*. Ah, the wild duck, by-the-bye! Let us talk about the wild duck a little, Hedvig.

HEDVIG. The poor wild duck! He doesn't want to see it any more either. Only think, he wanted to wring its neck!

GREGERS. Oh, he won't do that.

HEDVIG. No; but he said he would like to. And I think it was horrid of father to say it; for I pray for the wild duck every night, and ask that it may be preserved from death and all that is evil.

GREGERS *(looking at her)*. Do you say your prayers every night?

HEDVIG. Yes.

GREGERS. Who taught you to do that?

HEDVIG. I myself; one time when father was very ill, and had leeches on his neck, and said that death was staring him in the face.

GREGERS. Well?

HEDVIG. Then I prayed for him as I lay in bed; and since then I have always kept it up.

GREGERS. And now you pray for the wild duck too?

HEDVIG. I thought it was best to bring in the wild duck; for she was so weakly at first.

GREGERS. Do you pray in the morning, too?

HEDVIG. No, of course not.

GREGERS. Why not in the morning as well?

HEDVIG. In the morning it's light, you know, and there's nothing in particular to be afraid of.

GREGERS. And your father was going to wring the neck of the wild duck that you love so dearly?

HEDVIG. No; he said he ought to wring its neck, but he would spare it for my sake; and that was kind of father.

GREGERS *(coming a little nearer)*. But suppose *you* were to sacrifice the wild duck of your own free will for *his* sake.

HEDVIG *(rising)*. The wild duck!

GREGERS. Suppose you were to make a free-will offering, for his sake, of the dearest treasure you have in the world!

HEDVIG. Do you think *that* would do any good?

GREGERS. Try it, Hedvig.

HEDVIG *(softly, with flashing eyes)*. Yes, I will try it.

GREGERS. Have you really the courage for it, do you think?

HEDVIG. I'll ask grandfather to shoot the wild duck for me.

GREGERS. Yes, do. But not a word to your mother about it.

HEDVIG. Why not?

GREGERS. She doesn't understand us.

HEDVIG. The wild duck! I'll try it to-morrow morning.

(Gina comes in by the passage door.)

HEDVIG *(going towards her)*. Did you find him, mother?

GINA. No, but I heard as he had called and taken Relling with him.

GREGERS. Are you sure of that?

GINA. Yes, the porter's wife said so. Molvik went with them too, she said.

GREGERS. This evening, when his mind so sorely needs to wrestle in solitude . . . !

GINA *(takes off her things)*. Yes, men are strange creatures, so they are. The Lord only knows where Relling has dragged him to! I ran over to Madam Eriksen's, but they weren't *there.*

HEDVIG *(struggling to keep back her tears)*. Oh, if he should never come home any more!

GREGERS. He *will* come home again. I shall have news to give him to-morrow; and then you shall see *how* he comes home. You may rely upon that, Hedvig, and sleep in peace. Good-night. *(He goes out by the passage door.)*

HEDVIG *(throws herself sobbing on Gina's neck)*. Mother, mother!

GINA *(pats her shoulder and sighs)*. Ah yes; Relling was right, he was. That's what comes of it when crazy creatures go about present-ing the claims of the—what-you-may-call-it.

ACT FIFTH

Hialmar Ekdal's studio. Cold, grey, morning light. Wet snow lies upon the large panes of the sloping roof-window.

Gina comes from the kitchen with an apron and bib on, and carrying a dusting-brush and a duster; she goes towards the sitting-room door. At the same moment Hedvig comes hurriedly in from the passage.

GINA *(stops)*. Well?

HEDVIG. Oh, mother, I almost think he's down at Relling's . . .

GINA. There, you see!

HEDVIG. . . . because the porter's wife says she could hear that Relling had two people with him when he came home last night.

GINA. That's just what I thought.

HEDVIG. But it's no use his being there, if he won't come up to us.

GINA. I'll go down and speak to him at all events.

(Old Ekdal, in dressing-gown and slippers, and with a lighted pipe, appears at the door of his room.)

EKDAL. Hialmar . . . Isn't Hialmar at home?

GINA. No, he's gone out.

EKDAL. So early? And in such a tearing snowstorm? Well well; just as he pleases; I can take my morning walk alone. *(He slides the garret door aside; Hedvig helps him; he goes in; she closes it after him.)*

HEDVIG *(in an undertone)*. Only think, mother, when poor grandfather hears that father is going to leave us.

GINA. Oh, nonsense; grandfather mustn't hear anything about it. It was a heaven's mercy he wasn't at home yesterday in all that hurly-burly.

HEDVIG. Yes, but . . .

(Gregers comes in by the passage door.)

GREGERS. Well, have you any news of him?

GINA. They say he's down at Relling's.

GREGERS. At Relling's! Has he really been out with those creatures?

GINA. Yes, like enough.

GREGERS. When he ought to have been yearning for solitude, to collect and clear his thoughts . . .

GINA. Yes, you may well say so.

(Relling enters from the passage.)

HEDVIG *(going to him)*. Is father in your room?

GINA *(at the same time)*. Is he there?

RELLING. Yes, to be sure he is.

HEDVIG. And you never let us know!

RELLING. Yes; I'm a brute. But in the first place I had to look after the other brute; I mean our dæmonic friend, of course; and then I fell so dead asleep that . . .

GINA. What does Ekdal say to-day?

RELLING. He says nothing whatever.

HEDVIG. Doesn't he speak?

RELLING. Not a blessed word.

GREGERS. No no; I can understand that very well.

GINA. But what's he doing then?

RELLING. He's lying on the sofa, snoring.

GINA. Oh is he? Yes, Ekdal's a rare one to snore.

HEDVIG. Asleep? Can he sleep?

RELLING. Well, it certainly looks like it.

GREGERS. No wonder, after the spiritual conflict that has rent him . . .

GINA. And then he's never been used to gadding about out of doors at night.

HEDVIG. Perhaps it's a good thing that he's getting sleep, mother.

GINA. Of course it is; and we must take care we don't wake him up too early. Thank you, Relling. I must get the house cleaned up a bit now, and then . . . Come and help me, Hedvig.

(Gina and Hedvig go into the sitting-room.)

GREGERS *(turning to Relling)*. What is your explanation of the spiritual tumult that is now going on in Hialmar Ekdal?

RELLING. Devil a bit of a spiritual tumult have *I* noticed in him.

GREGERS. What! Not at such a crisis, when his whole life has been placed on a new foundation . . . ? How can you think that such an individuality as Hialmar's . . . ?

RELLING. Oh, individuality—he! If he ever had any tendency to the abnormal developments you call individuality, I can assure you it was rooted out of him while he was still in his teens.

GREGERS. That would be strange indeed,—considering the loving care with which he was brought up.

RELLING. By those two high-flown, hysterical maiden aunts, you mean?

GREGERS. Let me tell you that they were women who never forgot the claim of the ideal—but of course you will only jeer at me again.

RELLING. No, I'm in no humour for that. I know all about those ladies; for he has ladled out no end of rhetoric on the subject of his "two soul-mothers." But I don't think he has much to thank them for. Ekdal's misfortune is that in his own circle he has always been looked upon as a shining light . . .

GREGERS. Not without reason, surely. Look at the depth of his mind!

RELLING. *I* have never discovered it. That his father believed in it I don't so much wonder; the old lieutenant has been an ass all his days.

GREGERS. He has had a child-like mind all his days; that is what you cannot understand.

RELLING. Well, so be it. But then, when our dear, sweet Hialmar went to college, he at once passed for the great light of the future amongst his comrades too! He was handsome, the rascal—red and white—a shop-girl's dream of manly beauty; and with his super- ficially emotional temperament, and his sympathetic voice, and his talent for declaiming other people's verses and other people's thoughts . . .

GREGERS (*indignantly*). Is it Hialmar Ekdal you are talking about in this strain?

RELLING. Yes, with your permission; I am simply giving you an inside view of the idol you are grovelling before.

GREGERS. I should hardly have thought I was quite stone blind.

RELLING. Yes you are—or not far from it. You are a sick man, too, you see.

GREGERS. You are right there.

RELLING. Yes. Yours is a complicated case. First of all there is that plaguy integrity-fever; and then—what's worse—you are always in a delirium of hero-worship; you must always have something to adore, outside yourself.

GREGERS. Yes, I must certainly seek it outside myself.

RELLING. But you make such shocking mistakes about every new phœnix you think you have discovered. Here again you have come to a cotter's cabin with your claim of the ideal; and the people of the house are insolvent.

GREGERS. If you don't think better than that of Hialmar Ekdal, what pleasure can you find in being everlastingly with him?

RELLING. Well, you see, I'm supposed to be a sort of a doctor—save the mark! I can't but give a hand to the poor sick folk who live under the same roof with me.

GREGERS. Oh, indeed! Hialmar Ekdal is sick too, is he!

RELLING. Most people are, worse luck.

GREGERS. And what remedy are you applying in Hialmar's case?

RELLING. My usual one. I am cultivating the life-illusion[1] in him.

GREGERS. Life—illusion? I didn't catch what you said.

[1] "Livsløgnen," literally "the life-lie."

RELLING. Yes, I said illusion. For illusion, you know, is the stimulating principle.

GREGERS. May I ask with what illusion Hialmar is inoculated?

RELLING. No, thank you; I don't betray professional secrets to quack-salvers. You would probably go and muddle his case still more than you have already. But my method is infallible. I have applied it to Molvik as well. I have made him "dæmonic." That's the blister I have to put on *his* neck.

GREGERS. Is he not really dæmonic then?

RELLING. What the devil do you mean by dæmonic! It's only a piece of gibberish I've invented to keep up a spark of life in him. But for that, the poor harmless creature would have succumbed to self-contempt and despair many a long year ago. And the old lieutenant! But he has hit upon his own cure, you see.

GREGERS. Lieutenant Ekdal? What of him?

RELLING. Just think of the old bear-hunter shutting himself up in that dark garret to shoot rabbits! I tell you there is not a happier sportsman in the world than the old man pottering about in there among all that rubbish. The four or five withered Christmas-trees he has saved up are the same to him as the whole great fresh Høidal forest; the cock and the hens are big game-birds in the fir-tops; and the rabbits that flop about the garret floor are the bears he has to battle with—the mighty hunter of the mountains!

GREGERS. Poor unfortunate old man! Yes; he has indeed had to narrow the ideals of his youth.

RELLING. While I think of it, Mr. Werle, junior—don't use that foreign word: ideals. We have the excellent native word: lies.

GREGERS. Do you think the two things are related?

RELLING. Yes, just about as closely as typhus and putrid fever.

GREGERS. Dr. Relling, I shall not give up the struggle until I have rescued Hialmar from your clutches!

RELLING. So much the worse for him. Rob the average man of his life-illusion, and you rob him of his happiness at the same stroke. *(To Hedvig, who comes in from the sitting-room.)* Well, little wild-duck-mother, I'm just going down to see whether papa is still lying meditating upon that wonderful invention of his. (*Goes out by the passage door.*)

GREGERS (*approaches Hedvig*). I can see by your face that you have not yet done it.

HEDVIG. What? Oh, that about the wild duck! No.

GREGERS. I suppose your courage failed when the time came.

HEDVIG. No, that wasn't it. But when I awoke this morning and remembered what we had been talking about, it seemed so strange.

GREGERS. Strange?

HEDVIG. Yes, I don't know . . . Yesterday evening, at the moment, I thought there was something so delightful about it; but since I have slept and thought of it again, it somehow doesn't seem worth while.

GREGERS. Ah, I thought you could not have grown up quite unharmed in this house.

HEDVIG. I don't care about that, if only father would come up . . .

GREGERS. Oh, if only your eyes had been opened to that which gives life its value—if you possessed the true, joyous, fearless spirit of sacrifice, you would soon see *how* he would come up to you.—But I believe in you still, Hedvig. (*He goes out by the passage door.*)

(*Hedvig wanders about the room for a time; she is on the point of going into the kitchen when a knock is heard at the garret door. Hedvig goes over and opens it a little; old Ekdal comes out; she pushes the door to again.*)

EKDAL. H'm, it's not much fun to take one's morning walk alone.

HEDVIG. Wouldn't you like to go shooting, grandfather?

EKDAL. It's not the weather for it to-day. It's so dark there, you can scarcely see where you're going.

HEDVIG. Do you never want to shoot anything besides the rabbits?

EKDAL. Do you think the rabbits aren't good enough?

HEDVIG. Yes, but what about the wild duck?

EKDAL. Ho-ho! are you afraid I shall shoot your wild duck? Never in the world. Never.

HEDVIG. No, I suppose you couldn't; they say it's very difficult to shoot wild ducks.

EKDAL. Couldn't! Should rather think I could.

HEDVIG. How would you set about it, grandfather?—I don't mean with *my* wild duck, but with others?

EKDAL. I should take care to shoot them in the breast, you know; that's the surest place. And then you must shoot against the feathers, you see—not the way of the feathers.

HEDVIG. Do they die then, grandfather?

EKDAL. Yes, they die right enough—when you shoot properly. Well, I must go and brush up a bit. H'm—understand—h'm. *(Goes into his room.)*

(Hedvig waits a little, glances towards the sitting-room door, goes over to the bookcase, stands on tip-toe, takes the double-barrelled pistol down from the shelf, and looks at it. Gina, with brush and duster, comes from the sitting-room. Hedvig hastily lays down the pistol, unobserved.)

GINA. Don't stand raking amongst father's things, Hedvig.

HEDVIG *(goes away from the bookcase)*. I was only going to tidy up a little.

GINA. You'd better go into the kitchen, and see if the coffee's keeping hot; I'll take his breakfast on a tray, when I go down to him.

(Hedvig goes out. Gina begins to sweep and clean up the studio. Presently the passage door is opened with hesitation, and Hialmar Ekdal looks in. He has on his overcoat, but not his hat; he is unwashed, and his hair is dishevelled and unkempt. His eyes are dull and heavy.)

GINA *(standing with the brush in her hand, and looking at him)*. Oh, there now, Ekdal—so you've come after all?

HIALMAR *(comes in and answers in a toneless voice)*. I come—only to depart again immediately.

GINA. Yes, yes, I suppose so. But, Lord help us! what a sight you are!

HIALMAR. A sight?

GINA. And your nice winter coat too! Well, that's done for.

HEDVIG *(at the kitchen door)*. Mother, hadn't I better...? *(Sees Hialmar, gives a loud scream of joy, and runs to him.)* Oh, father, father!

HIALMAR *(turns away and makes a gesture of repulsion)*. Away, away, away! *(To Gina.)* Keep her away from me, I say!

GINA *(in a low tone)*. Go into the sitting-room, Hedvig.

(Hedvig does so without a word.)

HIALMAR *(fussily pulls out the table-drawer)*. I must have my books with me. Where are my books?

GINA. Which books?

HIALMAR. My scientific books, of course; the technical magazines I require for my invention.

GINA *(searches in the bookcase)*. Is it these here paper-covered ones?

HIALMAR. Yes, of course.

GINA *(lays a heap of magazines on the table)*. Shan't I get Hedvig to cut them for you?

HIALMAR. I don't require to have them cut for me.

(Short silence.)

GINA. Then you're still set on leaving us, Ekdal?

HIALMAR *(rummaging amongst the books)*. Yes, that is a matter of course, I should think.

GINA. Well, well.

HIALMAR *(vehemently)*. How can I live here, to be stabbed to the heart every hour of the day?

GINA. God forgive you for thinking such vile things of me.

HIALMAR. Prove . . . !

GINA. I think it's *you* as has got to prove.

HIALMAR. After a past like yours? There are certain claims—I must almost call them claims of the ideal . . .

GINA. But what about grandfather? What's to become of *him*, poor dear?

HIALMAR. I know my duty; my helpless father will come with me. I am going out into the town to make arrangements . . . H'm—*(hesitatingly)* has any one found my hat on the stairs?

GINA. No. Have you lost your hat?

HIALMAR. Of course I had it on when I came in last night; there's no doubt about that; but I couldn't find it this morning.

GINA. Lord help us! where *have* you been to with those two ne'er-do-weels?

HIALMAR. Oh, don't bother me about trifles. Do you suppose I am in the mood to remember details?

GINA. If only you haven't caught cold, Ekdal. *(Goes out into the kitchen.)*

HIALMAR *(talks to himself in a low tone of irritation, whilst he empties the table-drawer)*. You're a scoundrel, Relling!—You're a low fellow!—Ah, you shameless tempter!—I wish I could get some one to stick a knife into you.

(He lays some old letters on one side, finds the torn document of yesterday, takes it up and looks at the pieces; puts it down hurriedly as Gina enters.)

GINA (*sets a tray with coffee, etc., on the table*). Here's a drop of something hot, if you'd fancy it. And there's some bread and butter and a snack of salt meat.

HIALMAR (*glancing at the tray*). Salt meat? Never under this roof! It's true I have not had a mouthful of solid food for nearly twenty-four hours; but no matter.—My memoranda! The commencement of my autobiography! What has become of my diary, and all my important papers? (*Opens the sitting-room door but draws back.*) She is there too!

GINA. Good Lord! the child must be *somewhere!*

HIALMAR. Come out!

(*He makes room, Hedvig comes, scared, into the studio.*)

HIALMAR (*with his hand upon the door-handle, says to Gina*): In these, the last moments I spend in my former home, I wish to be spared from interlopers . . . (*Goes into the room.*)

HEDVIG (*with a bound towards her mother, asks softly, trembling*). Does that mean me?

GINA. Stay out in the kitchen, Hedvig; or, no—you'd best go into your own room. (*Speaks to Hialmar as she goes in to him.*) Wait a bit, Ekdal; don't rummage so in the drawers; *I* know where everything is.

HEDVIG (*stands a moment immovable, in terror and perplexity, biting her lips to keep back the tears; then she clenches her hands convulsively, and says softly*): The wild duck.

(*She steals over and takes the pistol from the shelf, opens the garret door a little way, creeps in, and draws the door to after her. Hialmar and Gina can be heard disputing in the sitting-room.*)

HIALMAR (*comes in with some manuscript books and old loose papers, which he lays upon the table*). That portmanteau is of no use. There are a thousand and one things I must drag with me.

GINA (*following with the portmanteau*). Why not leave all the rest for the present, and only take a shirt and a pair of woollen drawers with you?

HIALMAR. Whew!—all these exhausting preparations . . . !

(*Pulls off his overcoat and throws it upon the sofa.*)

GINA. And there's the coffee getting cold.

HIALMAR. H'm.

(Drinks a mouthful without thinking of it, and then another.)

GINA *(dusting the backs of the chairs)*. A nice job you'll have to find such another big garret for the rabbits.

HIALMAR. What! Am I to drag all those rabbits with me too?

GINA. You don't suppose grandfather can get on without his rabbits.

HIALMAR. He must just get used to doing without them. Have not *I* to sacrifice very much greater things than rabbits!

GINA *(dusting the bookcase)*. Shall I put the flute in the portmanteau for you?

HIALMAR. No. No flute for me. But give me the pistol!

GINA. Do you want to take the pigstol with you?

HIALMAR. Yes. My loaded pistol.

GINA *(searching for it)*. It's gone. He must have taken it in with him.

HIALMAR. Is he in the garret?

GINA. Yes, of course he's in the garret.

HIALMAR. H'm—poor lonely old man.

(He takes a piece of bread and butter, eats it, and finishes his cup of coffee.)

GINA. If we hadn't have let that room, you could have moved in there.

HIALMAR. And continued to live under the same roof with . . . ! Never, —never!

GINA. But couldn't you put up with the sitting-room for a day or two? You could have it all to yourself.

HIALMAR. Never within these walls!

GINA. Well then, down with Relling and Molvik.

HIALMAR. Don't mention those wretches' names to me! The very thought of them almost takes away my appetite.—Oh no, I must go out into the storm and the snow-drift,—go from house to house and seek shelter for my father and myself.

GINA. But you've got no hat, Ekdal! You've been and lost your hat, you know.

HIALMAR. Oh those two brutes, those slaves of all the vices! A hat must be procured. *(Takes another piece of bread and butter.)* Some arrangement must be made. For I have no mind to throw away my life, either. *(Looks for something on the tray.)*

GINA. What are you looking for?

HIALMAR. Butter.

GINA. I'll get some at once. *(Goes out into the kitchen.)*

HIALMAR *(calls after her)*. Oh it doesn't matter; dry bread is good enough for *me*.

GINA *(brings a dish of butter)*. Look here; this is fresh churned.
(She pours out another cup of coffee for him; he seats himself on the sofa, spreads more butter on the already buttered bread, and eats and drinks awhile in silence.)

HIALMAR. Could I, without being subject to intrusion—intrusion of *any* sort—could I live in the sitting-room there for a day or two?

GINA. Yes, to be sure you could, if you only would.

HIALMAR. For I see no possibility of getting all father's things out in such a hurry.

GINA. And besides, you've surely got to tell him first as you don't mean to live with us others no more.

HIALMAR *(pushes away his coffee cup)*. Yes, there is that too; I shall have to lay bare the whole tangled story to him ... I must turn matters over; I must have breathing-time; I cannot take all these burdens on my shoulders in a single day.

GINA. No, especially in such horrible weather as it is outside.

HIALMAR *(touching Werle's letter)*. I see that paper is still lying about here.

GINA. Yes, *I* haven't touched it.

HIALMAR. So far as I am concerned it is mere waste paper ...

GINA. Well, *I* have certainly no notion of making any use of it.

HIALMAR. ... but we had better not let it get lost all the same;—in all the upset when I move, it might easily ...

GINA. I'll take good care of it, Ekdal.

HIALMAR. The donation is in the first instance made to father, and it rests with him to accept or decline it.

GINA *(sighs)*. Yes, poor old father . . .

HIALMAR. To make quite safe . . . Where shall I find some gum?

GINA *(goes to the bookcase)*. Here's the gum-pot.

HIALMAR. And a brush?

GINA. The brush is here too. *(Brings him the things.)*

HIALMAR *(takes a pair of scissors)*. Just a strip of paper at the back . . . *(Clips and gums.)* Far be it from me to lay hands upon what is not my own—and least of all upon what belongs to a destitute old man—and to—the other as well.—There now. Let it lie there for a time; and when it is dry, take it away. I wish never to see that document again. Never!

(Gregers Werle enters from the passage.)

GREGERS *(somewhat surprised)*. What,—are you sitting here, Hialmar?

HIALMAR *(rises hurriedly)*. I had sunk down from fatigue.

GREGERS. You have been having breakfast, I see.

HIALMAR. The body sometimes makes its claims felt too.

GREGERS. What have you decided to do?

HIALMAR. For a man like me, there is only one course possible. I am just putting my most important things together. But it takes time, you know.

GINA *(with a touch of impatience)*. Am I to get the room ready for you, or am I to pack your portmanteau?

HIALMAR *(after a glance of annoyance at Gregers)*. Pack—and get the room ready!

GINA *(takes the portmanteau)*. Very well; then I'll put in the shirt and the other things.

(Goes into the sitting-room and draws the door to after her.)

GREGERS *(after a short silence)*. I never dreamed that this would be the end of it. Do you really feel it a necessity to leave house and home?

HIALMAR *(wanders about restlessly)*. What would you have me do? —I am not fitted to bear unhappiness, Gregers. I must feel secure and at peace in my surroundings.

GREGERS. But can you not feel that here? Just try it. I should have thought you had firm ground to build upon now—if only you start afresh. And remember, you have your invention to live for.

HIALMAR. Oh don't talk about my invention. It's perhaps still in the dim distance.

GREGERS. Indeed!

HIALMAR. Why, great heavens, what would you have me invent? Other people have invented almost everything already. It becomes more and more difficult every day . . .

GREGERS. And you have devoted so much labour to it.

HIALMAR. It was that blackguard Relling that urged me to it.

GREGERS. Relling?

HIALMAR. Yes, it was he that first made me realise my aptitude for making some notable discovery in photography.

GREGERS. Aha—it was Relling!

HIALMAR. Oh, I have been so truly happy over it! Not so much for the sake of the invention itself, as because Hedvig believed in it —believed in it with a child's whole eagerness of faith.—At least, I have been fool enough to go and imagine that she believed in it.

GREGERS. Can you really think that Hedvig has been false towards you?

HIALMAR. I can think anything now. It is Hedvig that stands in my way. She will blot out the sunlight from my whole life.

GREGERS. Hedvig! Is it Hedvig you are talking of? How should *she* blot out your sunlight?

HIALMAR *(without answering)*. How unutterably I have loved that child! How unutterably happy I have felt every time I came home to my humble room, and she flew to meet me, with her sweet little blinking eyes. Oh, confiding fool that I have been! I loved her unutterably;—and I yielded myself up to the dream, the delusion, that she loved me unutterably in return.

GREGERS. Do you call *that* a delusion?

HIALMAR. How should I know? I can get nothing out of Gina; and besides, she is totally blind to the ideal side of these complications. But to you I feel impelled to open my mind, Gregers. I cannot shake off this frightful doubt—perhaps Hedvig has never really and honestly loved me.

GREGERS. What would you say if she were to give you a proof of her love? *(Listens.)* What's that? I thought I heard the wild duck . . . ?

HIALMAR. It's the wild duck quacking. Father's in the garret.

GREGERS. Is he? *(His face lights up with joy.)* I say you may yet have proof that your poor misunderstood Hedvig loves you!

HIALMAR. Oh, what proof can she give me? I dare not believe in any assurances from that quarter.

GREGERS. Hedvig does not know what deceit means.

HIALMAR. Oh Gregers, that is just what I cannot be sure of. Who knows what Gina and that Mrs. Sørby may many a time have sat here whispering and tattling about? And Hedvig usually has her ears open, I can tell you. Perhaps the deed of gift was not such a surprise to her, after all. In fact, I'm not sure but that I noticed something of the sort.

GREGERS. What spirit is this that has taken possession of you?

HIALMAR. I have had my eyes opened. Just you notice;—you'll see, the deed of gift is only a beginning. Mrs. Sørby has always been a good deal taken up with Hedvig; and now she has the power to do whatever she likes for the child. They can take her from me whenever they please.

GREGERS. Hedvig will never, never leave you.

HIALMAR. Don't be so sure of that. If only they beckon to her and throw out a golden bait . . . ! And oh! I have loved her so unspeakably! I would have counted it my highest happiness to take her tenderly by the hand and lead her, as one leads a timid child through a great dark empty room!—I am cruelly certain now that the poor photographer in his humble attic has never really and truly been anything to her. She has only cunningly contrived to keep on a good footing with him until the time came.

GREGERS. You don't believe that yourself, Hialmar.

HIALMAR. That is just the terrible part of it—I don't know what to believe,—I never can know it. But can you really doubt that it must be as I say? Ho-ho, you have far too much faith in the claim of the ideal, my good Gregers! If those others came, with the glamour of wealth about them, and called to the child:—"Leave him: come to us: here life awaits you . . . !"

GREGERS *(quickly).* Well, what then?

HIALMAR. If I then asked her: Hedvig, are you willing to renounce that life for me? *(Laughs scornfully.)* No thank you! You would soon hear what answer I should get.

(A pistol shot is heard from within the garret.)

GREGERS *(loudly and joyfully).* Hialmar!

HIALMAR. There now; he must needs go shooting too.

GINA *(comes in).* Oh Ekdal, I can hear grandfather blazing away in the garret by hisself.

HIALMAR. I'll look in . . .

GREGERS *(eagerly, with emotion).* Wait a moment! Do you know what that was?

HIALMAR. Yes, of course I know.

GREGERS. No you don't know. But *I* do. That was the proof!

HIALMAR. What proof?

GREGERS. It was a child's free-will offering. She has got your father to shoot the wild duck.

HIALMAR. To shoot the wild duck!

GINA. Oh, think of that . . . !

HIALMAR. What was *that* for?

GREGERS. She wanted to sacrifice to you her most cherished possession; for then she thought you would surely come to love her again.

HIALMAR *(tenderly, with emotion).* Oh, poor child!

GINA. What things she does think of!

GREGERS. She only wanted your love again, Hialmar. She could not live without it.

GINA *(struggling with her tears).* There, you can see for yourself, Ekdal.

HIALMAR. Gina, where is she?

GINA *(sniffs).* Poor dear, she's sitting out in the kitchen, I dare say.

HIALMAR *(goes over, tears open the kitchen door, and says):* Hedvig, come, come in to me! *(Looks around.)* No, she's not here.

GINA. Then she must be in her own little room.

HIALMAR *(without).* No, she's not here either. *(Comes in.)* She must have gone out.

GINA. Yes, you wouldn't have her anywhere in the house.

HIALMAR. Oh, if she would only come home quickly, so that I can tell her . . . Everything will come right now, Gregers; now I believe we can begin life afresh.

GREGERS *(quietly).* I knew it; I knew the child would make amends. *(Old Ekdal appears at the door of his room; he is in full uniform, and is busy buckling on his sword.)*

HIALMAR *(astonished).* Father! Are you there?

GINA. Have you been firing in your room?

EKDAL *(resentfully, approaching).* So you go shooting alone, do you, Hialmar?

HIALMAR *(excited and confused).* Then it wasn't you that fired that shot in the garret?

EKDAL. *Me* that fired? H'm.

GREGERS *(calls out to Hialmar).* She has shot the wild duck herself!

HIALMAR. What can it mean? *(Hastens to the garret door, tears it aside, looks in and calls loudly):* Hedvig!

GINA *(runs to the door).* Good God, what's that!

HIALMAR *(goes in).* She's lying on the floor!

GREGERS. Hedvig! lying on the floor! *(Goes in to Hialmar.)*

GINA *(at the same time).* Hedvig! *(Inside the garret.)* No, no, no!

EKDAL. Ho-ho! does *she* go shooting too, now?

(Hialmar, Gina, and Gregers carry Hedvig into the studio; in her dangling right hand she holds the pistol fast clasped in her fingers.)

HIALMAR *(distracted).* The pistol has gone off. She has wounded herself. Call for help! Help!

GINA *(runs into the passage and calls down).* Relling! Relling! Doctor Relling; come up as quick as you can!

(Hialmar and Gregers lay Hedvig down on the sofa.)

EKDAL (*quietly*). The woods avenge themselves.

HIALMAR (*on his knees beside Hedvig*). She'll soon come to now. She's coming to . . . ; yes, yes, yes.

GINA (*who has come in again*). Where has she hurt herself? I can't see anything . . .

(*Relling comes hurriedly, and immediately after him Molvik; the latter without his waistcoat and necktie, and with his coat open.*)

RELLING. What's the matter here?

GINA. They say Hedvig has shot herself.

HIALMAR. Come and help us!

RELLING. Shot herself!

(*He pushes the table aside and begins to examine her.*)

HIALMAR (*kneeling and looking anxiously up at him*). It can't be dangerous? Speak, Relling! She is scarcely bleeding at all. It can't be dangerous?

RELLING. How did it happen?

HIALMAR. Oh, we don't know . . . !

GINA. She wanted to shoot the wild duck.

RELLING. The wild duck?

HIALMAR. The pistol must have gone off.

RELLING. H'm. Indeed.

EKDAL. The woods avenge themselves. But I'm not afraid, all the same.

(*Goes into the garret and closes the door after him.*)

HIALMAR. Well, Relling,—why don't you say something?

RELLING. The ball has entered the breast.

HIALMAR. Yes, but she's coming to!

RELLING. Surely you can see that Hedvig is dead.

GINA (*bursts into tears*). Oh my child, my child.

GREGERS (*huskily*). In the depths of the sea . . .

HIALMAR (*jumps up*). No, no, she *must* live! Oh, for God's sake, Relling—only a moment—only just till I can tell her how unspeakably I loved her all the time!

RELLING. The bullet has gone through her heart. Internal hemorrhage. Death must have been instantaneous.

HIALMAR. And I! I hunted her from me like an animal! And she crept terrified into the garret and died for love of me! *(Sobbing.)* I can never atone to her! I can never tell her ... ! *(Clenches his hands and cries, upwards.)* O thou above ... ! If thou *be* indeed! Why hast thou done this thing to me?

GINA. Hush, hush, you mustn't go on that awful way. We had no right to keep her, I suppose.

MOLVIK. The child is not dead, but sleepeth.

RELLING. Bosh!

HIALMAR *(becomes calm, goes over to the sofa, folds his arms, and looks at Hedvig)*. There she lies so stiff and still.

RELLING *(tries to loosen the pistol)*. She's holding it so tight, so tight.

GINA. No, no, Relling, don't break her fingers; let the pigstol be.

HIALMAR. She shall take it with her.

GINA. Yes, let her. But the child mustn't lie here for a show. She shall go to her own room, so she shall. Help me, Ekdal.

(Hialmar and Gina take Hedvig between them.)

HIALMAR *(as they are carrying her)*. Oh Gina, Gina, can you survive this!

GINA. We must help each other to bear it. For *now* at least she belongs to both of us.

MOLVIK *(stretches out his arms and mumbles)*. Blessed be the Lord; to earth thou shalt return; to earth thou shalt return ...

GREGERS *(whispers)*. Hold your tongue, you fool; you're drunk.

(Hialmar and Gina carry the body out through the kitchen door. Relling shuts it after them. Molvik slinks out into the passage.)

RELLING *(goes over to Gregers and says)*: No one shall ever convince me that the pistol went off by accident.

GREGERS *(who has stood terrified, with convulsive twitchings)*. Who can say how the dreadful thing happened?

RELLING. The powder has burnt the body of her dress. She must have pressed the pistol against her breast and fired.

GREGERS. Hedvig has not died in vain. Did you not see how sorrow set free what is noble in him?

RELLING. Most people are ennobled by the actual presence of death. But how long do you suppose this nobility will last in *him?*

GREGERS. Why should it not endure and increase throughout his life?

RELLING. Before a year is over, little Hedvig will be nothing to him but a pretty theme for declamation.

GREGERS. How dare you say that of Hialmar Ekdal?

RELLING. We will talk of this again, when the grass has first withered on her grave. Then you'll hear him spouting about "the child too early torn from her father's heart"; then you'll see him steep himself in a syrup of sentiment and self-admiration and self-pity. Just you wait!

GREGERS. If you are right and I am wrong, then life is not worth living.

RELLING. Oh, life would be quite tolerable, after all, if only we could be rid of the confounded duns that keep on pestering us, in our poverty, with the claim of the ideal.

GREGERS *(looking straight before him).* In that case, I am glad that my destiny is what it is.

RELLING. May I inquire,—what *is* your destiny?

GREGERS *(going).* To be the thirteenth at table.

RELLING. The devil it is.

THE END

HEDDA GABLER

TRANSLATED BY
EDMUND GOSSE
AND
WILLIAM ARCHER

CHARACTERS

GEORGE TESMAN
*Holder of a scholarship for research in the
History of Civilisation*

HEDDA GABLER TESMAN
His wife

MISS JULIANA TESMAN
His aunt

MRS. ELVSTED

JUDGE BRACK

EILERT LØVBORG

BERTA
Servant at the Tesmans'

*The scene of the action is Tesman's villa,
in the west end of Christiania (Oslo)*

Pronunciation of names: Gabler = *Gahbler;*
ø in Løvborg = *u* as in *fur*

ACT FIRST

*A spacious, handsome, and tastefully furnished drawing-room, deco-
rated in dark colours. In the back, a wide doorway with curtains drawn
back, leading into a smaller room decorated in the same style as the
drawing-room. In the right-hand wall of the front room, a folding
door leading out to the hall. In the opposite wall, on the left, a glass
door, also with curtains drawn back. Through the panes can be seen
part of a veranda outside, and trees covered with autumn foliage. An
oval table, with a cover on it, and surrounded by chairs, stands well
forward. In front, by the wall on the right, a wide stove of dark porce-
lain, a high-backed arm-chair, a cushioned foot-rest, and two footstools.
A settee, with a small round table in front of it, fills the upper right-
hand corner. In front, on the left, a little way from the wall, a sofa.
Further back than the glass door, a piano. On either side of the doorway at the back a whatnot with terra-cotta and majolica ornaments.—
Against the back wall of the inner room a sofa, with a table, and one
or two chairs. Over the sofa hangs the portrait of a handsome elderly
man in a General's uniform. Over the table a hanging lamp, with an
opal glass shade.—A number of bouquets are arranged about the
drawing-room, in vases and glasses. Others lie upon the tables. The
floors in both rooms are covered with thick carpets.—Morning light.
The sun shines in through the glass door.*

Miss Juliana Tesman, with her bonnet on and carrying a parasol, comes in from the hall, followed by Berta, who carries a bouquet wrapped in paper. Miss Tesman is a comely and pleasant-looking lady of about sixty-five. She is nicely but simply dressed in a grey walking-costume. Berta is a middle-aged woman of plain and rather countrified appearance.

MISS TESMAN *(stops close to the door, listens, and says softly)*: Upon my word, I don't believe they are stirring yet!

BERTA *(also softly)*. I told you so, Miss. Remember how late the steamboat got in last night. And then, when they got home!—good Lord, what a lot the young mistress had to unpack before she could get to bed.

MISS TESMAN. Well well—let them have their sleep out. But let us see that they get a good breath of the fresh morning air when they do appear.

(She goes to the glass door and throws it open.)

BERTA *(beside the table, at a loss what to do with the bouquet in her hand)*. I declare there isn't a bit of room left. I think I'll put it down here, Miss.

(She places it on the piano.)

MISS TESMAN. So you've got a new mistress now, my dear Berta. Heaven knows it was a wrench to me to part with you.

BERTA *(on the point of weeping)*. And do you think it wasn't hard for me too, Miss? After all the blessed years I've been with you and Miss Rina.

MISS TESMAN. We must make the best of it, Berta. There was nothing else to be done. George can't do without you, you see—he absolutely can't. He has had you to look after him ever since he was a little boy.

BERTA. Ah but, Miss Julia, I can't help thinking of Miss Rina lying helpless at home there, poor thing. And with only that new girl too! *She'll* never learn to take proper care of an invalid.

MISS TESMAN. Oh, I shall manage to train her. And of course, you know, I shall take most of it upon myself. You needn't be uneasy about my poor sister, my dear Berta.

BERTA. Well, but there's another thing, Miss. I'm so mortally afraid I shan't be able to suit the young mistress.

MISS TESMAN. Oh well—just at first there may be one or two things . . .

BERTA. Most like she'll be terrible grand in her ways.

MISS TESMAN. Well, you can't wonder at that—General Gabler's daughter! Think of the sort of life she was accustomed to in her father's time. Don't you remember how we used to see her riding down the road along with the General? In that long black habit—and with feathers in her hat?

BERTA. Yes indeed—I remember well enough!—But, good Lord, I should never have dreamt in those days that she and Master George would make a match of it.

MISS TESMAN. Nor I.—But by-the-bye, Berta—while I think of it: in future you mustn't say Master George. You must say Dr. Tesman.

BERTA. Yes, the young mistress spoke of that too—last night—the moment they set foot in the house. Is it true then, Miss?

MISS TESMAN. Yes, indeed it is. Only think, Berta—some foreign university has made him a doctor—while he has been abroad, you understand. I hadn't heard a word about it, until he told me himself upon the pier.

BERTA. Well well, he's clever enough for anything, *he* is. But I didn't think he'd have gone in for doctoring people too.

MISS TESMAN. No no, it's not that sort of doctor he is. *(Nods significantly.)* But let me tell you, we may have to call him something still grander before long.

BERTA. You don't say so! What can *that* be, Miss?

MISS TESMAN *(smiling).* H'm—wouldn't you like to know! *(With emotion.)* Ah, dear dear—if my poor brother could only look up from his grave now, and see what his little boy has grown into! *(Looks around.)* But bless me, Berta—why have you done *this*? Taken the chintz covers off all the furniture?

BERTA. The mistress told me to. She can't abide covers on the chairs, she says.

MISS TESMAN. Are they going to make this their everyday sitting-room then?

BERTA. Yes, that's what I understood—from the mistress. Master George—the doctor—he said nothing.

(George Tesman comes from the right into the inner room, humming to himself, and carrying an unstrapped empty portmanteau. He is a middle-sized, young-looking man of thirty-three, rather stout, with a round, open, cheerful face, fair hair and beard. He wears spectacles, and is somewhat carelessly dressed in comfortable indoor clothes.)

MISS TESMAN. Good morning, good morning, George.

TESMAN *(in the doorway between the rooms)*. Aunt Julia! Dear Aunt Julia! *(Goes up to her and shakes hands warmly.)* Come all this way—so early! Eh?

MISS TESMAN. Why, of course I had to come and see how you were getting on.

TESMAN. In spite of your having had no proper night's rest?

MISS TESMAN. Oh, that makes no difference to me.

TESMAN. Well, I suppose you got home all right from the pier? Eh?

MISS TESMAN. Yes, quite safely, thank goodness. Judge Brack was good enough to see me right to my door.

TESMAN. We were so sorry we couldn't give you a seat in the carriage. But you saw what a fearful pile of boxes Hedda had to bring with her.

MISS TESMAN. Yes, she had certainly plenty of boxes.

BERTA *(to Tesman)*. Shall I go in and see if there's anything I can do for the mistress?

TESMAN. No thank you, Berta—you needn't. She said she would ring if she wanted anything.

BERTA *(going towards the right)*. Very well.

TESMAN. But look here—take this portmanteau with you.

BERTA *(taking it)*. I'll put it in the attic.

(She goes out by the hall door.)

TESMAN. Fancy, Auntie—I had the whole of that portmanteau chock full of copies of documents. You wouldn't believe how much I have picked up from all the archives I have been examining—curious old details that no one has had any idea of . . .

MISS TESMAN. Yes, you don't seem to have wasted your time on your wedding trip, George.

TESMAN. No, that I haven't. But do take off your bonnet, Auntie. Look here! Let me untie the strings—eh?

MISS TESMAN *(while he does so)*. Well well—this is just as if you were still at home with us.

TESMAN *(with the bonnet in his hand, looks at it from all sides)*. Why, what a gorgeous bonnet you've been investing in!

MISS TESMAN. I bought it on Hedda's account.

TESMAN. On Hedda's account? Eh?

MISS TESMAN. Yes, so that Hedda needn't be ashamed of me if we happened to go out together.

TESMAN *(patting her cheek)*. You always think of everything, Aunt Julia. *(Lays the bonnet on a chair beside the table.)* And now, look here—suppose we sit comfortably on the sofa and have a little chat, till Hedda comes.

(They seat themselves. She places her parasol in the corner of the sofa.)

MISS TESMAN *(takes both his hands and looks at him)*. What a delight it is to have you again, as large as life, before my very eyes, George! My George—my poor brother's own boy!

TESMAN. And it's a delight for me, too, to see you again, Aunt Julia! You, who have been father and mother in one to me.

MISS TESMAN. Oh yes, I know you will always keep a place in your heart for your old aunts.

TESMAN. And what about Aunt Rina? No improvement—eh?

MISS TESMAN. Oh no—we can scarcely look for any improvement in her case, poor thing. There she lies, helpless, as she has lain for all these years. But heaven grant I may not lose her yet awhile! For if I did, I don't know what I should make of my life, George—especially now that I haven't you to look after any more.

TESMAN (*patting her back*). There there there ... !

MISS TESMAN (*suddenly changing her tone*). And to think that here are *you* a married man, George!—And that *you* should be the one to carry off Hedda Gabler—the beautiful Hedda Gabler! Only think of it—she, that was so beset with admirers!

TESMAN (*hums a little and smiles complacently*). Yes, I fancy I have several good friends about town who would like to stand in my shoes—eh?

MISS TESMAN. And then this fine long wedding-tour you have had! More than five—nearly six months ...

TESMAN. Well, for me it has been a sort of tour of research as well. I have had to do much grubbing among old records—and to read no end of books too, Auntie.

MISS TESMAN. Oh yes, I suppose so. (*More confidentially, and lowering her voice a little.*) But listen now, George,—have you nothing—nothing special to tell me?

TESMAN. As to our journey?

MISS TESMAN. Yes.

TESMAN. No, I don't know of anything except what I have told you in my letters. I had a doctor's degree conferred on me—but that I told you yesterday.

MISS TESMAN. Yes, yes, you did. But what I mean is—haven't you any —any—expectations ... ?

TESMAN. Expectations?

MISS TESMAN. Why you know, George—I'm your old auntie!

TESMAN. Why, of course I have expectations.

MISS TESMAN. Ah!

TESMAN. I have every expectation of being a professor one of these days.

MISS TESMAN. Oh yes, a professor ...

TESMAN. Indeed, I may say I am certain of it. But my dear Auntie—you know all about that already!

MISS TESMAN *(laughing to herself)*. Yes, of course I do. You are quite right there. *(Changing the subject.)* But we were talking about your journey. It must have cost a great deal of money, George?

TESMAN. Well, you see—my handsome travelling-scholarship went a good way.

MISS TESMAN. But I can't understand how you can have made it go far enough for two.

TESMAN. No, that's not so easy to understand—eh?

MISS TESMAN. And especially travelling with a lady—they tell me that makes it ever so much more expensive.

TESMAN. Yes, of course—it makes it a little more expensive. But Hedda *had* to have this trip, Auntie! She really *had* to. Nothing else would have done.

MISS TESMAN. No no, I suppose not. A wedding-tour seems to be quite indispensable nowadays.—But tell me now—have you gone thoroughly over the house yet?

TESMAN. Yes, you may be sure I have. I have been afoot ever since daylight.

MISS TESMAN. And what do you think of it all?

TESMAN. I'm delighted! Quite delighted! Only I can't think what we are to do with two empty rooms between this inner parlour and Hedda's bedroom.

MISS TESMAN *(laughing)*. Oh my dear George, I daresay you may find some use for them—in the course of time.

TESMAN. Why of course you are quite right, Aunt Julia! You mean as my library increases—eh?

MISS TESMAN. Yes, quite so, my dear boy. It was your library I was thinking of.

TESMAN. I am specially pleased on Hedda's account. Often and often, before we were engaged, she said that she would never care to live anywhere but in Secretary Falk's villa.[1]

---

[1] In the original, "Statsrådinde Falks villa"—showing that it had belonged to the widow of a cabinet minister.

MISS TESMAN. Yes, it was lucky that this very house should come into the market, just after you had started.

TESMAN. Yes, Aunt Julia, the luck was on our side, wasn't it—eh?

MISS TESMAN. But the expense, my dear George! You will find it very expensive, all this.

TESMAN (*looks at her, a little cast down*). Yes, I suppose I shall, Aunt!

MISS TESMAN. Oh, frightfully!

TESMAN. How much do you think? In round numbers?—Eh?

MISS TESMAN. Oh, I can't even guess until all the accounts come in.

TESMAN. Well, fortunately, Judge Brack has secured the most favourable terms for me,—so he said in a letter to Hedda.

MISS TESMAN. Yes, don't be uneasy, my dear boy.—Besides, I have given security for the furniture and all the carpets.

TESMAN. Security? You? My dear Aunt Julia—what sort of security could *you* give?

MISS TESMAN. I have given a mortgage on our annuity.

TESMAN (*jumps up*). What! On your—and Aunt Rina's annuity!

MISS TESMAN. Yes, I knew of no other plan, you see.

TESMAN (*placing himself before her*). Have you gone out of your senses, Auntie! Your annuity—it's all that you and Aunt Rina have to live upon.

MISS TESMAN. Well well—don't get so excited about it. It's only a matter of form you know—Judge Brack assured me of that. It was he that was kind enough to arrange the whole affair for me. A mere matter of form, he said.

TESMAN. Yes, that may be all very well. But nevertheless . . .

MISS TESMAN. You will have your own salary to depend upon now. And, good heavens, even if we did have to pay up a little . . . ! To eke things out a bit at the start . . . ! Why, it would be nothing but a pleasure to us.

TESMAN. Oh Auntie—will you never be tired of making sacrifices for me!

MISS TESMAN (*rises and lays her hands on his shoulders*). Have I any

other happiness in this world except to smooth your way for you,
my dear boy? You, who have had neither father nor mother to depend on. And now we have reached the goal, George! Things have
looked black enough for us, sometimes; but, thank heaven, now
you have nothing to fear.

TESMAN. Yes, it is really marvellous how everything has turned out
for the best.

MISS TESMAN. And the people who opposed you—who wanted to bar
the way for you—now you have them at your feet. They have fallen,
George. Your most dangerous rival—his fall was the worst.—And
now he has to lie on the bed he has made for himself—poor mis-
guided creature.

TESMAN. Have you heard anything of Eilert? Since I went away, I
mean.

MISS TESMAN. Only that he is said to have published a new book.

TESMAN. What! Eilert Løvborg! Recently—eh?

MISS TESMAN. Yes, so they say. Heaven knows whether it can be worth
anything! Ah, when *your* new book appears—that will be another
story, George! What is it to be about?

TESMAN. It will deal with the domestic industries of Brabant during
the Middle Ages.

MISS TESMAN. Fancy—to be able to write on such a subject as that!

TESMAN. However, it may be some time before the book is ready. I
have all these collections to arrange first, you see.

MISS TESMAN. Yes, collecting and arranging—no one can beat you at
that. There you are my poor brother's own son.

TESMAN. I am looking forward eagerly to setting to work at it; especially now that I have my own delightful home to work in.

MISS TESMAN. And, most of all, now that you have got the wife of your
heart, my dear George.

TESMAN (*embracing her*). Oh yes, yes, Aunt Julia. Hedda—she is the
best part of it all! (*Looks towards the doorway.*) I believe I hear
her coming—eh?

(*Hedda enters from the left through the inner room. She is a woman of nine-and-twenty. Her face and figure show refinement and distinction. Her complexion is pale and opaque. Her steel-grey eyes express a cold, unruffled repose. Her hair is of an agreeable medium brown, but not particularly abundant. She is dressed in a tasteful, somewhat loose-fitting morning gown.)*

MISS TESMAN *(going to meet Hedda).* Good morning, my dear Hedda! Good morning, and a hearty welcome!

HEDDA *(holds out her hand).* Good morning, dear Miss Tesman! So early a call! That is kind of you.

MISS TESMAN *(with some embarrassment).* Well—has the bride slept well in her new home?

HEDDA. Oh yes, thanks. Passably.

TESMAN *(laughing).* Passably! Come, that's good, Hedda! You were sleeping like a stone when I got up.

HEDDA. Fortunately. Of course one has always to accustom one's self to new surroundings, Miss Tesman—little by little. *(Looking towards the left.)* Oh—there the servant has gone and opened the veranda door, and let in a whole flood of sunshine.

MISS TESMAN *(going towards the door).* Well, then we will shut it.

HEDDA. No no, not that! Tesman, please draw the curtains. That will give a softer light.

TESMAN *(at the door).* All right—all right.—There now, Hedda, now you have both shade and fresh air.

HEDDA. Yes, fresh air we certainly must have, with all these stacks of flowers . . . But—won't you sit down, Miss Tesman?

MISS TESMAN. No, thank you. Now that I have seen that everything is all right here—thank heaven!—I must be getting home again. My sister is lying longing for me, poor thing.

TESMAN. Give her my very best love, Auntie; and say I shall look in and see her later in the day.

MISS TESMAN. Yes, yes, I'll be sure to tell her. But by-the-bye, George —*(feeling in her dress pocket)*—I had almost forgotten—I have something for you here.

TESMAN. What is it, Auntie? Eh?

MISS TESMAN (*produces a flat parcel wrapped in newspaper and hands it to him*). Look here, my dear boy.

TESMAN (*opening the parcel*). Well, I declare!—Have you really saved them for me, Aunt Julia! Hedda! isn't this touching—eh?

HEDDA (*beside the whatnot on the right*). Well, what is it?

TESMAN. My old morning-shoes! My slippers.

HEDDA. Indeed. I remember you often spoke of them while we were abroad.

TESMAN. Yes, I missed them terribly. (*Goes up to her.*) Now you shall see them, Hedda!

HEDDA (*going towards the stove*). Thanks, I really don't care about it.

TESMAN (*following her*). Only think—ill as she was, Aunt Rina embroidered these for me. Oh you can't think how many associations cling to them.

HEDDA (*at the table*). Scarcely for me.

MISS TESMAN. Of course not for Hedda, George.

TESMAN. Well, but now that she belongs to the family, I thought . . .

HEDDA (*interrupting*). We shall never get on with this servant, Tesman.

MISS TESMAN. Not get on with Berta?

TESMAN. Why, dear, what puts *that* in your head? Eh?

HEDDA (*pointing*). Look there! She has left her old bonnet lying about on a chair.

TESMAN (*in consternation, drops the slippers on the floor*). Why, Hedda . . .

HEDDA. Just fancy, if any one should come in and see it!

TESMAN. But Hedda—that's Aunt Julia's bonnet.

HEDDA. Is it!

MISS TESMAN (*taking up the bonnet*). Yes, indeed it's mine. And, what's more, it's not old, Madam Hedda.

HEDDA. I really did not look closely at it, Miss Tesman.

MISS TESMAN (*trying on the bonnet*). Let me tell you it's the first time I have worn it—the very first time.

TESMAN. And a very nice bonnet it is too—quite a beauty!

MISS TESMAN. Oh, it's no such great thing, George. *(Looks around her.)* My parasol . . . ? Ah, here. *(Takes it.)* For this is mine too— *(mutters)*—not Berta's.

TESMAN. A new bonnet and a new parasol! Only think, Hedda!

HEDDA. Very handsome indeed.

TESMAN. Yes, isn't it? Eh? But Auntie, take a good look at Hedda before you go! See how handsome *she* is!

MISS TESMAN. Oh, my dear boy, there's nothing new in *that*. Hedda was always lovely.

(She nods and goes towards the right.)

TESMAN *(following)*. Yes, but have you noticed what splendid condition she is in? How she has filled out on the journey?

HEDDA *(crossing the room)*. Oh, do be quiet . . . !

MISS TESMAN *(who has stopped and turned)*. Filled out?

TESMAN. Of course you don't notice it so much now that she has that dress on. But I, who can see . . .

HEDDA *(at the glass door, impatiently)*. Oh, you can't see anything.

TESMAN. It must be the mountain air in the Tyrol . . .

HEDDA *(curtly, interrupting)*. I am exactly as I was when I started.

TESMAN. So you insist; but I'm quite certain you are not. Don't you agree with me, Auntie?

MISS TESMAN *(who has been gazing at her with folded hands)*. Hedda is lovely—lovely—lovely. *(Goes up to her, takes her head between both hands, draws it downwards, and kisses her hair.)* God bless and preserve Hedda Tesman—for George's sake.

HEDDA *(gently freeing herself)*. Oh—! Let me go.

MISS TESMAN *(in quiet emotion)*. I shall not let a day pass without coming to see you.

TESMAN. No you won't, will you, Auntie? Eh?

MISS TESMAN. Good-bye—good-bye!

(She goes out by the hall door. Tesman accompanies her. The door remains half open. Tesman can be heard repeating his message to Aunt Rina and his thanks for the slippers.

In the meantime, Hedda walks about the room, raising her arms

*and clenching her hands as if in desperation. Then she flings back
the curtains from the glass door, and stands there looking out.
Presently Tesman returns and closes the door behind him.)*

TESMAN *(picks up the slippers from the floor).* What are you looking
at, Hedda?

HEDDA *(once more calm and mistress of herself).* I am only looking
at the leaves. They are so yellow—so withered.

TESMAN *(wraps up the slippers and lays them on the table).* Well you
see, we are well into September now.

HEDDA *(again restless).* Yes, to think of it!—Already in—in September.

TESMAN. Don't you think Aunt Julia's manner was strange, dear?
Almost solemn? Can you imagine what was the matter with her?
Eh?

HEDDA. I scarcely know her, you see. Is she not often like that?

TESMAN. No, not as she was to-day.

HEDDA *(leaving the glass door).* Do you think she was annoyed about
the bonnet?

TESMAN. Oh, scarcely at all. Perhaps a little, just at the moment...

HEDDA. But what an idea, to pitch her bonnet about in the drawing-
room! No one does that sort of thing.

TESMAN. Well you may be sure Aunt Julia won't do it again.

HEDDA. In any case, I shall manage to make my peace with her.

TESMAN. Yes, my dear, good Hedda, if you only would.

HEDDA. When you call this afternoon, you might invite her to spend
the evening here.

TESMAN. Yes, that I will. And there's one thing more you could do
that would delight her heart.

HEDDA. What is it?

TESMAN. If you could only prevail on yourself to say *du*[1] to her. For
my sake, Hedda? Eh?

HEDDA. No no, Tesman—you really mustn't ask that of me. I have

[1] *Du* is the familiar form for *you*. Tesman is asking Hedda to be less formal, more
affectionate.

told you so already. I shall try to call her "Aunt"; and you must be satisfied with that.

TESMAN. Well well. Only I think now that you belong to the family, you . . .

HEDDA. H'm—I can't in the least see why . . .

(She goes up towards the middle doorway.)

TESMAN *(after a pause)*. Is there anything the matter with you, Hedda? Eh?

HEDDA. I'm only looking at my old piano. It doesn't go at all well with all the other things.

TESMAN. The first time I draw my salary, we'll see about exchanging it.

HEDDA. No, no—no exchanging. I don't want to part with it. Suppose we put it there in the inner room, and then get another here in its place. When it's convenient, I mean.

TESMAN *(a little taken aback)*. Yes—of course we could do that.

HEDDA *(takes up the bouquet from the piano)*. These flowers were not here last night when we arrived.

TESMAN. Aunt Julia must have brought them for you.

HEDDA *(examining the bouquet)*. A visiting-card. *(Takes it out and reads)*: "Shall return later in the day." Can you guess whose card it is?

TESMAN. No. Whose? Eh?

HEDDA. The name is "Mrs. Elvsted."

TESMAN. Is it really? Sheriff Elvsted's wife? Miss Rysing that was.

HEDDA. Exactly. The girl with the irritating hair, that she was always showing off. An old flame of yours I've been told.

TESMAN *(laughing)*. Oh, that didn't last long; and it was before I knew you, Hedda. But fancy her being in town!

HEDDA. It's odd that she should call upon us. I have scarcely seen her since we left school.

TESMAN. I haven't seen her either for—heaven knows how long. I wonder how she can endure to live in such an out-of-the-way hole —eh?

HEDDA *(after a moment's thought, says suddenly)*. Tell me, Tesman

—isn't it somewhere near there that he—that—Eilert Løvborg is living?

TESMAN. Yes, he is somewhere in that part of the country.

(Berta enters by the hall door.)

BERTA. That lady, ma'am, that brought some flowers a little while ago, is here again. *(Pointing.)* The flowers you have in your hand, ma'am.

HEDDA. Ah, is she? Well, please show her in.

(Berta opens the door for Mrs. Elvsted, and goes out herself.—Mrs. Elvsted is a woman of fragile figure, with pretty, soft features. Her eyes are light blue, large, round, and somewhat prominent, with a startled, inquiring expression. Her hair is remarkably light, almost flaxen, and unusually abundant and wavy. She is a couple of years younger than Hedda. She wears a dark visiting dress, tasteful, but not quite in the latest fashion.)

HEDDA *(receives her warmly)*. How do you do, my dear Mrs. Elvsted? It's delightful to see you again.

MRS. ELVSTED *(nervously, struggling for self-control)*. Yes, it's a very long time since we met.

TESMAN *(gives her his hand)*. And we too—eh?

HEDDA. Thanks for your lovely flowers . . .

MRS. ELVSTED. Oh, not at all . . . I would have come straight here yesterday afternoon; but I heard that you were away . . .

TESMAN. Have you just come to town? Eh?

MRS. ELVSTED. I arrived yesterday, about midday. Oh, I was quite in despair when I heard that you were not at home.

HEDDA. In despair! How so?

TESMAN. Why, my dear Mrs. Rysing—I mean Mrs. Elvsted . . .

HEDDA. I hope that you are not in any trouble?

MRS. ELVSTED. Yes, I am. And I don't know another living creature here that I can turn to.

HEDDA *(laying the bouquet on the table)*. Come—let us sit here on the sofa . . .

MRS. ELVSTED. Oh, I am too restless to sit down.

HEDDA. Oh no, you're not. Come here.

(She draws Mrs. Elvsted down upon the sofa and sits at her side.)

TESMAN. Well? What is it, Mrs. Elvsted . . . ?

HEDDA. Has anything particular happened to you at home?

MRS. ELVSTED. Yes—and no. Oh—I am so anxious you should not misunderstand me . . .

HEDDA. Then your best plan is to tell us the whole story, Mrs. Elvsted.

TESMAN. I suppose that's what you have come for—eh?

MRS. ELVSTED. Yes, yes—of course it is. Well then, I must tell you— if you don't already know—that Eilert Løvborg is in town, too.

HEDDA. Løvborg . . . !

TESMAN. What! Has Eilert Løvborg come back? Fancy that, Hedda!

HEDDA. Well well—I hear it.

MRS. ELVSTED. He has been here a week already. Just fancy—a whole week! In this terrible town, alone! With so many temptations on all sides.

HEDDA. But my dear Mrs. Elvsted—how does *he* concern you so much?

MRS. ELVSTED *(looks at her with a startled air, and says rapidly)*. He was the children's tutor.

HEDDA. Your children's?

MRS. ELVSTED. My husband's. I have none.

HEDDA. Your step-children's, then?

MRS. ELVSTED. Yes.

TESMAN *(somewhat hesitatingly)*. Then was he—I don't know how to express it—was he—regular enough in his habits to be fit for the post? Eh?

MRS. ELVSTED. For the last two years his conduct has been irreproachable.

TESMAN. Has it indeed? Fancy that, Hedda!

HEDDA. I hear it.

MRS. ELVSTED. Perfectly irreproachable, I assure you! In every respect. But all the same—now that I know he is here—in this great town— and with a large sum of money in his hands—I can't help being in mortal fear for him.

TESMAN. Why did he not remain where he was? With you and your husband? Eh?

MRS. ELVSTED. After his book was published he was too restless and unsettled to remain with us.

TESMAN. Yes, by-the-bye, Aunt Julia told me he had published a new book.

MRS. ELVSTED. Yes, a big book, dealing with the march of civilisation —in broad outline, as it were. It came out about a fortnight ago.

And since it has sold so well, and been so much read—and made such a sensation . . .

TESMAN. Has it indeed? It must be something he has had lying by since his better days.

MRS. ELVSTED. Long ago, you mean?

TESMAN. Yes.

MRS. ELVSTED. No, he has written it all since he has been with us— within the last year.

TESMAN. Isn't that good news, Hedda? Think of that.

MRS. ELVSTED. Ah yes, if only it would last!

HEDDA. Have you seen him here in town?

MRS. ELVSTED. No, not yet. I have had the greatest difficulty in finding out his address. But this morning I discovered it at last.

HEDDA (*looks searchingly at her*). Do you know, it seems to me a little odd of your husband—h'm . . .

MRS. ELVSTED (*starting nervously*). Of my husband! What?

HEDDA. That he should send *you* to town on such an errand—that he does not come himself and look after his friend.

MRS. ELVSTED. Oh no, no—my husband has no time. And besides, I—I had some shopping to do.

HEDDA (*with a slight smile*). Ah, that is a different matter.

MRS. ELVSTED (*rising quickly and uneasily*). And now I beg and implore you, Mr. Tesman—receive Eilert Løvborg kindly if he comes to you! And that he is sure to do. You see you were such great friends in the old days. And then you are interested in the same studies—the same branch of science—so far as I can understand.

TESMAN. We used to be, at any rate.

MRS. ELVSTED. That is why I beg so earnestly that you—you too—will keep a sharp eye upon him. Oh, you will promise me that, Mr. Tesman—won't you?

TESMAN. With the greatest of pleasure, Mrs. Rysing . . .

HEDDA. Elvsted.

TESMAN. I assure you I shall do all I possibly can for Eilert. You may rely upon me.

MRS. ELVSTED. Oh, how very, very kind of you! (*Presses his hands.*) Thanks, thanks, thanks! (*Frightened.*) You see, my husband is so very fond of him!

HEDDA (*rising*). You ought to write to him, Tesman. Perhaps he may not care to come to you of his own accord.

TESMAN. Well, perhaps it would be the right thing to do, Hedda? Eh?

HEDDA. And the sooner the better. Why not at once?

MRS. ELVSTED (*imploringly*). Oh, if you only would!

TESMAN. I'll write this moment. Have you his address, Mrs.—Mrs. Elvsted?

MRS. ELVSTED. Yes. *(Takes a slip of paper from her pocket, and hands it to him.)* Here it is.

TESMAN. Good, good. Then I'll go in . . . *(Looks about him.)* By-the-bye,—my slippers? Oh, here.

(Takes the packet, and is about to go.)

HEDDA. Be sure you write him a cordial, friendly letter. And a good long one too.

TESMAN. Yes, I will.

MRS. ELVSTED. But please, please don't say a word to show that I have suggested it.

TESMAN. No, how could you think I would? Eh?

(He goes out to the right, through the inner room.)

HEDDA *(goes up to Mrs. Elvsted, smiles, and says in a low voice).* There! We have killed two birds with one stone.

MRS. ELVSTED. What do you mean?

HEDDA. Could you not see that I wanted him to go?

MRS. ELVSTED. Yes, to write the letter . . .

HEDDA. And that I might speak to you alone.

MRS. ELVSTED *(confused).* About the same thing?

HEDDA. Precisely.

MRS. ELVSTED *(apprehensively).* But there *is* nothing more, Mrs. Tesman! Absolutely nothing!

HEDDA. Oh yes, but there is. There is a great deal more—I can see that. Sit here—and we'll have a cosy, confidential chat.

(She forces Mrs. Elvsted to sit in the easy-chair beside the stove, and seats herself on one of the footstools.)

MRS. ELVSTED *(anxiously, looking at her watch).* But, my dear Mrs. Tesman—I was really on the point of going.

HEDDA. Oh, you can't be in such a hurry.—Well? Now tell me something about your life at home.

MRS. ELVSTED. Oh, that is just what I care least to speak about.

HEDDA. But to me, dear . . . ? Why, weren't we schoolfellows?

MRS. ELVSTED. Yes, but you were in the class above me. Oh, how dreadfully afraid of you I was then!

HEDDA. Afraid of me?

MRS. ELVSTED. Yes, dreadfully. For when we met on the stairs you used always to pull my hair.

HEDDA. Did I, really?

MRS. ELVSTED. Yes, and once you said you would burn it off my head.

HEDDA. Oh that was all nonsense, of course.

MRS. ELVSTED. Yes, but I was so silly in those days.—And since then, too—we have drifted so far—far apart from each other. Our circles have been so entirely different.

HEDDA. Well then, we must try to drift together again. Now listen! At school we said *du* to each other; and we called each other by our Christian names . . .

MRS. ELVSTED. No, I am sure you must be mistaken.

HEDDA. No, not at all! I can remember quite distinctly. So now we are going to renew our old friendship. *(Draws the footstool closer to Mrs. Elvsted.)* There now! *(Kisses her cheek.)* You must say *du* to me and call me Hedda.

MRS. ELVSTED *(presses and pats her hands)*. Oh, how good and kind you are! I am not used to such kindness.

HEDDA. There, there, there! And I shall say *du* to you, as in the old days, and call you my dear Thora.

MRS. ELVSTED. My name is Thea.

HEDDA. Why, of course! I meant Thea. *(Looks at her compassionately.)* So you are not accustomed to goodness and kindness, Thea? Not in your own home?

MRS. ELVSTED. Oh, if I only had a home! But I haven't any; I have never had a home.

HEDDA *(looks at her for a moment)*. I almost suspected as much.

MRS. ELVSTED *(gazing helplessly before her)*. Yes—yes—yes.

HEDDA. I don't quite remember—was it not as housekeeper that you first went to Mr. Elvsted's?

MRS. ELVSTED. I really went as governess. But his wife—his late wife—was an invalid,—and rarely left her room. So I had to look after the housekeeping as well.

HEDDA. And then—at last—you became mistress of the house.

MRS. ELVSTED *(sadly)*. Yes, I did.

HEDDA. Let me see—about how long ago was that?

MRS. ELVSTED. My marriage?

HEDDA. Yes.

MRS. ELVSTED. Five years ago.

HEDDA. To be sure; it must be that.

MRS. ELVSTED. Oh those five years...! Or at all events the last two or three of them! Oh, if you[1] could only imagine...

HEDDA *(giving her a little slap on the hand). De?* Fie, Thea!

MRS. ELVSTED. Yes, yes, I will try... Well, if—you could only imagine and understand...

HEDDA *(lightly)*. Eilert Løvborg has been in your neighbourhood about three years, hasn't he?

MRS. ELVSTED *(looks at her doubtfully)*. Eilert Løvborg? Yes—he has.

HEDDA. Had you known him before, in town here?

MRS. ELVSTED. Scarcely at all. I mean—I knew him by name, of course.

HEDDA. But you saw a good deal of him in the country?

MRS. ELVSTED. Yes, he came to us every day. You see, he gave the children lessons; for in the long run I couldn't manage it all myself.

HEDDA. No, that's clear.—And your husband...? I suppose he is often away from home?

MRS. ELVSTED. Yes. Being sheriff, you know, he has to travel about a good deal in his district.

HEDDA *(leaning against the arm of the chair)*. Thea—my poor, sweet Thea—now you must tell me everything—exactly as it stands.

MRS, ELVSTED. Well then, you must question me.

HEDDA. What sort of a man is your husband, Thea? I mean—you know—in everyday life. Is he kind to you?

[1] Mrs. Elvsted here uses the formal pronoun *De,* whereupon Hedda rebukes her. In her next speech Mrs. Elvsted says *du.*

MRS. ELVSTED (*evasively*) I am sure he means well in everything.

HEDDA. I should think he must be altogether too old for you. There is at least twenty years' difference between you, is there not?

MRS. ELVSTED (*irritably*). Yes, that is true, too. Everything about him is repellent to me! We have not a thought in common. We have no single point of sympathy—he and I.

HEDDA. But is he not fond of you all the same? In his own way?

MRS. ELVSTED. Oh I really don't know. I think he regards me simply as a useful property. And then it doesn't cost much to keep me. I am not expensive.

HEDDA. That is stupid of you.

MRS. ELVSTED (*shakes her head*). It cannot be otherwise—not with him. I don't think he really cares for any one but himself—and perhaps a little for the children.

HEDDA. And for Eilert Løvborg, Thea.

MRS. ELVSTED (*looking at her*). For Eilert Løvborg? What puts that into your head?

HEDDA. Well, my dear—I should say, when he sends you after him all the way to town ... (*Smiling almost imperceptibly.*) And besides, you said so yourself, to Tesman.

MRS. ELVSTED (*with a little nervous twitch*). Did I? Yes, I suppose I did. (*Vehemently, but not loudly.*) No—I may just as well make a clean breast of it at once! For it must all come out in any case.

HEDDA. Why, my dear Thea ... ?

MRS. ELVSTED. Well, to make a long story short: My husband did not know that I was coming.

HEDDA. What! Your husband didn't know it!

MRS. ELVSTED. No, of course not. For the matter, he was away from home himself—he was travelling. Oh, I could bear it no longer, Hedda! I couldn't indeed—so utterly alone as I should have been in future.

HEDDA. Well? And then?

MRS. ELVSTED. So I put together some of my things—what I needed most—as quickly as possible. And then I left the house.

HEDDA. Without a word?

MRS. ELVSTED. Yes—and took the train straight to town.

HEDDA. Why, my dear, good Thea—to think of you daring to do it!

MRS. ELVSTED (*rises and moves about the room*). What else could I possibly do?

HEDDA. But what do you think your husband will say when you go home again?

MRS. ELVSTED (*at the table, looks at her*). Back to *him?*

HEDDA. Of course.

MRS. ELVSTED. I shall never go back to him again.

HEDDA (*rising and going towards her*). Then you have left your home —for good and all?

MRS. ELVSTED. Yes. There was nothing else to be done.

HEDDA. But then—to take flight so openly.

MRS. ELVSTED. Oh, it's impossible to keep things of that sort secret.

HEDDA. But what do you think people will say of you, Thea?

MRS. ELVSTED. They may say what they like, for aught *I* care. (*Seats herself wearily and sadly on the sofa.*) I have done nothing but what I *had* to do.

HEDDA (*after a short silence*). And what are your plans now? What do you think of doing?

MRS. ELVSTED. I don't know yet. I only know this, that I *must* live here, where Eilert Løvborg is—if I am to live at all.

HEDDA (*takes a chair from the table, seats herself beside her, and strokes her hands*). My dear Thea—how did this—this friendship— between you and Eilert Løvborg come about?

MRS. ELVSTED. Oh it grew up gradually. I gained a sort of influence over him.

HEDDA. Indeed?

MRS. ELVSTED. He gave up his old habits. Not because I asked him to, for I never dared do that. But of course he saw how repulsive they were to me; and so he dropped them.

HEDDA (*concealing an involuntary smile of scorn*). Then you have reclaimed him—as the saying goes—my little Thea.

MRS. ELVSTED. So he says himself, at any rate. And he, on his side, has made a real human being of me—taught me to think, and to understand so many things.

HEDDA. Did he give *you* lessons too, then?

MRS. ELVSTED. No, not exactly lessons. But he talked to me—talked about such an infinity of things. And then came the lovely, happy time when I began to share in his work—when he allowed me to help him!

HEDDA. Oh he did, did he?

MRS. ELVSTED. Yes! He never wrote anything without my assistance.

HEDDA. You were two good comrades, in fact?

MRS. ELVSTED *(eagerly)*. Comrades! Yes, fancy, Hedda—that is the very word he used!—Oh, I ought to feel perfectly happy; and yet I cannot; for I don't know how long it will last.

HEDDA. Are you no surer of him than that?

MRS. ELVSTED *(gloomily)*. A woman's shadow stands between Eilert Løvborg and me.

HEDDA *(looks at her anxiously)*. Who can *that* be?

MRS. ELVSTED. I don't know. Some one he knew in his—in his past. Some one he has never been able wholly to forget.

HEDDA. What has he told you—about this?

MRS. ELVSTED. He has only once—quite vaguely—alluded to it.

HEDDA. Well! And what did he say?

MRS. ELVSTED. He said that when they parted, she threatened to shoot him with a pistol.

HEDDA *(with cold composure)*. Oh nonsense! No one does that sort of thing here.

MRS. ELVSTED. No. And that is why I think it must have been that red-haired singing-woman whom he once . . .

HEDDA. Yes, very likely.

MRS. ELVSTED. For I remember they used to say of her that she carried loaded firearms.

HEDDA. Oh—then of course it must have been she.

MRS. ELVSTED *(wringing her hands)*. And now just fancy, Hedda—I hear that this singing-woman—that she is in town again! Oh, I don't know what to do . . .

HEDDA *(glancing towards the inner room).* Hush! Here comes Tesman. *(Rises and whispers.)* Thea—all this must remain between you and me.

MRS. ELVSTED *(springing up).* Oh yes—yes! For heaven's sake . . . !

(George Tesman, with a letter in his hand, comes from the right through the inner room.)

TESMAN. There now—the epistle is finished.

HEDDA. That's right. And now Mrs. Elvsted is just going. Wait a moment—I'll go with you to the garden gate.

TESMAN. Do you think Berta could post the letter, Hedda dear?

HEDDA *(takes it).* I will tell her to.

(Berta enters from the hall.)

BERTA. Judge Brack wishes to know if Mrs. Tesman will receive him.

HEDDA. Yes, ask Judge Brack to come in. And look here—put this letter in the post.

BERTA *(taking the letter).* Yes, ma'am.

(She opens the door for Judge Brack and goes out herself. Brack is a man of forty-five; thick-set, but well-built and elastic in his movements. His face is roundish with an aristocratic profile. His hair is short, still almost black, and carefully dressed. His eyes are lively and sparkling. His eyebrows thick. His moustaches are also thick, with short-cut ends. He wears a well-cut walking-suit, a little too youthful for his age. He uses an eye-glass, which he now and then lets drop.)

JUDGE BRACK *(with his hat in his hand, bowing).* May one venture to call so early in the day?

HEDDA. Of course one may.

TESMAN *(presses his hand).* You are welcome at any time. *(Introducing him.)* Judge Brack—Miss Rysing . . .

HEDDA. Oh . . . !

BRACK *(bowing).* Ah—delighted . . .

HEDDA *(looks at him and laughs).* It's nice to have a look at you by daylight, Judge!

BRACK. Do you find me—altered?

HEDDA. A little younger, I think.

BRACK. Thank you so much.

TESMAN. But what do you think of Hedda—eh? Doesn't she look flourishing? She has actually . . .

HEDDA. Oh, do leave me alone. You haven't thanked Judge Brack for all the trouble he has taken . . .

BRACK. Oh, nonsense—it was a pleasure to me . . .

HEDDA. Yes, you are a friend indeed. But here stands Thea all impatience to be off—so *au revoir,* Judge. I shall be back again presently. *(Mutual salutations. Mrs. Elvsted and Hedda go out by the hall door.)*

BRACK. Well,—is your wife tolerably satisfied . . .

TESMAN. Yes, we can't thank you sufficiently. Of course she talks of a little re-arrangement here and there; and one or two things are still wanting. We shall have to buy some additional trifles.

BRACK. Indeed!

TESMAN. But we won't trouble you about these things. Hedda says she herself will look after what is wanting.—Shan't we sit down? Eh?

BRACK. Thanks, for a moment. *(Seats himself beside the table.)* There is something I wanted to speak to you about, my dear Tesman.

TESMAN. Indeed? Ah, I understand! *(Seating himself.)* I suppose it's the serious part of the frolic that is coming now. Eh?

BRACK. Oh, the money question is not so very pressing; though, for that matter, I wish we had gone a little more economically to work.

TESMAN. But that would never have done, you know! Think of Hedda, my dear fellow! You, who know her so well . . . I couldn't possibly ask her to put up with a shabby style of living!

BRACK. No, no—that is just the difficulty.

TESMAN. And then—fortunately—it can't be long before I receive my appointment.

BRACK. Well, you see—such things are often apt to hang fire for a time.

TESMAN. Have you heard anything definite? Eh?

BRACK. Nothing exactly definite... *(Interrupting himself.)* But by-the-bye—I have one piece of news for you.

TESMAN. Well?

BRACK. Your old friend, Eilert Løvborg, has returned to town.

TESMAN. I know that already.

BRACK. Indeed! How did you learn it?

TESMAN. From that lady who went out with Hedda.

BRACK. Really? What was her name? I didn't quite catch it.

TESMAN. Mrs. Elvsted.

BRACK. Aha—Sheriff Elvsted's wife? Of course—he has been living up in their regions.

TESMAN. And fancy—I'm delighted to hear that he is quite a reformed character!

BRACK. So they say.

TESMAN. And then he has published a new book—eh?

BRACK. Yes, indeed he has.

TESMAN. And I hear it has made some sensation!

BRACK. Quite an unusual sensation.

TESMAN. Fancy—isn't that good news! A man of such extraordinary talents... I felt so grieved to think that he had gone irretrievably to ruin.

BRACK. That was what everybody thought.

TESMAN. But I cannot imagine what he will take to now! How in the world will he be able to make his living? Eh?

(During the last words, Hedda has entered by the hall door.)

HEDDA *(to Brack, laughing with a touch of scorn).* Tesman is for ever worrying about how people are to make their living.

TESMAN. Well you see, dear—we were talking about poor Eilert Løvborg.

HEDDA *(glancing at him rapidly).* Oh, indeed? *(Seats herself in the arm-chair beside the stove and asks indifferently):* What is the matter with *him?*

TESMAN. Well—no doubt he has run through all his property long ago; and he can scarcely write a new book every year—eh? So I really can't see what is to become of him.

BRACK. Perhaps I can give you some information on that point.

TESMAN. Indeed!

BRACK. You must remember that his relations have a good deal of influence.

TESMAN. Oh, his relations, unfortunately, have entirely washed their hands of him.

BRACK. At one time they called him the hope of the family.

TESMAN. At one time, yes! But he has put an end to all that.

HEDDA. Who knows? *(With a slight smile.)* I hear they have reclaimed him up at Sheriff Elvsted's . . .

BRACK. And then this book that he has published . . .

TESMAN. Well well, I hope to goodness they may find something for him to do. I have just written to him. I asked him to come and see us this evening, Hedda dear.

BRACK. But my dear fellow, you are booked for my bachelors' party this evening. You promised on the pier last night.

HEDDA. Had you forgotten, Tesman?

TESMAN. Yes, I had utterly forgotten.

BRACK. But it doesn't matter, for you may be sure he won't come.

TESMAN. What makes you think that? Eh?

BRACK *(with a little hesitation, rising and resting his hands on the back of his chair)*. My dear Tesman—and you too, Mrs. Tesman—I think I ought not to keep you in the dark about something that—that . . .

TESMAN. That concerns Eilert . . . ?

BRACK. Both you and him.

TESMAN. Well, my dear Judge, out with it.

BRACK. You must be prepared to find your appointment deferred longer than you desired or expected.

TESMAN *(jumping up uneasily)*. Is there some hitch about it? Eh?

BRACK. The nomination may perhaps be made conditional on the result of a competition . . .

TESMAN. Competition! Think of that, Hedda!

HEDDA *(leans further back in the chair)*. Aha—aha!

TESMAN. But who can my competitor be? Surely not . . . ?

BRACK. Yes, precisely—Eilert Løvborg.

TESMAN *(clasping his hands)*. No, no—it's quite inconceivable! Quite impossible! Eh?

BRACK. H'm—that is what it may come to, all the same.

TESMAN. Well but, Judge Brack—it would show the most incredible lack of consideration for me. *(Gesticulates with his arms.)* For—just think—I'm a married man! We have married on the strength of these prospects, Hedda and I; and run deep into debt; and borrowed money from Aunt Julia too. Good heavens, they had as good as promised me the appointment. Eh?

BRACK. Well, well, well—no doubt you will get it in the end; only after a contest.

HEDDA *(immovable in her arm-chair)*. Fancy, Tesman, there will be a sort of sporting interest in that.

TESMAN. Why, my dearest Hedda, how can you be so indifferent about it.

HEDDA *(as before)*. I am not at all indifferent. I am most eager to see who wins.

BRACK. In any case, Mrs. Tesman, it is best that you should know how matters stand. I mean—before you set about the little purchases I hear you are threatening.

HEDDA. This can make no difference.

BRACK. Indeed! Then I have no more to say. Good-bye! *(To Tesman.)* I shall look in on my way back from my afternoon walk, and take you home with me.

TESMAN. Oh yes, yes—your news has quite upset me.

HEDDA *(reclining, holds out her hand)*. Good-bye, Judge; and be sure you call in the afternoon.

BRACK. Many thanks. Good-bye, good-bye!

TESMAN *(accompanying him to the door)*. Good-bye, my dear Judge! You must really excuse me . . .

(Judge Brack goes out by the hall door.)

TESMAN *(crosses the room)*. Oh Hedda—one should never rush into adventures. Eh?

HEDDA *(looks at him, smiling)*. Do *you* do *that?*

TESMAN. Yes, dear—there is no denying—it *was* adventurous to go and marry and set up house upon mere expectations.

HEDDA. Perhaps you are right there.

TESMAN. Well—at all events, we have our delightful home, Hedda! Fancy, the home we both dreamed of—the home we were in love with, I may almost say. Eh?

HEDDA *(rising slowly and wearily)*. It was part of our compact that we were to go into society—to keep open house.

TESMAN. Yes, if you only knew how I had been looking forward to it! Fancy—to see you as hostess—in a select circle! Eh? Well, well, well—for the present we shall have to get on without society, Hedda—only to invite Aunt Julia now and then.—Oh, I intended you to lead such an utterly different life, dear ...!

HEDDA. Of course I cannot have my man in livery just yet.

TESMAN. Oh no, unfortunately. It would be out of the question for us to keep a footman, you know.

HEDDA. And the saddle-horse I was to have had ...

TESMAN *(aghast)*. The saddle-horse!

HEDDA. ... I suppose I must not think of that now.

TESMAN. Good heavens, no!—that's as clear as daylight.

HEDDA *(goes up the room)*. Well, I shall have one thing at least to kill time with in the meanwhile.

TESMAN *(beaming)*. Oh thank heaven for that! What is it, Hedda? Eh?

HEDDA *(in the middle doorway, looks at him with covert scorn)*. My pistols, George.

TESMAN *(in alarm)*. Your pistols!

HEDDA *(with cold eyes)*. General Gabler's pistols.

(She goes out through the inner room, to the left.)

TESMAN *(rushes up to the middle doorway and calls after her)*. No, for heaven's sake, Hedda darling—don't touch those dangerous things! For my sake, Hedda! Eh?

ACT SECOND

The room at the Tesmans' as in the first Act, except that the piano has been removed, and an elegant little writing-table with book-shelves put in its place. A smaller table stands near the sofa on the left. Most of the bouquets have been taken away. Mrs. Elvsted's bouquet is upon the large table in front.—It is afternoon.

Hedda, dressed to receive callers, is alone in the room. She stands by the open glass door, loading a revolver. The fellow to it lies in an open pistol-case on the writing-table.

HEDDA *(looks down the garden, and calls).* So you are here again, Judge!

BRACK *(is heard calling from a distance).* As you see, Mrs. Tesman!

HEDDA *(raises the pistol and points).* Now I'll shoot you, Judge Brack.

BRACK *(calling unseen).* No, no, no! Don't stand aiming at me!

HEDDA. This is what comes of sneaking in by the back way.[1]

(She fires.)

BRACK *(nearer).* Are you out of your senses . . . !

HEDDA. Dear me—did I happen to hit you?

[1] "Bagveje" means both "back ways" and "underhand courses."

BRACK *(still outside).* I wish you would let these pranks alone!

HEDDA. Come in then, Judge.

(Judge Brack, dressed as though for a men's party, enters by the glass door. He carries a light overcoat over his arm.)

BRACK. What the deuce—haven't you tired of that sport, yet? What are you shooting at?

HEDDA. Oh, I am only firing in the air.

BRACK *(gently takes the pistol out of her hand).* Allow me, madam! *(Looks at it.)* Ah—I know this pistol well! *(Looks around.)* Where is the case? Ah, here it is. *(Lays the pistol in it, and shuts it.)* Now we won't play at that game any more to-day.

HEDDA. Then what in heaven's name would you have me do with myself?

BRACK. Have you had no visitors?

HEDDA *(closing the glass door).* Not one. I suppose all our set are still out of town.

BRACK. And is Tesman not at home either?

HEDDA *(at the writing-table, putting the pistol-case in a drawer which she shuts).* No. He rushed off to his aunt's directly after lunch; he didn't expect you so early.

BRACK. H'm—how stupid of me not to have thought of that!

HEDDA *(turning her head to look at him).* Why stupid?

BRACK. Because if I had thought of it I should have come a little—earlier.

HEDDA *(crossing the room).* Then you would have found no one to receive you; for I have been in my room changing my dress ever since lunch.

BRACK. And is there no sort of little chink that we could hold a parley through?

HEDDA. You have forgotten to arrange one.

BRACK. That was another piece of stupidity.

HEDDA. Well, we must just settle down here—and wait. Tesman is not likely to be back for some time yet.

BRACK. Never mind; I shall not be impatient.

(Hedda seats herself in the corner of the sofa. Brack lays his over-coat over the back of the nearest chair, and sits down, but keeps his hat in his hand. A short silence. They look at each other.)

HEDDA. Well?

BRACK *(in the same tone)*. Well?

HEDDA. I spoke first.

BRACK *(bending a little forward)*. Come, let us have a cosy little chat, Mrs.—Hedda.

HEDDA *(leaning further back in the sofa)*. Does it not seem like a whole eternity since our last talk? Of course I don't count those few words yesterday evening and this morning.

BRACK. You mean since our last confidential talk? Our last *tête-à-tête?*

HEDDA. Well yes—since you put it so.

BRACK. Not a day has passed but I have wished that you were home again.

HEDDA. And I have done nothing but wish the same thing.

BRACK. You? Really, Mrs. Hedda? And I thought you had been enjoying your tour so much!

HEDDA. Oh yes, you may be sure of that!

BRACK. But Tesman's letters spoke of nothing but happiness.

HEDDA. Oh, *Tesman.* You see, he thinks nothing so delightful as grubbing in libraries and making copies of old parchments, or whatever you call them.

BRACK *(with a spice of malice)*. Well, that is his vocation in life—or part of it at any rate.

HEDDA. Yes, of course; and no doubt when it's your vocation ... But *I!* Oh, my dear Mr. Brack, how mortally bored I have been.

BRACK *(sympathetically)*. Do you really say so? In downright earnest?

HEDDA. Yes, you can surely understand it ... ! To go for six whole months without meeting a soul that knew anything of *our* circle, or could talk about the things we are interested in.

BRACK. Yes, yes—I too should feel that a deprivation.

HEDDA. And then, what I found most intolerable of all ...

BRACK. Well?

HEDDA. . . . was being everlastingly in the company of—one and the same person . . .

BRACK *(with a nod of assent)*. Morning, noon, and night, yes—at all possible times and seasons.

HEDDA. I said "everlastingly."

BRACK. Just so. But I should have thought, with our excellent Tesman, one could . . .

HEDDA. Tesman is—a specialist, my dear Judge.

BRACK. Undeniably.

HEDDA. And specialists are not at all amusing to travel with. Not in the long run at any rate.

BRACK. Not even—the specialist one happens to *love?*

HEDDA. Faugh—don't use that sickening word!

BRACK *(taken aback)*. What do you say, Mrs. Hedda?

HEDDA *(half laughing, half irritated)*. You should just try it! To hear of nothing but the history of civilisation, morning, noon, and night . . .

BRACK. Everlastingly.

HEDDA. Yes yes yes! And then all this about the domestic industry of the Middle Ages . . . ! That's the most disgusting part of it!

BRACK *(looks searchingly at her)*. But tell me—in that case, how am I to understand your . . . ? H'm . . .

HEDDA. My accepting George Tesman, you mean?

BRACK. Well, let us put it so.

HEDDA. Good heavens, do you see anything so wonderful in that?

BRACK. Yes and no—Mrs. Hedda.

HEDDA. I had positively danced myself tired, my dear Judge. My day was done . . . *(With a slight shudder.)* Oh no—I won't say that; nor think it either!

BRACK. You have assuredly no reason to.

HEDDA. Oh, reasons . . . *(Watching him closely.)* And George Tesman —after all, you must admit that he is correctness itself.

BRACK. His correctness and respectability are beyond all question.

HEDDA. And I don't see anything absolutely ridiculous about him.—Do you?

BRACK. Ridiculous? N—no—I shouldn't exactly say so . . .

HEDDA. Well—and his powers of research, at all events, are untiring. —I see no reason why he should not one day come to the front, after all.

BRACK *(looks at her hesitatingly)*. I thought that you, like every one else, expected him to attain the highest distinction.

HEDDA *(with an expression of fatigue)*. Yes, so I did.—And then, since he was bent, at all hazards, on being allowed to provide for me—I really don't know why I should not have accepted his offer?

BRACK. No—if you look at it in *that* light . . .

HEDDA. It was more than my other adorers were prepared to do for me, my dear Judge.

BRACK *(laughing)*. Well, I can't answer for all the rest; but as for myself, you know quite well that I have always entertained a—a certain respect for the marriage tie—for marriage as an institution, Mrs. Hedda.

HEDDA *(jestingly)*. Oh, I assure you I have never cherished any hopes with respect to *you*.

BRACK. All I require is a pleasant and intimate interior, where I can make myself useful in every way, and am free to come and go as —as a trusted friend . . .

HEDDA. Of the master of the house, do you mean?

BRACK *(bowing)*. Frankly—of the mistress first of all; but of course of the master too, in the second place. Such a triangular friendship —if I may call it so—is really a great convenience for all parties, let me tell you.

HEDDA. Yes, I have many a time longed for some one to make a third on our travels. Oh—those railway-carriage *tête-à-têtes* . . . !

BRACK. Fortunately your wedding journey is over now.

HEDDA *(shaking her head)*. Not by a long—long way. I have only arrived at a station on the line.

BRACK. Well, then the passengers jump out and move about a little, Mrs. Hedda.

HEDDA. I never jump out.

BRACK. Really?

HEDDA. No—because there is always some one standing by to . . .

BRACK *(laughing)*. To look at your ankles, do you mean?

HEDDA. Precisely.

BRACK. Well but, dear me . . .

HEDDA *(with a gesture of repulsion)*. I won't have it. I would rather keep my seat where I happen to be—and continue the *tête-à-tête*.

BRACK. But suppose a third person were to jump in and join the couple.

HEDDA. Ah—*that* is quite another matter!

BRACK. A trusted, sympathetic friend . . .

HEDDA. . . . with a fund of conversation on all sorts of lively topics . . .

BRACK. . . . and not the least bit of a specialist!

HEDDA *(with an audible sigh)*. Yes, that would be a relief indeed.

BRACK *(hears the front door open, and glances in that direction)*. The triangle is completed.

HEDDA *(half aloud)*. And on goes the train.

(George Tesman, in a grey walking-suit, with a soft felt hat, enters from the hall. He has a number of unbound books under his arm and in his pockets.)

TESMAN *(goes up to the table beside the corner settee)*. Ouf—what a load for a warm day—all these books. *(Lays them on the table.)* I'm positively perspiring, Hedda. Hallo—are you there already, my dear Judge? Eh? Berta didn't tell me.

BRACK *(rising)*. I came in through the garden.

HEDDA. What books have you got there?

TESMAN *(stands looking them through)*. Some new books on my special subjects—quite indispensable to me.

HEDDA. Your special subjects?

BRACK. Yes, books on his special subjects, Mrs. Tesman.

(Brack and Hedda exchange a confidential smile.)

HEDDA. Do you need still more books on your special subjects?

TESMAN. Yes, my dear Hedda, one can never have too many of them. Of course one must keep up with all that is written and published.

HEDDA. Yes, I suppose one must.

TESMAN *(searching among his books)*. And look here—I have got hold of Eilert Løvborg's new book too. *(Offering it to her.)* Perhaps you would like to glance through it, Hedda? Eh?

HEDDA. No, thank you. Or rather—afterwards perhaps.

TESMAN. I looked into it a little on the way home.

BRACK. Well, what do you think of it—as a specialist?

TESMAN. I think it shows quite remarkable soundness of judgment. He never wrote like that before. *(Putting the books together.)* Now I shall take all these into my study. I'm longing to cut the leaves . . . ! And then I must change my clothes. *(To Brack.)* I suppose we needn't start just yet? Eh?

BRACK. Oh, dear no—there is not the slightest hurry.

TESMAN. Well then, I will take my time. *(Is going with his books, but stops in the doorway and turns.)* By-the-bye, Hedda—Aunt Julia is not coming this evening.

HEDDA. Not coming? Is it that affair of the bonnet that keeps her away?

TESMAN. Oh, not at all. How could you think such a thing of Aunt Julia? Just fancy . . . ! The fact is, Aunt Rina is very ill.

HEDDA. She always is.

TESMAN. Yes, but to-day she is much worse than usual, poor dear.

HEDDA. Oh, then it's only natural that her sister should remain with her. I must bear my disappointment.

TESMAN. And you can't imagine, dear, how delighted Aunt Julia seemed to be—because you had come home looking so flourishing!

HEDDA *(half aloud, rising)*. Oh, those everlasting Aunts!

TESMAN. What?

HEDDA *(going to the glass door)*. Nothing.

TESMAN. Oh, all right.

(He goes through the inner room, out to the right.)

BRACK. What bonnet were you talking about?

HEDDA. Oh, it was a little episode with Miss Tesman this morning. She had laid down her bonnet on the chair there—*(looks at him and smiles)*—and I pretended to think it was the servant's.

BRACK *(shaking his head)*. Now my dear Mrs. Hedda, how could you do such a thing? To that excellent old lady, too!

HEDDA *(nervously crossing the room)*. Well, you see—these impulses come over me all of a sudden; and I *cannot* resist them. *(Throws herself down in the easy-chair by the stove.)* Oh, I don't know how to explain it.

BRACK *(behind the easy-chair)*. You are not really happy—that is at the bottom of it.

HEDDA *(looking straight before her)*. I know of no reason why I should be—happy. Perhaps you can give me one?

BRACK. Well—amongst other things, because you have got exactly the home you had set your heart on.

HEDDA *(looks up at him and laughs)*. Do you too believe in that legend?

BRACK. Is there nothing in it, then?

HEDDA. Oh yes, there is *something* in it.

BRACK. Well?

HEDDA. There is *this* in it, that I made use of Tesman to see me home from evening parties last summer . . .

BRACK. I, unfortunately, had to go quite a different way.

HEDDA. That's true. I know you were going a different way last summer.

BRACK *(laughing)*. Oh fie, Mrs. Hedda! Well, then—you and Tesman . . . ?

HEDDA. Well, we happened to pass here one evening; Tesman, poor fellow, was writhing in the agony of having to find conversation; so I took pity on the learned man . . .

BRACK *(smiles doubtfully)*. *You* took pity? H'm . . .

HEDDA. Yes, I really did. And so—to help him out of his torment— I happened to say, in pure thoughtlessness, that I should like to live in this villa.

BRACK. No more than that?

HEDDA. Not *that* evening.

BRACK. But afterwards?

HEDDA. Yes, my thoughtlessness had consequences, my dear Judge.

BRACK. Unfortunately that too often happens, Mrs. Hedda.

HEDDA. Thanks! So you see it was this enthusiasm for Secretary Falk's villa that first constituted a bond of sympathy between George Tesman and me. From *that* came our engagement and our marriage, and our wedding journey, and all the rest of it. Well, well, my dear Judge—as you make your bed so you must lie, I could almost say.

BRACK. This is exquisite! And you really cared not a rap about it all the time?

HEDDA. No, heaven knows I didn't.

BRACK. But now? Now that we have made it so homelike for you?

HEDDA. Uh—the rooms all seem to smell of lavender and dried rose-leaves.—But perhaps it's Aunt Julia that has brought that scent with her.

BRACK *(laughing)*. No, I think it must be a legacy from the late Mrs. Secretary Falk.

HEDDA. Yes, there is an odour of mortality about it. It reminds me of a bouquet—the day after the ball. *(Clasps her hands behind her head, leans back in her chair and looks at him.)* Oh, my dear Judge —you cannot imagine how horribly I shall bore myself here.

BRACK. Why should not you, too, find some sort of vocation in life, Mrs. Hedda?

HEDDA. A vocation—that should attract me?

BRACK. If possible, of course.

HEDDA. Heaven knows what sort of a vocation that could be. I often wonder whether . . . *(Breaking off.)* But that would never do either.

BRACK. Who can tell? Let me hear what it is.

HEDDA. Whether I might not get Tesman to go into politics, I mean.

BRACK *(laughing)*. Tesman? No really now, political life is not the life for him—not at all in his line.

HEDDA. No, I daresay not.—But if I could get him into it all the same?

BRACK. Why—what satisfaction could you find in that? If he is not fitted for that sort of thing, why should you want to drive him into it?

HEDDA. Because I am bored, I tell you! *(After a pause.)* So you think it quite out of the question that Tesman should ever get into the ministry?

BRACK. H'm—you see, my dear Mrs. Hedda—to get into the ministry, he would have to be a tolerably rich man.

HEDDA *(rising impatiently)*. Yes, there we have it! It is this genteel poverty I have managed to drop into . . . ! *(Crosses the room.) That* is what makes life so pitiable! So utterly ludicrous!—For that's what it is.

BRACK. Now *I* should say the fault lay elsewhere.

HEDDA. Where, then?

BRACK. You have never gone through any really stimulating experience.

HEDDA. Anything serious, you mean?

BRACK. Yes, you may call it so. But now you may perhaps have one in store.

HEDDA *(tossing her head)*. Oh, you're thinking of the annoyances about this wretched professorship! But that must be Tesman's own affair. I assure you I shall not waste a thought upon it.

BRACK. No, no, I daresay not. But suppose now that what people call —in elegant language—a solemn responsibility were to come upon you? *(Smiling.)* A new responsibility, Mrs. Hedda?

HEDDA *(angrily)*. Be quiet! Nothing of that sort will ever happen!

BRACK *(warily)*. We will speak of this again a year hence—at the very outside.

HEDDA *(curtly)*. I have no turn for anything of the sort, Judge Brack. No responsibilities for me!

BRACK. Are you so unlike the generality of women as to have no turn for duties which . . . ?

HEDDA *(beside the glass door)*. Oh, be quiet, I tell you!—I often think there is only one thing in the world I have any turn for.

BRACK *(drawing near to her)*. And what is that, if I may ask?

HEDDA *(stands looking out)*. Boring myself to death. Now you know it. *(Turns, looks towards the inner room, and laughs.)* Yes, as I thought! Here comes the Professor.

BRACK *(softly, in a tone of warning)*. Come, come, come, Mrs. Hedda! *(George Tesman, dressed for the party, with his gloves and hat in his hand, enters from the right through the inner room.)*

TESMAN. Hedda, has no message come from Eilert Løvborg? Eh?

HEDDA. No.

TESMAN. Then you'll see he'll be here presently.

BRACK. Do you really think he will come?

TESMAN. Yes, I am almost sure of it. For what you were telling us this morning must have been a mere floating rumour.

BRACK. You think so?

TESMAN. At any rate, Aunt Julia said she did not believe for a moment that he would ever stand in my way again. Fancy that!

BRACK. Well then, that's all right.

TESMAN *(placing his hat and gloves on a chair on the right)*. Yes, but you must really let me wait for him as long as possible.

BRACK. We have plenty of time yet. None of my guests will arrive before seven or half-past.

TESMAN. Then meanwhile we can keep Hedda company, and see what happens. Eh?

HEDDA *(placing Brack's hat and overcoat upon the corner settee)*. And at the worst Mr. Løvborg can remain here with me.

BRACK *(offering to take his things)*. Oh, allow me, Mrs. Tesman!— What do you mean by "At the worst"?

HEDDA. If he won't go with you and Tesman.

TESMAN *(looks dubiously at her)*. But, Hedda dear—do you think it would quite do for him to remain with you? Eh? Remember, Aunt Julia can't come.

HEDDA. No, but Mrs. Elvsted is coming. We three can have a cup of tea together.

TESMAN. Oh yes, *that* will be all right.

BRACK *(smiling)*. And that would perhaps be the safest plan for him.

HEDDA. Why so?

BRACK. Well, you know, Mrs. Tesman, how you used to gird at my little bachelor parties. You declared they were adapted only for men of the strictest principles.

HEDDA. But no doubt Mr. Løvborg's principles are strict enough now. A converted sinner . . .

(Berta appears at the hall door.)

BERTA. There's a gentleman asking if you are at home, ma'am . . .

HEDDA. Well, show him in.

TESMAN *(softly)*. I'm sure it is he! Fancy that!

(Eilert Løvborg enters from the hall. He is slim and lean; of the same age as Tesman, but looks older and somewhat worn out. His hair and beard are of a blackish brown, his face long and pale, but with patches of colour on the cheekbones. He is dressed in a well-cut black visiting suit, quite new. He has dark gloves and a silk hat. He stops near the door, and makes a rapid bow, seeming somewhat embarrassed.)

TESMAN *(goes up to him and shakes him warmly by the hand)*. Well, my dear Eilert—so at last we meet again!

EILERT LØVBORG *(speaks in a subdued voice)*. Thanks for your letter, Tesman. *(Approaching Hedda.)* Will you too shake hands with me, Mrs. Tesman?

HEDDA *(taking his hand)*. I am glad to see you, Mr. Løvborg. *(With a motion of her hand.)* I don't know whether you two gentle-men . . . ?

LØVBORG *(bowing slightly)*. Judge Brack, I think.

BRACK *(doing likewise)*. Oh yes,—in the old days . . .

TESMAN *(to Løvborg, with his hands on his shoulders)*. And now you must make yourself entirely at home, Eilert! Mustn't he, Hedda?—For I hear you are going to settle in town again? Eh?

LØVBORG. Yes, I am.

TESMAN. Quite right, quite right. Let me tell you, I have got hold of your new book; but I haven't had time to read it yet.

LØVBORG. You may spare yourself the trouble.

TESMAN. Why so?

LØVBORG. Because there is very little in it.

TESMAN. Just fancy—how can you say so?

BRACK. But it has been very much praised, I hear.

LØVBORG. That was what I wanted; so I put nothing into the book but what every one would agree with.

BRACK. Very wise of you.

TESMAN. Well but, my dear Eilert . . . !

LØVBORG. For now I mean to win myself a position again—to make a fresh start.

TESMAN (*a little embarrassed*). Ah, that is what you wish to do? Eh?

LØVBORG (*smiling, lays down his hat, and draws a packet, wrapped in paper, from his coat pocket*). But when this one appears, George Tesman, you will have to read it. For *this* is the real book—the book I have put my true self into.

TESMAN. Indeed? And what is it?

LØVBORG. It is the continuation.

TESMAN. The continuation? Of what?

LØVBORG. Of the book.

TESMAN. Of the new book?

LØVBORG. Of course.

TESMAN. Why, my dear Eilert—does it not come down to our own days?

LØVBORG. Yes, it does; and this one deals with the future.

TESMAN. With the future! But, good heavens, we know nothing of the future!

LØVBORG. No; but there is a thing or two to be said about it all the same. (*Opens the packet.*) Look here . . .

TESMAN. Why, that's not your handwriting.

LØVBORG. I dictated it. (*Turning over the pages.*) It falls into two sections. The first deals with the civilising forces of the future. And here is the second—(*running through the pages towards the end*)—forecasting the probable line of development.

TESMAN. How odd now! I should never have thought of writing any-thing of that sort.

HEDDA *(at the glass door, drumming on the pane)*. H'm ... I daresay not.

LØVBORG *(replacing the manuscript in its paper and laying the packet on the table)*. I brought it, thinking I might read you a little of it this evening.

TESMAN. That was very good of you, Eilert. But this evening ... ? *(Looking at Brack.)* I don't quite see how we can manage it ...

LØVBORG. Well then, some other time. There is no hurry.

BRACK. I must tell you, Mr. Løvborg—there is a little gathering at my house this evening—mainly in honour of Tesman, you know ...

LØVBORG *(looking for his hat)*. Oh—then I won't detain you ...

BRACK. No, but listen—will you not do me the favour of joining us?

LØVBORG *(curtly and decidedly)*. No, I can't—thank you very much.

BRACK. Oh, nonsense—do! We shall be quite a select little circle. And I assure you we shall have a "lively time," as Mrs. Hed—as Mrs. Tesman says.

LØVBORG. I have no doubt of it. But nevertheless ...

BRACK. And then you might bring your manuscript with you, and read it to Tesman at my house. I could give you a room to yourselves.

TESMAN. Yes, think of that, Eilert,—why shouldn't you? Eh?

HEDDA *(interposing)*. But, Tesman, if Mr. Løvborg would really rather not! I am sure Mr. Løvborg is much more inclined to remain here and have supper with me.

LØVBORG *(looking at her)*. With you, Mrs. Tesman?

HEDDA. And with Mrs. Elvsted.

LØVBORG. Ah ... *(Lightly.)* I saw her for a moment this morning.

HEDDA. Did you? Well, she is coming this evening. So you see you are almost bound to remain, Mr. Løvborg, or she will have no one to see her home.

LØVBORG. That's true. Many thanks, Mrs. Tesman—in that case I will remain.

HEDDA. Then I have one or two orders to give the servant ...

(She goes to the hall door and rings. Berta enters. Hedda talks to her in a whisper, and points towards the inner room. Berta nods and goes out again.)

TESMAN *(at the same time, to Løvborg)*. Tell me, Eilert—is it this new subject—the future—that you are going to lecture about?

LØVBORG. Yes.

TESMAN. They told me at the bookseller's that you are going to deliver a course of lectures this autumn.

LØVBORG. That is my intention. I hope you won't take it ill, Tesman.

TESMAN. Oh no, not in the least! But . . . ?

LØVBORG. I can quite understand that it must be disagreeable to you.

TESMAN *(cast down)*. Oh, I can't expect you, out of consideration for me, to . . .

LØVBORG. But I shall wait till you have received your appointment.

TESMAN. Will you wait? Yes but—yes but—are you not going to compete with me? Eh?

LØVBORG. No; it is only the moral victory I care for.

TESMAN. Why, bless me—then Aunt Julia was right after all! Oh yes —I knew it! Hedda! Just fancy—Eilert Løvborg is not going to stand in our way!

HEDDA *(curtly)*. *Our* way? Pray leave *me* out of the question.

(She goes up towards the inner room, where Berta is placing a tray with decanters and glasses on the table. Hedda nods approval, and comes forward again. Berta goes out.)

TESMAN *(at the same time)*. And you, Judge Brack—what do you say to this? Eh?

BRACK. Well, I say that a moral victory—h'm—may be all very fine . . .

TESMAN. Yes, certainly. But all the same . . .

HEDDA *(looking at Tesman with a cold smile)*. You stand there looking as if you were thunderstruck . . .

TESMAN. Yes—so I am—I almost think . . .

BRACK. Don't you see, Mrs. Tesman, a thunderstorm has just passed over?

HEDDA *(pointing towards the inner room).* Will you not take a glass of cold punch, gentlemen?

BRACK *(looking at his watch).* A stirrup-cup? Yes, it wouldn't come amiss.

TESMAN. A capital idea, Hedda! Just the thing! Now that the weight has been taken off my mind . . .

HEDDA. Will you not join them, Mr. Løvborg?

LØVBORG *(with a gesture of refusal).* No, thank you. Nothing for me.

BRACK. Why bless me—cold punch is surely not poison.

LØVBORG. Perhaps not for every one.

HEDDA. I will keep Mr. Løvborg company in the meantime.

TESMAN. Yes, yes, Hedda dear, do.

(He and Brack go into the inner room, seat themselves, drink punch, smoke cigarettes, and carry on a lively conversation during what follows. Eilert Løvborg remains standing beside the stove. Hedda goes to the writing-table.)

HEDDA *(raising her voice a little).* Do you care to look at some photographs, Mr. Løvborg? You know Tesman and I made a tour in the Tyrol on our way home?

(She takes up an album, and places it on the table beside the sofa, in the further corner of which she seats herself. Eilert Løvborg approaches, stops, and looks at her. Then he takes a chair and seats himself to her left, with his back towards the inner room.)

HEDDA *(opening the album).* Do you see this range of mountains, Mr. Løvborg? It's the Ortler group. Tesman has written the name underneath. Here it is: "The Ortler group near Meran."

LØVBORG *(who has never taken his eyes off her, says softly and slowly):* Hedda—Gabler!

HEDDA *(glancing hastily at him).* Ah! Hush!

LØVBORG *(repeats softly).* Hedda Gabler!

HEDDA *(looking at the album).* That was my name in the old days— when we two knew each other.

LØVBORG. And I must teach myself never to say Hedda Gabler again —never, as long as I live.

HEDDA *(still turning over the pages)*. Yes, you must. And I think you ought to practise in time. The sooner the better, I should say.

LØVBORG *(in a tone of indignation)*. Hedda Gabler married? And married to—George Tesman!

HEDDA. Yes, so the world goes.

LØVBORG. Oh, Hedda, Hedda—how could you[1] throw yourself away!

HEDDA *(looks sharply at him)*. What? I can't allow this!

LØVBORG. What do you mean?

(Tesman comes into the room and goes towards the sofa.)

HEDDA *(hears him coming and says in an indifferent tone)*. And this is a view from the Val d'Ampezzo, Mr. Løvborg. Just look at these peaks! *(Looks affectionately up at Tesman.)* What's the name of these curious peaks, dear?

TESMAN. Let me see. Oh, those are the Dolomites.

HEDDA. Yes, that's it!—Those are the Dolomites, Mr. Løvborg.

TESMAN. Hedda dear,—I only wanted to ask whether I shouldn't bring you a little punch after all? For yourself at any rate—eh?

HEDDA. Yes, do, please; and perhaps a few biscuits.

TESMAN. No cigarettes?

HEDDA. No.

TESMAN. Very well.

(He goes into the inner room and out to the right. Brack sits in the inner room, and keeps an eye from time to time on Hedda and Løvborg.)

LØVBORG *(softly, as before)*. Answer me, Hedda—how could you go and do this?

HEDDA *(apparently absorbed in the album)*. If you continue to say *du* to me I won't talk to you.

LØVBORG. May I not say *du* even when we are alone?

HEDDA. No. You may think it; but you mustn't say it.

LØVBORG. Ah, I understand. It is an offence against George Tesman, whom you[2]—love.

---

[1] He uses the familiar *du*.

[2] From this point onward Løvborg uses the formal *De*.

HEDDA *(glances at him and smiles)*. Love? What an idea!

LØVBORG. You don't love him then!

HEDDA. But I won't hear of any sort of unfaithfulness! Remember that.

LØVBORG. Hedda—answer me one thing . . .

HEDDA. Hush!

(Tesman enters with a small tray from the inner room.)

TESMAN. Here you are! Isn't this tempting?

(He puts the tray on the table.)

HEDDA. Why do you bring it yourself?

TESMAN *(filling the glasses)*. Because I think it's such fun to wait upon you, Hedda.

HEDDA. But you have poured out two glasses. Mr. Løvborg said he wouldn't have any . . .

TESMAN. No, but Mrs. Elvsted will soon be here, won't she?

HEDDA. Yes, by-the-bye—Mrs. Elvsted . . .

TESMAN. Had you forgotten her? Eh?

HEDDA. We were so absorbed in these photographs. *(Shows him a picture.)* Do you remember this little village?

TESMAN. Oh, it's that one just below the Brenner Pass. It was there we passed the night . . .

HEDDA. . . . and met that lively party of tourists.

TESMAN. Yes, that was the place. Fancy—if we could only have had *you* with us, Eilert! Eh?

(He returns to the inner room and sits beside Brack.)

LØVBORG. Answer me this one thing, Hedda . . .

HEDDA. Well?

LØVBORG. Was there no love in your friendship for *me* either? Not a spark—not a tinge of love in it?

HEDDA. I wonder if there was? To me it seems as though we were two good comrades—two thoroughly intimate friends. *(Smilingly.)* You especially were frankness itself.

LØVBORG. It was you that made me so.

HEDDA. As I look back upon it all, I think there was really something beautiful, something fascinating—something daring—in—in that secret intimacy—that comradeship which no living creature so much as dreamed of.

LØVBORG. Yes, yes, Hedda! Was there not?—When I used to come to your father's in the afternoon—and the General sat over at the window reading his papers—with his back towards us . . .

HEDDA. And we two on the corner sofa . . .

LØVBORG. Always with the same illustrated paper before us . . .

HEDDA. For want of an album, yes.

LØVBORG. Yes, Hedda, and when I made my confessions to you—told you about myself, things that at that time no one else knew! There I would sit and tell you of my escapades—my days and nights of devilment. Oh, Hedda—what was the power in you that forced me to confess these things?

HEDDA. Do you think it was any power in me?

LØVBORG. How else can I explain it? And all those—those round-about questions you used to put to me . . .

HEDDA. Which you understood so particularly well . . .

LØVBORG. How could you sit and question me like that? Question me quite frankly . . .

HEDDA. In roundabout terms, please observe.

LØVBORG. Yes, but frankly nevertheless. Cross-question me about—all that sort of thing?

HEDDA. And how could you answer, Mr. Løvborg?

LØVBORG. Yes, that is just what I can't understand—in looking back upon it. But tell me now, Hedda—was there not love at the bottom of our friendship? On your side, did you not feel as though you might purge my stains away—if I made you my confessor? Was it not so?

HEDDA. No, not quite.

LØVBORG. What was your motive, then?

HEDDA. Do you think it quite incomprehensible that a young girl—when it can be done—without any one knowing . . .

LØVBORG. Well?

HEDDA. . . . should be glad to have a peep, now and then, into a world which . . .

LØVBORG. Which . . . ?

HEDDA. . . . which she is forbidden to know anything about?

LØVBORG. So *that* was it?

HEDDA. Partly. Partly—I almost think.

LØVBORG. Comradeship in the thirst for life. But why should not *that*, at any rate, have continued?

HEDDA. The fault was yours.

LØVBORG. It was you that broke with me.

HEDDA. Yes, when our friendship threatened to develop into something more serious. Shame upon you, Eilert Løvborg! How could you think of wronging your—your frank comrade?

LØVBORG *(clenching his hands)*. Oh, why did you not carry out your threat? Why did you not shoot me down?

HEDDA. Because I have such a dread of scandal.

LØVBORG. Yes, Hedda, you are a coward at heart.

HEDDA. A terrible coward. *(Changing her tone.)* But it was a lucky thing for you. And now you have found ample consolation at the Elvsteds'.

LØVBORG. I know what Thea has confided to you.

HEDDA. And perhaps you have confided to her something about us?

LØVBORG. Not a word. She is too stupid to understand anything of that sort.

HEDDA. Stupid?

LØVBORG. She is stupid about matters of that sort.

HEDDA. And I am cowardly. *(Bends over towards him, without looking him in the face, and says more softly):* But now I will confide something to *you.*

LØVBORG *(eagerly)*. Well?

HEDDA. The fact that I dared not shoot you down . . .

LØVBORG. Yes!

HEDDA. . . . *that* was not my most arrant cowardice—that evening.

LØVBORG *(looks at her a moment, understands, and whispers passion-*

ately). Oh, Hedda! Hedda Gabler! Now I begin to see a hidden reason beneath our comradeship! You[1] and I . . . ! After all, then, it was your craving for life . . .

HEDDA *(softly, with a sharp glance).* Take care! Believe nothing of the sort!

(Twilight has begun to fall. The hall door is opened from without by Berta.)

HEDDA *(closes the album with a bang and calls smilingly):* Ah, at last! My darling Thea—come along!

(Mrs. Elvsted enters from the hall. She is in evening dress. The door is closed behind her.)

HEDDA *(on the sofa, stretches out her arms towards her).* My sweet Thea—you can't think how I have been longing for you!

(Mrs. Elvsted, in passing, exchanges slight salutations with the gentlemen in the inner room, then goes up to the table and gives Hedda her hand. Eilert Løvborg has risen. He and Mrs. Elvsted greet each other with a silent nod.)

MRS. ELVSTED. Ought I to go in and talk to your husband for a moment?

HEDDA. Oh, not at all. Leave those two alone. They will soon be going.

MRS. ELVSTED. Are they going out?

HEDDA. Yes, to a supper-party.

MRS. ELVSTED *(quickly, to Løvborg).* Not *you?*

LØVBORG. No.

HEDDA. Mr. Løvborg remains with us.

MRS. ELVSTED *(takes a chair and is about to seat herself at his side).* Oh, how nice it is here!

HEDDA. No, thank you, my little Thea. Not *there!* You'll be good enough to come over here to me. I will sit between you.

MRS. ELVSTED. Yes, just as you please.

(She goes round the table and seats herself on the sofa on Hedda's right. Løvborg re-seats himself on his chair.)

[1] In this speech he once more says *du.* Hedda addresses him throughout as *De.*

LØVBORG (*after a short pause, to Hedda*). Is not she lovely to look at?

HEDDA (*lightly stroking her hair*). Only to look at?

LØVBORG. Yes. For *we* two—she and I—*we* are two real comrades. We have absolute faith in each other; so we can sit and talk with perfect frankness . . .

HEDDA. Not round about, Mr. Løvborg?

LØVBORG. Well . . .

MRS. ELVSTED (*softly clinging close to Hedda*). Oh, how happy I am, Hedda! For, only think, he says I have inspired him too.

HEDDA (*looks at her with a smile*). Ah! Does he say that, dear?

LØVBORG. And then she is so brave, Mrs. Tesman!

MRS. ELVSTED. Good heavens—am I brave?

LØVBORG. Exceedingly—where your comrade is concerned.

HEDDA. Ah yes—courage! If one only had *that!*

LØVBORG. What then? What do you mean?

HEDDA. Then life would perhaps be liveable, after all. (*With a sudden change of tone.*) But now, my dearest Thea, you really must have a glass of cold punch.

MRS. ELVSTED. No, thanks—I never take anything of that kind.

HEDDA. Well then, *you*, Mr. Løvborg.

LØVBORG. Nor I, thank you.

MRS. ELVSTED. No, he doesn't either.

HEDDA (*looks fixedly at him*). But if I say you *shall?*

LØVBORG. It would be no use.

HEDDA (*laughing*). Then I, poor creature, have no sort of power over you?

LØVBORG. Not in *that* respect.

HEDDA. But seriously, I think you ought to—for your own sake.

MRS. ELVSTED. Why, Hedda . . . ?

LØVBORG. How so?

HEDDA. Or rather on account of other people.

LØVBORG. Indeed?

HEDDA. Otherwise people might be apt to suspect that—in your heart of hearts—you did not feel quite secure—quite confident in yourself.

MRS. ELVSTED (*softly*). Oh please, Hedda . . . !

LØVBORG. People may suspect what they like—for the present.

MRS. ELVSTED (*joyfully*). Yes, let them!

HEDDA. I saw it plainly in Judge Brack's face a moment ago.

LØVBORG. What did you see?

HEDDA. His contemptuous smile, when you dared not go with them into the inner room.

LØVBORG. Dared not? Of course I preferred to stop here and talk to *you*.

MRS. ELVSTED. What could be more natural, Hedda?

HEDDA. But the Judge could not guess that. And I saw, too, the way he smiled and glanced at Tesman when you dared not accept his invitation to this wretched little supper-party of his.

LØVBORG. Dared not! Do you say I dared not?

HEDDA. *I* don't say so. But that was how Judge Brack understood it.

LØVBORG. Well, let him.

HEDDA. Then you are not going with them?

LØVBORG. I will stay here with you and Thea.

MRS. ELVSTED. Yes, Hedda—how can you doubt that?

HEDDA *(smiles and nods approvingly to Løvborg)*. Firm as a rock!
Faithful to your principles, now and for ever! Ah, that is how a man
should be! *(Turns to Mrs. Elvsted and caresses her.)* Well now, what
did I tell you, when you came to us this morning in such a state of
distraction . . .

LØVBORG *(surprised)*. Distraction!

MRS. ELVSTED *(terrified)*. Hedda—oh Hedda . . . !

HEDDA. You can see for yourself! You haven't the slightest reason to
be in such a mortal terror . . . *(Interrupting herself.)* There! Now
we can all three enjoy ourselves!

LØVBORG *(who has given a start)*. Ah—what is all this, Mrs. Tesman?

MRS. ELVSTED. Oh my God, Hedda! What are you saying? What are
you doing?

HEDDA. Don't get excited! That horrid Judge Brack is sitting watching
you.

LØVBORG. So she was in mortal terror! On my account!

MRS. ELVSTED *(softly and piteously)*. Oh, Hedda—now you have ruined
everything!

LØVBORG *(looks fixedly at her for a moment. His face is distorted)*.
So *that* was my comrade's frank confidence in me?

MRS. ELVSTED *(imploringly)*. Oh, my dearest friend—only let me tell
you . . .

LØVBORG *(takes one of the glasses of punch, raises it to his lips, and
says in a low, husky voice)*. Your health, Thea!

(He empties the glass, puts it down, and takes the second.)

MRS. ELVSTED *(softly)*. Oh, Hedda, Hedda—how *could* you do this?

HEDDA. *I* do it? *I?* Are you crazy?

LØVBORG. Here's to your health too, Mrs. Tesman. Thanks for the
truth. Hurrah for the truth!

(He empties the glass and is about to re-fill it.)

HEDDA *(lays her hand on his arm)*. Come, come—no more for the
present. Remember you are going out to supper.

MRS. ELVSTED. No, no, no!

HEDDA. Hush! They are sitting watching you.

LØVBORG (*putting down the glass*). Now, Thea—tell me the truth . . .

MRS. ELVSTED. Yes.

LØVBORG. Did your husband know that you had come after me?

MRS. ELVSTED (*wringing her hands*). Oh, Hedda—do you hear what he is asking?

LØVBORG. Was it arranged between you and him that you were to come to town and look after me? Perhaps it was the Sheriff himself that urged you to come? Aha, my dear—no doubt he wanted my help in his office! Or was it at the card-table that he missed me?

MRS. ELVSTED (*softly, in agony*). Oh, Løvborg, Løvborg . . . !

LØVBORG (*seizes a glass and is on the point of filling it*). Here's a glass for the old Sheriff too!

HEDDA (*preventing him*). No more just now. Remember, you have to read your manuscript to Tesman.

LØVBORG (*calmly, putting down the glass*). It was stupid of me all this, Thea—to take it in this way, I mean. Don't be angry with me, my dear, dear comrade. You shall see—both you and the others—that if I was fallen once—now I have risen again! Thanks to *you*, Thea.

MRS. ELVSTED (*radiant with joy*). Oh, heaven be praised . . . !

(*Brack has in the meantime looked at his watch. He and Tesman rise and come into the drawing-room.*)

BRACK (*takes his hat and overcoat*). Well, Mrs. Tesman, our time has come.

HEDDA. I suppose it has.

LØVBORG (*rising*). Mine too, Judge Brack.

MRS. ELVSTED (*softly and imploringly*). Oh, Løvborg, don't do it!

HEDDA (*pinching her arm*). They can hear you!

MRS. ELVSTED (*with a suppressed shriek*). Ow!

LØVBORG (*to Brack*). You were good enough to invite me.

BRACK. Well, are you coming after all?

LØVBORG. Yes, many thanks.

BRACK. I'm delighted . . .

LØVBORG *(to Tesman, putting the parcel of MS. in his pocket).* I should like to show you one or two things before I send it to the printers.

TESMAN. Fancy—that will be delightful. But, Hedda dear, how is Mrs. Elvsted to get home? Eh?

HEDDA. Oh, that can be managed somehow.

LØVBORG *(looking towards the ladies).* Mrs. Elvsted? Of course, I'll come again and fetch her. *(Approaching.)* At ten or thereabouts, Mrs. Tesman? Will that do?

HEDDA. Certainly. That will do capitally.

TESMAN. Well, then, that's all right. But you must not expect *me* so early, Hedda.

HEDDA. Oh, you may stop as long—as long as ever you please.

MRS. ELVSTED *(trying to conceal her anxiety).* Well then, Mr. Løvborg —I shall remain here until you come.

LØVBORG *(with his hat in his hand).* Pray do, Mrs. Elvsted.

BRACK. And now off goes the excursion train, gentlemen! I hope we shall have a lively time, as a certain fair lady puts it.

HEDDA. Ah, if only the fair lady could be present unseen . . . !

BRACK. Why unseen?

HEDDA. In order to hear a little of your liveliness at first hand, Judge Brack.

BRACK *(laughing).* I should not advise the fair lady to try it.

TESMAN *(also laughing).* Come, you're a nice one, Hedda! Fancy that!

BRACK. Well, good-bye, good-bye, ladies.

LØVBORG *(bowing).* About ten o'clock, then.

(Brack, Løvborg, and Tesman go out by the hall door. At the same time, Berta enters from the inner room with a lighted lamp, which she places on the drawing-room table; she goes out by the way she came.)

MRS. ELVSTED *(who has risen and is wandering restlessly about the room).* Hedda—Hedda—what will come of all this?

HEDDA. At ten o'clock—he will be here. I can see him already—with vine-leaves in his hair—flushed and fearless . . .

MRS. ELVSTED. Oh, I hope he may.

HEDDA. And then, you see—then he will have regained control over himself. Then he will be a free man for all his days.

MRS. ELVSTED. Oh God!—if he would only come as you see him now!

HEDDA. He will come as I see him—so, and not otherwise! *(Rises and approaches Thea.)* You may doubt him as long as you please; *I* believe in him. And now we will try . . .

MRS. ELVSTED. You have some hidden motive in this, Hedda!

HEDDA. Yes, I have. I want for once in my life to have power to mould a human destiny.

MRS. ELVSTED. Have you not the power?

HEDDA. I have not—and have never had it.

MRS. ELVSTED. Not your husband's?

HEDDA. Do you think *that* is worth the trouble? Oh, if you could only understand how poor I am. And fate has made *you* so rich! *(Clasps her passionately in her arms.)* I think I must burn your hair off, after all.

MRS. ELVSTED. Let me go! Let me go! I am afraid of you, Hedda.

BERTA *(in the middle doorway)*. Tea is laid in the dining-room, ma'am.

HEDDA. Very well. We are coming.

MRS. ELVSTED. No, no, no! I would rather go home alone! At once!

HEDDA. Nonsense! First you shall have a cup of tea, you little stupid. And then—at ten o'clock—Eilert Løvborg will be here—with vine-leaves in his hair.

(She drags Mrs. Elvsted almost by force towards the middle doorway).

ACT THIRD

The room at the Tesmans'. The curtains are drawn over the middle doorway, and also over the glass door. The lamp, half turned down, and with a shade over it, is burning on the table. In the stove, the door of which stands open, there has been a fire, which is now nearly burnt out.

Mrs. Elvsted, wrapped in a large shawl, and with her feet upon a foot-rest, sits close to the stove, sunk back in the arm-chair. Hedda, fully dressed, lies sleeping upon the sofa, with a sofa-blanket over her.

MRS. ELVSTED (*after a pause, suddenly sits up in her chair, and listens eagerly. Then she sinks back again wearily, moaning to herself*). Not yet!—Oh God—oh God—not yet!

(*Berta slips cautiously in by the hall door. She has a letter in her hand.*)

MRS. ELVSTED (*turns and whispers eagerly*). Well—has any one come?

BERTA (*softly*). Yes, a girl has just brought this letter.

MRS. ELVSTED (*quickly, holding out her hand*). A letter! Give it to me!

BERTA. No, it's for Dr. Tesman, ma'am.

MRS. ELVSTED. Oh, indeed.

BERTA. It was Miss Tesman's servant that brought it. I'll lay it here on the table.

MRS. ELVSTED. Yes, do.

BERTA (*laying down the letter*). I think I had better put out the lamp. It's smoking.

MRS. ELVSTED. Yes, put it out. It must soon be daylight now.

BERTA (*putting out the lamp*). It is daylight already, ma'am.

MRS. ELVSTED. Yes, broad day! And no one come back yet . . . !

BERTA. Lord bless you, ma'am—I guessed how it would be.

MRS. ELVSTED. You guessed?

BERTA. Yes, when I saw that a certain person had come back to town —and that he went off with them. For we've heard enough about that gentleman before now.

MRS. ELVSTED. Don't speak so loud. You will waken Mrs. Tesman.

BERTA (*looks towards the sofa and sighs*). No, no—let her sleep, poor thing. Shan't I put some wood on the fire?

MRS. ELVSTED. Thanks, not for me.

BERTA. Oh, very well.

(*She goes softly out by the hall door.*)

HEDDA (*is wakened by the shutting of the door, and looks up*). What's that . . . ?

MRS. ELVSTED. It was only the servant . . .

HEDDA (*looking about her*). Oh, we're here . . . ! Yes, now I remember. (*Sits erect upon the sofa, stretches herself, and rubs her eyes.*) What o'clock is it, Thea?

MRS. ELVSTED (*looks at her watch*). It's past seven.

HEDDA. When did Tesman come home?

MRS. ELVSTED. He has not come.

HEDDA. Not come home *yet?*

MRS. ELVSTED (*rising*). No one has come.

HEDDA. Think of our watching and waiting here till four in the morning . . .

MRS. ELVSTED (*wringing her hands*). And *how* I watched and waited for him!

HEDDA *(yawns, and says with her hand before her mouth)*. Well well
—we might have spared ourselves the trouble.

MRS. ELVSTED. Did you get a little sleep?

HEDDA. Oh yes; I believe I have slept pretty well. Have you not?

MRS. ELVSTED. Not for a moment. I couldn't, Hedda!—not to save
my life.

HEDDA *(rises and goes towards her)*. There there there! There's
nothing to be so alarmed about. I understand quite well what has
happened.

MRS. ELVSTED. Well, what do you think? Won't you tell me?

HEDDA. Why, of course it has been a very late affair at Judge
Brack's . . .

MRS. ELVSTED. Yes, yes—that is clear enough. But all the same . . .

HEDDA. And then, you see, Tesman hasn't cared to come home and
ring us up in the middle of the night. *(Laughing.)* Perhaps he
wasn't inclined to show himself either—immediately after a jollifica-
tion.

MRS. ELVSTED. But in that case—where can he have gone?

HEDDA. Of course he has gone to his Aunts' and slept there. They
have his old room ready for him.

MRS. ELVSTED. No, he can't be with *them;* for a letter has just come
for him from Miss Tesman. There it lies.

HEDDA. Indeed? *(Looks at the address.)* Why yes, it's addressed in
Aunt Julia's own hand. Well then, he has remained at Judge Brack's.
And as for Eilert Løvborg—he is sitting, with vine-leaves in his
hair, reading his manuscript.

MRS. ELVSTED. Oh Hedda, you are just saying things you don't believe
a bit.

HEDDA. You really are a little blockhead, Thea.

MRS. ELVSTED. Oh yes, I suppose I am.

HEDDA. And how mortally tired you look.

MRS. ELVSTED. Yes, I *am* mortally tired.

HEDDA. Well then, you must do as I tell you. You must go into my
room and lie down for a little while.

MRS. ELVSTED. Oh no, no—I shouldn't be able to sleep.

HEDDA. I am sure you would.

MRS. ELVSTED. Well, but your husband is certain to come soon now; and then I want to know at once . . .

HEDDA. I shall take care to let you know when he comes.

MRS. ELVSTED. Do you promise me, Hedda?

HEDDA. Yes, rely upon me. Just you go in and have a sleep in the meantime.

MRS. ELVSTED. Thanks; then I'll try to.

(She goes off through the inner room.

Hedda goes up to the glass door and draws back the curtains. The broad daylight streams into the room. Then she takes a little hand-glass from the writing-table, looks at herself in it, and arranges her hair. Next she goes to the hall door and presses the bell-button.

Berta presently appears at the hall door.)

BERTA. Did you want anything, ma'am?

HEDDA. Yes; you must put some more wood in the stove. I am shivering.

BERTA. Bless me—I'll make up the fire at once. *(She rakes the embers together and lays a piece of wood upon them; then stops and listens.)* That was a ring at the front door, ma'am.

HEDDA. Then go to the door. I will look after the fire.

BERTA. It'll soon burn up.

(She goes out by the hall door.

Hedda kneels on the foot-rest and lays some more pieces of wood in the stove.

After a short pause, George Tesman enters from the hall. He looks tired and rather serious. He steals on tiptoe towards the middle doorway and is about to slip through the curtains.)

HEDDA *(at the stove, without looking up)*. Good morning.

TESMAN *(turns)*. Hedda! *(Approaching her.)* Good heavens—are you up so early? Eh?

HEDDA. Yes, I am up very early this morning.

TESMAN. And I never doubted you were still sound asleep! Fancy that, Hedda!

HEDDA. Don't speak so loud. Mrs. Elvsted is resting in my room.

TESMAN. Has Mrs. Elvsted been here all night?

HEDDA. Yes, since no one came to fetch her.

TESMAN. Ah, to be sure.

HEDDA *(closes the door of the stove and rises)*. Well, did you enjoy yourselves at Judge Brack's?

TESMAN. Have you been anxious about me? Eh?

HEDDA. No, I should never think of being anxious. But I asked if you had enjoyed yourself.

TESMAN. Oh yes,—for once in a way. Especially the beginning of the evening; for then Eilert read me part of his book. We arrived more than an hour too early—fancy that! And Brack had all sorts of arrangements to make—so Eilert read to me.

HEDDA *(seating herself by the table on the right)*. Well? Tell me, then . . .

TESMAN *(sitting on a footstool near the stove)*. Oh Hedda, you can't conceive what a book that is going to be! I believe it is one of the most remarkable things that have ever been written. Fancy that!

HEDDA. Yes yes; I don't care about that . . .

TESMAN. I must make a confession to you, Hedda. When he had finished reading—a horrid feeling came over me.

HEDDA. A horrid feeling?

TESMAN. I felt jealous of Eilert for having had it in him to write such a book. Only think, Hedda!

HEDDA. Yes, yes, I am thinking!

TESMAN. And then how pitiful to think that he—with all his gifts— should be irreclaimable, after all.

HEDDA. I suppose you mean that he has more courage than the rest?

TESMAN. No, not at all—I mean that he is incapable of taking his pleasures in moderation.

HEDDA. And what came of it all—in the end?

TESMAN. Well, to tell the truth, I think it might best be described as an orgy, Hedda.

HEDDA. Had he vine-leaves in his hair?

TESMAN. Vine-leaves? No, I saw nothing of the sort. But he made a long, rambling speech in honour of the woman who had inspired him in his work—that was the phrase he used.

HEDDA. Did he name her?

TESMAN. No, he didn't; but I can't help thinking he meant Mrs. Elvsted. You may be sure he did.

HEDDA. Well—where did you part from him?

TESMAN. On the way to town. We broke up—the last of us at any rate —all together; and Brack came with us to get a breath of fresh air. And then, you see, we agreed to take Eilert home; for he had had far more than was good for him.

HEDDA. I daresay.

TESMAN. But now comes the strange part of it, Hedda; or, I should rather say, the melancholy part of it. I declare I am almost ashamed —on Eilert's account—to tell you . . .

HEDDA. Oh, go on . . . !

TESMAN. Well, as we were getting near town, you see, I happened to drop a little behind the others. Only for a minute or two—fancy that!

HEDDA. Yes yes yes, but . . . ?

TESMAN. And then, as I hurried after them—what do you think I found by the wayside? Eh?

HEDDA. Oh, how should I know!

TESMAN. You mustn't speak of it to a soul, Hedda! Do you hear! Promise me, for Eilert's sake. (Draws a parcel, wrapped in paper, from his coat pocket.) Fancy, dear—I found this.

HEDDA. Is not that the parcel he had with him yesterday?

TESMAN. Yes, it is the whole of his precious, irreplaceable manuscript! And he had gone and lost it, and knew nothing about it. Only fancy, Hedda! So deplorably . . .

HEDDA. But why did you not give him back the parcel at once?

TESMAN. I didn't dare to—in the state he was then in . . .

HEDDA. Did you not tell any of the others that you had found it?

TESMAN. Oh, far from it! You can surely understand that, for Eilert's sake, I wouldn't do that.

HEDDA. So no one knows that Eilert Løvborg's manuscript is in your possession?

TESMAN. No. And no one *must* know it.

HEDDA. Then what did you say to him afterwards?

TESMAN. I didn't talk to him at all; for when we got in among the streets, he and two or three of the others gave us the slip and disappeared. Fancy that!

HEDDA. Indeed! They must have taken him home then.

TESMAN. Yes, so it would appear. And Brack, too, left us.

HEDDA. And what have you been doing with yourself since?

TESMAN. Well, I and some of the others went home with one of the party, a jolly fellow, and took our morning coffee with him; or perhaps I should rather call it our night coffee—eh? But now, when I have rested a little, and given Eilert, poor fellow, time to have his sleep out, I must take this back to him.

HEDDA *(holds out her hand for the packet)*. No—don't give it to him! Not in such a hurry, I mean. Let me read it first.

TESMAN. No, my dearest Hedda, I mustn't, I really mustn't.

HEDDA. You must not?

TESMAN. No—for you can imagine what a state of despair he will be in when he wakens and misses the manuscript. He has no copy of it, you must know! He told me so.

HEDDA *(looking searchingly at him)*. Can such a thing not be reproduced? Written over again?

TESMAN. No, I don't think that would be possible. For the inspiration, you see . . .

HEDDA. Yes, yes—I suppose it depends on that . . . *(Lightly.)* But, by-the-bye—here is a letter for you.

TESMAN. Fancy . . . !

HEDDA *(handing it to him)*. It came early this morning.

TESMAN. It's from Aunt Julia! What can it be? *(He lays the packet on the other footstool, opens the letter, runs his eye through it, and jumps up.)* Oh, Hedda—she says that poor Aunt Rina is dying!

HEDDA. Well, we were prepared for that.

TESMAN. And that if I want to see her again, I must make haste. I'll run in to them at once.

HEDDA *(suppressing a smile)*. Will you run?

TESMAN. Oh, my dearest Hedda—if you could only make up your mind to come with me! Just think!

HEDDA *(rises and says wearily, repelling the idea)*. No, no, don't ask me. I *will* not look upon sickness and death. I loathe all sorts of ugliness.

TESMAN. Well, well, then . . . ! *(Bustling around.)* My hat . . . ? My overcoat . . . ? Oh, in the hall . . . I do hope I mayn't come too late, Hedda! Eh?

HEDDA. Oh, if you run . . .

(Berta appears at the hall door.)

BERTA. Judge Brack is at the door, and wishes to know it he may come in.

TESMAN. At this time! No, I can't possibly see him.

HEDDA. But I can. *(To Berta.)* Ask Judge Brack to come in.

(Berta goes out.)

HEDDA *(quickly, whispering)*. The parcel, Tesman!

(She snatches it up from the stool.)

TESMAN. Yes, give it to me!

HEDDA. No, no, I will keep it till you come back.

(She goes to the writing-table and places it in the bookcase. Tesman stands in a flurry of haste, and cannot get his gloves on.

Judge Brack enters from the hall.)

HEDDA *(nodding to him)*. You are an early bird, I must say.

BRACK. Yes, don't you think so? *(To Tesman.)* Are you on the move, too?

TESMAN. Yes, I *must* rush off to my aunts'. Fancy—the invalid one is lying at death's door, poor creature.

BRACK. Dear me, is she indeed? Then on no account let me detain you. At such a critical moment . . .

TESMAN. Yes, I must really rush . . . Good-bye! Good-bye!

(He hastens out by the hall door.)

HEDDA *(approaching).* You seem to have made a particularly lively night of it at your rooms, Judge Brack.

BRACK. I assure you I have not had my clothes off, Mrs. Hedda.

HEDDA. Not you, either?

BRACK. No, as you may see. But what has Tesman been telling you of the night's adventures?

HEDDA. Oh, some tiresome story. Only that they went and had coffee somewhere or other.

BRACK. I have heard about that coffee-party already. Eilert Løvborg was not with them, I fancy?

HEDDA. No, they had taken him home before that.

BRACK. Tesman too?

HEDDA. No, but some of the others, he said.

BRACK *(smiling).* George Tesman is really an ingenuous creature, Mrs. Hedda.

HEDDA. Yes, heaven knows he is. Then is there something behind all this?

BRACK. Yes, perhaps there may be.

HEDDA. Well then, sit down, my dear Judge, and tell your story in comfort.

(She seats herself to the left of the table. Brack sits near her, at the long side of the table.)

HEDDA. Now then?

BRACK. I had special reasons for keeping track of my guests—or rather of some of my guests—last night.

HEDDA. Of Eilert Løvborg among the rest, perhaps?

BRACK. Frankly—yes.

HEDDA. Now you make me really curious . . .

BRACK. Do you know where he and one or two of the others finished the night, Mrs. Hedda?

HEDDA. If it is not quite unmentionable, tell me.

BRACK. Oh no, it's not at all unmentionable. Well, they put in an appearance at a particularly animated soirée.

HEDDA. Of the lively kind?

BRACK. Of the very liveliest . . .

HEDDA. Tell me more of this, Judge Brack . . .

BRACK. Løvborg, as well as the others, had been invited in advance. I knew all about it. But he had declined the invitation; for now, as you know, he has become a new man.

HEDDA. Up at the Elvsteds', yes. But he went after all, then?

BRACK. Well, you see, Mrs. Hedda—unhappily the spirit moved him at my rooms last evening . . .

HEDDA. Yes, I hear he found inspiration.

BRACK. Pretty violent inspiration. Well, I fancy that altered his purpose; for we menfolk are unfortunately not always so firm in our principles as we ought to be.

HEDDA. Oh, I am sure *you* are an exception, Judge Brack. But as to Løvborg . . . ?

BRACK. To make a long story short—he landed at last in Mademoiselle Diana's rooms.

HEDDA. Mademoiselle Diana's?

BRACK. It was Mademoiselle Diana that was giving the soirée, to a select circle of her admirers and her lady friends.

HEDDA. Is she a red-haired woman?

BRACK. Precisely.

HEDDA. A sort of a—singer?

BRACK. Oh yes—in her leisure moments. And moreover a mighty huntress—of men—Mrs. Hedda. You have no doubt heard of her. Eilert Løvborg was one of her most enthusiastic protectors—in the days of his glory.

HEDDA. And how did all this end?

BRACK. Far from amicably, it appears. After a most tender meeting, they seem to have come to blows . . .

HEDDA. Løvborg and she?

BRACK. Yes. He accused her or her friends of having robbed him. He declared that his pocket-book had disappeared—and other things as well. In short, he seems to have made a furious disturbance.

HEDDA. And what came of it all?

BRACK. It came to a general scrimmage, in which the ladies as well as the gentlemen took part. Fortunately the police at last appeared on the scene.

HEDDA. The police too?

BRACK. Yes. I fancy it will prove a costly frolic for Eilert Løvborg, crazy being that he is.

HEDDA. How so?

BRACK. He seems to have made a violent resistance—to have hit one of the constables on the head and torn the coat off his back. So they had to march him off to the police-station with the rest.

HEDDA. How have you learnt all this?

BRACK. From the police themselves.

HEDDA *(gazing straight before her)*. So that is what happened. Then he had no vine-leaves in his hair.

BRACK. Vine-leaves, Mrs. Hedda?

HEDDA *(changing her tone)*. But tell me now, Judge—what is your real reason for tracking out Eilert Løvborg's movements so carefully?

BRACK. In the first place, it could not be entirely indifferent to me if it should appear in the police-court that he came straight from my house.

HEDDA. Will the matter come into court then?

BRACK. Of course. However, I should scarcely have troubled so much about that. But I thought that, as a friend of the family, it was my duty to supply you and Tesman with a full account of his nocturnal exploits.

HEDDA. Why so, Judge Brack?

BRACK. Why, because I have a shrewd suspicion that he intends to use you as a sort of blind.

HEDDA. Oh, how can you think such a thing!

BRACK. Good heavens, Mrs. Hedda—we have eyes in our head. Mark my words! This Mrs. Elvsted will be in no hurry to leave town again.

HEDDA. Well, even if there should be anything between them, I suppose there are plenty of other places where they could meet.

BRACK. Not a single *home*. Henceforth, as before, every respectable house will be closed against Eilert Løvborg.

HEDDA. And so ought mine to be, you mean?

BRACK. Yes. I confess it would be more than painful to me if this personage were to be made free of your house. How superfluous, how intrusive, he would be, if he were to force his way into . . .

HEDDA. . . . into the triangle?

BRACK. Precisely. It would simply mean that I should find myself homeless.

HEDDA (*looks at him with a smile*). So you want to be the one cock in the basket—that is your aim.

BRACK (*nods slowly and lowers his voice*). Yes, that is my aim. And for that I will fight—with every weapon I can command.

HEDDA (*her smile vanishing*). I see you are a dangerous person—when it comes to the point.

BRACK. Do you think so?

HEDDA. I am beginning to think so. And I am exceedingly glad to think—that you have no sort of hold over me.

BRACK (*laughing equivocally*). Well well, Mrs. Hedda—perhaps you are right there. If I had, who knows what I might be capable of?

HEDDA. Come come now, Judge Brack! That sounds almost like a threat.

BRACK (*rising*). Oh, not at all! The triangle, you know, ought, if possible, to be spontaneously constructed.

HEDDA. There I agree with you.

BRACK. Well, now I have said all I had to say; and I had better be getting back to town. Good-bye, Mrs. Hedda.

(*He goes towards the glass door.*)

HEDDA (*rising*). Are you going through the garden?

BRACK. Yes, it's a short cut for me.

HEDDA. And then it is a back way, too.

BRACK. Quite so. I have no objection to back ways. They may be piquant enough at times.

HEDDA. When there is ball practice going on, you mean?

BRACK *(in the doorway, laughing to her).* Oh, people don't shoot their tame poultry, I fancy.

HEDDA *(also laughing).* Oh no, when there is only one cock in the basket . . .

(They exchange laughing nods of farewell. He goes. She closes the door behind him.

Hedda, who has become quite serious, stands for a moment looking out. Presently she goes and peeps through the curtain over the middle doorway. Then she goes to the writing-table, takes Løvborg's packet out of the bookcase, and is on the point of looking through its contents. Berta is heard speaking loudly in the hall. Hedda turns and listens. Then she hastily locks up the packet in the drawer, and lays the key on the inkstand.

Eilert Løvborg, with his greatcoat on and his hat in his hand, tears open the hall door. He looks somewhat confused and irritated.)

LØVBORG *(looking towards the hall).* And I tell you I must and will come in! There!

(He closes the door, turns, sees Hedda, at once regains his self-control, and bows.)

HEDDA *(at the writing-table).* Well, Mr. Løvborg, this is rather a late hour to call for Thea.

LØVBORG. You mean rather an early hour to call on you. Pray pardon me.

HEDDA. How do you know that she is still here?

LØVBORG. They told me at her lodgings that she had been out all night.

HEDDA *(going to the oval table).* Did you notice anything about the people of the house when they said that?

LØVBORG *(looks inquiringly at her).* Notice anything about them?

HEDDA. I mean, did they seem to think it odd?

LØVBORG *(suddenly understanding).* Oh yes, of course! I am dragging her down with me! However, I didn't notice anything.—I suppose Tesman is not up yet?

HEDDA. No—I think not . . .

LØVBORG. When did he come home?

HEDDA. Very late.

LØVBORG. Did he tell you anything?

HEDDA. Yes, I gathered that you had had an exceedingly jolly evening at Judge Brack's.

LØVBORG. Nothing more?

HEDDA. I don't think so. However, I was so dreadfully sleepy . . .

(Mrs. Elvsted enters through the curtains of the middle doorway.)

MRS. ELVSTED *(going towards him)*. Ah, Løvborg! At last . . . !

LØVBORG. Yes, at last. And too late!

MRS. ELVSTED *(looks anxiously at him)*. What is too late?

LØVBORG. Everything is too late now. It is all over with me.

MRS. ELVSTED. Oh no, no—don't say that!

LØVBORG. You will say the same when you hear . . .

MRS. ELVSTED. I won't hear anything!

HEDDA. Perhaps you would prefer to talk to her alone? If so, I will leave you.

LØVBORG. No, stay—you too. I beg you to stay.

MRS. ELVSTED. Yes, but I won't hear anything, I tell you.

LØVBORG. It is not last night's adventures that I want to talk about.

MRS. ELVSTED. What is it then . . . ?

LØVBORG. I want to say that now our ways must part.

MRS. ELVSTED. Part!

HEDDA *(involuntarily).* I knew it!

LØVBORG. You can be of no more service to me, Thea.

MRS. ELVSTED. How can you stand there and say that! No more service to you! Am I not to help you now, as before? Are we not to go on working together?

LØVBORG. Henceforward I shall do no work.

MRS. ELVSTED *(despairingly).* Then what am I to do with my life?

LØVBORG. You must try to live your life as if you had never known me.

MRS. ELVSTED. But you know I cannot do that!

LØVBORG. Try if you cannot, Thea. You must go home again . . .

MRS. ELVSTED *(in vehement protest).* Never in this world! Where you are, there will I be also! I will not let myself be driven away like this! I will remain here! I will be with you when the book appears.

HEDDA *(half aloud, in suspense).* Ah yes—the book!

LØVBORG *(looks at her).* My book and Thea's; for *that* is what it is.

MRS. ELVSTED. Yes, I feel that it is. And that is why I have a right to be with you when it appears! I will see with my own eyes how respect and honour pour in upon you afresh. And the happiness— the happiness—oh, I must share it with you!

LØVBORG. Thea—our book will never appear.

HEDDA. Ah!

MRS. ELVSTED. Never appear!

LØVBORG. *Can* never appear.

MRS. ELVSTED *(in agonised foreboding).* Løvborg—what have you done with the manuscript?

HEDDA *(looks anxiously at him).* Yes, the manuscript . . . ?

MRS. ELVSTED. Where is it?

LØVBORG. Oh Thea—don't ask me about it!

MRS. ELVSTED. Yes, yes, I *will* know. I demand to be told at once.

LØVBORG. The manuscript . . . Well then—I have torn the manuscript into a thousand pieces.

MRS. ELVSTED *(shrieks)*. Oh no, no . . . !

HEDDA *(involuntarily)*. But that's not . . .

LØVBORG *(looks at her)*. Not true, you think?

HEDDA *(collecting herself)*. Oh well, of course—since you say so. But it sounded so improbable . . .

LØVBORG. It is true, all the same.

MRS. ELVSTED *(wringing her hands)*. Oh God—oh God, Hedda—torn his own work to pieces!

LØVBORG. I have torn my own life to pieces. So why should I not tear my life-work too . . . ?

MRS. ELVSTED. And you did this last night?

LØVBORG. Yes, I tell you! Tore it into a thousand pieces—and scattered them on the fiord—far out. There there is cool sea-water at any rate —let them drift upon it—drift with the current and the wind. And then presently they will sink—deeper and deeper—as I shall, Thea.

MRS. ELVSTED. Do you know, Løvborg, that what you have done with the book—I shall think of it to my dying day as though you had killed a little child.

LØVBORG. Yes, you are right. It is a sort of child-murder.

MRS. ELVSTED. How could you, then . . . ! Did not the child belong to me too?

HEDDA *(almost inaudibly)*. Ah, the child . . .

MRS. ELVSTED *(breathing heavily)*. It is all over then. Well well, now I will go, Hedda.

HEDDA. But you are not going away from town?

MRS. ELVSTED. Oh, I don't know what I shall do. I see nothing but darkness before me.

(She goes out by the hall door.)

HEDDA *(stands waiting for a moment)*. So you are not going to see her home, Mr. Løvborg?

LØVBORG. I? Through the streets? Would you have people see her walking with me?

HEDDA. Of course I don't know what else may have happened last
night. But is it so utterly irretrievable?

LØVBORG. It will not end with last night—I know that perfectly well.
And the thing is that now I have no taste for that sort of life either.
I won't begin it anew. She has broken my courage and my power
of braving life out.

HEDDA *(looking straight before her).* So that pretty little fool has had
her fingers in a man's destiny. *(Looks at him.)* But all the same,
how could you treat her so heartlessly.

LØVBORG. Oh, don't say that it was heartless!

HEDDA. To go and destroy what has filled her whole soul for months
and years. You do not call that heartless!

LØVBORG. To you I can tell the truth, Hedda.

HEDDA. The truth?

LØVBORG. First promise me—give me your word—that what I now
confide to you Thea shall never know.

HEDDA. I give you my word.

LØVBORG. Good. Then let me tell you that what I said just now was
untrue.

HEDDA. About the manuscript?

LØVBORG. Yes. I have not torn it to pieces—nor thrown it into the
fiord.

HEDDA. No, no . . . But—where is it then?

LØVBORG. I have destroyed it none the less—utterly destroyed it,
Hedda!

HEDDA. I don't understand.

LØVBORG. Thea said that what I had done seemed to her like a child-
murder.

HEDDA. Yes, so she said.

LØVBORG. But to kill his child—that is not the worst thing a father
can do to it.

HEDDA. Not the worst?

LØVBORG. No. I wanted to spare Thea from hearing the worst.

HEDDA. Then what is the worst?

LØVBORG. Suppose now, Hedda, that a man—in the small hours of the morning—came home to the child's mother after a night of riot and debauchery, and said: "Listen—I have been here and there—in this place and in that. And I have taken our child with me—to this place and to that. And I have lost the child—utterly lost it. The devil knows into what hands it may have fallen—who may have had their clutches on it."

HEDDA. Well—but when all is said and done, you know—this was only a book . . .

LØVBORG. Thea's pure soul was in that book.

HEDDA. Yes, so I understand.

LØVBORG. And you can understand, too, that for her and me together no future is possible.

HEDDA. What path do you mean to take then?

LØVBORG. None. I will only try to make an end of it all—the sooner the better.

HEDDA (*a step nearer him*). Eilert Løvborg—listen to me.—Will you not try to—to do it beautifully?

LØVBORG. Beautifully? (*Smiling.*) With vine-leaves in my hair, as you used to dream in the old days . . . ?

HEDDA. No, no. I have lost my faith in the vine-leaves. But beautifully nevertheless! For once in a way!—Good-bye! You must go now—and do not come here any more.

LØVBORG. Good-bye, Mrs. Tesman. And give George Tesman my love. (*He is on the point of going.*)

HEDDA. No, wait! I must give you a memento to take with you. (*She goes to the writing-table and opens the drawer and the pistol-case; then returns to Løvborg with one of the pistols.*)

LØVBORG (*looks at her*). This? Is *this* the memento?

HEDDA (*nodding slowly*). Do you recognise it? It was aimed at you once.

LØVBORG. You should have used it then.

HEDDA. Take it—and do *you* use it now.

LØVBORG (*puts the pistol in his breast pocket*). Thanks!

HEDDA.   And beautifully, Eilert Løvborg. Promise me that!

LØVBORG.   Good-bye, Hedda Gabler.

(*He goes out by the hall door.*

Hedda listens for a moment at the door. Then she goes up to the writing-table, takes out the packet of manuscript, peeps under the cover, draws a few of the sheets half out, and looks at them. Next she goes over and seats herself in the arm-chair beside the stove, with the packet in her lap. Presently she opens the stove door, and then the packet.)

HEDDA (*throws one of the quires into the fire and whispers to herself*).
Now I am burning your child, Thea!—Burning it, curly-locks! (*Throwing one or two more quires into the stove.*) Your child and Eilert Løvborg's. (*Throws the rest in.*) I am burning—I am burning your child.

ACT FOURTH

The same rooms at the Tesmans'. It is evening. The drawing-room is in darkness. The back room is lighted by the hanging lamp over the table. The curtains over the glass door are drawn close.

Hedda, dressed in black, walks to and fro in the dark room. Then she goes into the back room and disappears for a moment to the left. She is heard to strike a few chords on the piano. Presently she comes in sight again, and returns to the drawing-room.

Berta enters from the right, through the inner room, with a lighted lamp, which she places on the table in front of the corner settee in the drawing-room. Her eyes are red with weeping, and she has black ribbons in her cap. She goes quietly and circumspectly out to the right. Hedda goes up to the glass door, lifts the curtain a little aside, and looks out into the darkness. Shortly afterwards, Miss Tesman, in mourning, with a bonnet and veil on, comes in from the hall. Hedda goes towards her and holds out her hand.

MISS TESMAN. Yes, Hedda, here I am, in mourning and forlorn; for now my poor sister has at last found peace.

HEDDA. I have heard the news already, as you see. Tesman sent me a card.

MISS TESMAN. Yes, he promised me he would. But nevertheless I thought that to Hedda—here in the house of life—I ought myself to bring the tidings of death.

HEDDA. That was very kind of you.

MISS TESMAN. Ah, Rina ought not to have left us just *now*. This is not the time for Hedda's house to be a house of mourning.

HEDDA *(changing the subject)*. She died quite peacefully, did she not, Miss Tesman?

MISS TESMAN. Oh, her end was so calm, so beautiful. And then she had the unspeakable happiness of seeing George once more—and bidding him good-bye.—Has he not come home yet?

HEDDA. No. He wrote that he might be detained. But won't you sit down?

MISS TESMAN. No thank you, my dear, dear Hedda. I should like to, but I have so much to do. I must prepare my dear one for her rest as well as I can. She shall go to her grave looking her best.

HEDDA. Can I not help you in any way?

MISS TESMAN. Oh, you must not think of it! Hedda Tesman must have no hand in such mournful work. Nor let her thoughts dwell on it either—not at this time.

HEDDA. One is not always mistress of one's thoughts . . .

MISS TESMAN *(continuing)*. Ah yes, it is the way of the world. At home we shall be sewing a shroud; and here there will soon be sewing too, I suppose—but of another sort, thank God!

(George Tesman enters by the hall door.)

HEDDA. Ah, you have come at last!

TESMAN. You here, Aunt Julia? With Hedda? Fancy that!

MISS TESMAN. I was just going, my dear boy. Well, have you done all you promised?

TESMAN. No; I'm really afraid I have forgotten half of it. I must come to you again to-morrow. To-day my brain is all in a whirl. I can't keep my thoughts together.

MISS TESMAN. Why, my dear George, you mustn't take it in this way.

TESMAN. Mustn't . . . ? How do you mean?

MISS TESMAN. Even in your sorrow you must rejoice, as I do—rejoice that she is at rest.

TESMAN. Oh yes, yes—you are thinking of Aunt Rina.

HEDDA. You will feel lonely now, Miss Tesman.

MISS TESMAN. Just at first, yes. But that will not last very long, I hope. I daresay I shall soon find an occupant for poor Rina's little room.

TESMAN. Indeed? Who do you think will take it? Eh?

MISS TESMAN. Oh, there's always some poor invalid or other in want of nursing, unfortunately.

HEDDA. Would you really take such a burden upon you again?

MISS TESMAN. A burden! Heaven forgive you, child—it has been no burden to me.

HEDDA. But suppose you had a total stranger on your hands . . .

MISS TESMAN. Oh, one soon makes friends with sick folk; and it's such an absolute necessity for me to have some one to live for. Well, heaven be praised, there may soon be something in this house, too, to keep an old aunt busy.

HEDDA. Oh, don't trouble about anything here.

TESMAN. Yes, just fancy what a nice time we three might have together, if . . . ?

HEDDA. If . . . ?

TESMAN *(uneasily)*. Oh, nothing. It will all come right. Let us hope so—eh?

MISS TESMAN. Well well, I daresay you two want to talk to each other. *(Smiling.)* And perhaps Hedda may have something to tell you too, George. Good-bye! I must go home to Rina. *(Turning at the door.)* How strange it is to think that now Rina is with me and with my poor brother as well!

TESMAN. Yes, fancy that, Aunt Julia! Eh?

(Miss Tesman goes out by the hall door.)

HEDDA *(follows Tesman coldly and searchingly with her eyes)*. I almost believe your Aunt Rina's death affects *you* more than it does your Aunt Julia.

TESMAN. Oh, it's not that alone. It's Eilert I am so terribly uneasy about.

HEDDA *(quickly)*. Is there anything new about him?

TESMAN. I looked in at his rooms this afternoon, intending to tell him the manuscript was in safe keeping.

HEDDA. Well, did you not find him?

TESMAN. No. He wasn't at home. But afterwards I met Mrs. Elvsted, and she told me that he had been here early this morning.

HEDDA. Yes, directly after you had gone.

TESMAN. And he said that he had torn his manuscript to pieces—eh?

HEDDA. Yes, so he declared.

TESMAN. Why, good heavens, he must have been completely out of his mind! And I suppose you thought it best not to give it back to him, Hedda?

HEDDA. No, he did not get it.

TESMAN. But of course you told him that we had it?

HEDDA. No. *(Quickly.)* Did you tell Mrs. Elvsted?

TESMAN. No; I thought I had better not. But you ought to have told *him.* Fancy, if, in desperation, he should go and do himself some injury! Let me have the manuscript, Hedda! I will take it to him at once. Where is it?

HEDDA *(cold and immovable, leaning on the arm-chair)*. I have not got it.

TESMAN. Have not got it? What in the world do you mean?

HEDDA. I have burnt it—every line of it.

TESMAN *(with a violent movement of terror)*. Burnt! Burnt Eilert's manuscript!

HEDDA. Don't scream so. The servant might hear you.

TESMAN. Burnt! Why, good God . . . ! No, no, no! It's impossible!

HEDDA. It is so, nevertheless.

TESMAN. Do you know what you have done, Hedda? It's unlawful appropriation of lost property. Fancy that! Just ask Judge Brack, and he'll tell you what it is.

HEDDA. I advise you not to speak of it—either to Judge Brack, or to any one else.

TESMAN. But how could you do anything so unheard-of? What put it into your head? What possessed you? Answer me that—eh?

HEDDA *(suppressing an almost imperceptible smile)*. I did it for your sake, George.

TESMAN. For my sake!

HEDDA. This morning, when you told me about what he had read to you . . .

TESMAN. Yes yes—what then?

HEDDA. You acknowledged that you envied him his work.

TESMAN. Oh, of course I didn't mean that literally.

HEDDA. No matter—I could not bear the idea that any one should throw you into the shade.

TESMAN *(in an outburst of mingled doubt and joy)*. Hedda! Oh, is this true? But—but—I never knew you show your love like that before. Fancy that!

HEDDA. Well, I may as well tell you that—just at this time . . . *(Impatiently, breaking off.)* No, no; you can ask Aunt Julia. *She* will tell you, fast enough.

TESMAN. Oh, I almost think I understand you, Hedda! *(Clasps his hands together.)* Great heavens! do you really mean it! Eh?

HEDDA. Don't shout so. The servant might hear.

TESMAN *(laughing in irrepressible glee)*. The servant! Why, how absurd you are, Hedda. It's only my old Berta! Why, I'll tell Berta myself.

HEDDA *(clenching her hands together in desperation)*. Oh, it is killing me,—it is killing me, all this!

TESMAN. What is, Hedda? Eh?

HEDDA *(coldly, controlling herself)*. All this—absurdity—George.

TESMAN. Absurdity! Do you see anything absurd in my being overjoyed at the news! But after all—perhaps I had better not say anything to Berta.

HEDDA. Oh . . . why not that too?

TESMAN. No, no, not yet! But I must certainly tell Aunt Julia. And then that you have begun to call me George too! Fancy that! Oh, Aunt Julia will be so happy—so happy!

HEDDA. When she hears that I have burnt Eilert Løvborg's manuscript
—for your sake?

TESMAN. No, by-the-bye—that affair of the manuscript—of course
nobody must know about that. But that you love me so much,[1]
Hedda—Aunt Julia must really share my joy in that! I wonder,
now, whether this sort of thing is usual in young wives? Eh?

HEDDA. I think you had better ask Aunt Julia that question too.

TESMAN. I will indeed, some time or other. *(Looks uneasy and down-cast again.)* And yet the manuscript—the manuscript! Good God!
it is terrible to think what will become of poor Eilert now.

*(Mrs. Elvsted, dressed as in the first Act, with hat and cloak, enters
by the hall door.)*

MRS. ELVSTED *(greets them hurriedly, and says in evident agitation).*
Oh, dear Hedda, forgive my coming again.

HEDDA. What is the matter with you, Thea?

TESMAN. Something about Eilert Løvborg again—eh?

MRS. ELVSTED. Yes! I am dreadfully afraid some misfortune has hap-pened to him.

HEDDA *(seizes her arm).* Ah,—do you think so?

TESMAN. Why, good Lord—what makes you think that, Mrs. Elvsted?

MRS. ELVSTED. I heard them talking of him at my boarding-house—
just as I came in. Oh, the most incredible rumours are afloat about
him to-day.

TESMAN. Yes, fancy, so I heard too! And I can bear witness that he
went straight home to bed last night. Fancy that!

HEDDA. Well, what did they say at the boarding-house?

MRS. ELVSTED. Oh, I couldn't make out anything clearly. Either they
knew nothing definite, or else . . . They stopped talking when they
saw me; and I did not dare to ask.

TESMAN *(moving about uneasily).* We must hope—we must hope that
you misunderstood them, Mrs. Elvsted.

MRS. ELVSTED. No, no; I am sure it was of him they were talking. And
I heard something about the hospital or . . .

[1] Literally, "That you burn for me."

TESMAN. The hospital?

HEDDA. No—surely that cannot be!

MRS. ELVSTED. Oh, I was in such mortal terror! I went to his lodgings and asked for him there.

HEDDA. *You* could make up your mind to that, Thea!

MRS. ELVSTED. What else could I do? I really could bear the suspense no longer.

TESMAN. But you didn't find him either—eh?

MRS. ELVSTED. No. And the people knew nothing about him. He hadn't been home since yesterday afternoon, they said.

TESMAN. Yesterday! Fancy, how could they say that?

MRS. ELVSTED. Oh, I am sure something terrible must have happened to him.

TESMAN. Hedda dear—how would it be if I were to go and make inquiries . . . ?

HEDDA. No, no—don't you mix yourself up in this affair.

(Judge Brack, with his hat in his hand, enters by the hall door, which Berta opens, and closes behind him. He looks grave and bows in silence.)

TESMAN. Oh, is that you, my dear Judge? Eh?

BRACK. Yes. It was imperative I should see you this evening.

TESMAN. I can see you have heard the news about Aunt Rina?

BRACK. Yes, that among other things.

TESMAN. Isn't it sad—eh?

BRACK. Well, my dear Tesman, that depends on how you look at it.

TESMAN *(looks doubtfully at him)*. Has anything else happened?

BRACK. Yes.

HEDDA *(in suspense)*. Anything sad, Judge Brack?

BRACK. That, too, depends on how you look at it, Mrs. Tesman.

MRS. ELVSTED *(unable to restrain her anxiety)*. Oh! It is something about Eilert Løvborg!

BRACK *(with a glance at her)*. What makes you think that, Madam? Perhaps you have already heard something . . . ?

MRS. ELVSTED *(in confusion)*. No, nothing at all, but . . .

TESMAN. Oh, for heaven's sake, tell us!

BRACK *(shrugging his shoulders)*. Well, I regret to say Eilert Løvborg has been taken to the hospital. He is lying at the point of death.

MRS. ELVSTED *(shrieks)*. Oh God! oh God . . . !

TESMAN. To the hospital! And at the point of death!

HEDDA *(involuntarily)*. So soon then . . .

MRS. ELVSTED *(wailing)*. And we parted in anger, Hedda!

HEDDA *(whispers)*. Thea—Thea—be careful!

MRS. ELVSTED *(not heeding her)*. I must go to him! I must see him alive!

BRACK. It is useless, Madam. No one will be admitted.

MRS. ELVSTED. Oh, at least tell me what has happened to him? What is it?

TESMAN. You don't mean to say that he has himself . . . Eh?

HEDDA. Yes, I am sure he has.

TESMAN. Hedda, how can you . . . ?

BRACK *(keeping his eyes fixed upon her).* Unfortunately you have guessed quite correctly, Mrs. Tesman.

MRS. ELVSTED. Oh, how horrible!

TESMAN. Himself, then! Fancy that!

HEDDA. Shot himself!

BRACK. Rightly guessed again, Mrs. Tesman.

MRS. ELVSTED *(with an effort at self-control).* When did it happen, Mr. Brack?

BRACK. This afternoon—between three and four.

TESMAN. But, good Lord, where did he do it? Eh?

BRACK *(with some hesitation).* Where? Well—I suppose at his lodgings.

MRS. ELVSTED. No, that cannot be; for I was there between six and seven.

BRACK. Well then, somewhere else. I don't know exactly. I only know that he was found . . . He had shot himself—in the breast.

MRS. ELVSTED. Oh, how terrible! That he should die like that!

HEDDA *(to Brack).* Was it in the breast?

BRACK. Yes—as I told you.

HEDDA. Not in the temple?

BRACK. In the breast, Mrs. Tesman.

HEDDA. Well, well—the breast is a good place, too.

BRACK. How do you mean, Mrs. Tesman?

HEDDA *(evasively).* Oh, nothing—nothing.

TESMAN. And the wound is dangerous, you say—eh?

BRACK. Absolutely mortal. The end has probably come by this time.

MRS. ELVSTED. Yes, yes, I feel it. The end! The end! Oh, Hedda . . . !

TESMAN. But tell me, how have you learnt all this?

BRACK *(curtly).* Through one of the police. A man I had some business with.

HEDDA *(in a clear voice).* At last a deed worth doing!

TESMAN *(terrified).* Good heavens, Hedda! what are you saying?

HEDDA. I say there is beauty in this.

BRACK. H'm, Mrs. Tesman . . .

TESMAN. Beauty! Fancy that!

MRS. ELVSTED. Oh, Hedda, how can you talk of beauty in such an act!

HEDDA. Eilert Løvborg has himself made up his account with life. He has had the courage to do—the one right thing.

MRS. ELVSTED. No, you must never think *that* was how it happened! It must have been in delirium that he did it.

TESMAN. In despair!

HEDDA. That he did not. I am certain of that.

MRS. ELVSTED. Yes, yes! In delirium! Just as when he tore up our manuscript.

BRACK *(starting)*. The manuscript? Has he torn that up?

MRS. ELVSTED. Yes, last night.

TESMAN *(whispers softly)*. Oh, Hedda, we shall never get over this.

BRACK. H'm, very extraordinary.

TESMAN *(moving about the room)*. To think of Eilert going out of the world in this way! And not leaving behind him the book that would have immortalised his name . . .

MRS. ELVSTED. Oh, if only it could be put together again!

TESMAN. Yes, if it only could! I don't know what I would not give . . .

MRS. ELVSTED. Perhaps it can, Mr. Tesman.

TESMAN. What do you mean?

MRS. ELVSTED *(searches in the pocket of her dress)*. Look here. I have kept all the loose notes he used to dictate from.

HEDDA *(a step forward)*. Ah . . . !

TESMAN. You have kept them, Mrs. Elvsted! Eh?

MRS. ELVSTED. Yes, I have them here. I put them in my pocket when I left home. Here they still are . . .

TESMAN. Oh, do let me see them!

MRS. ELVSTED *(hands him a bundle of papers)*. But they are in such disorder—all mixed up.

TESMAN. Fancy, if we could make something out of them, after all! Perhaps if we two put our heads together . . .

MRS. ELVSTED. Oh yes, at least let us try . . .

TESMAN. We *will* manage it! We *must!* I will dedicate my life to this task.

HEDDA. You, George? Your life?

TESMAN. Yes, or rather all the time I can spare. My own collections must wait in the meantime. Hedda—you understand, eh? I owe this to Eilert's memory.

HEDDA. Perhaps.

TESMAN. And so, my dear Mrs. Elvsted, we will give our whole minds to it. There is no use in brooding over what can't be undone —eh? We must try to control our grief as much as possible, and . . .

MRS. ELVSTED. Yes, yes, Mr. Tesman, I will do the best I can.

TESMAN. Well then, come here. I can't rest until we have looked through the notes. Where shall we sit? Here? No, in there, in the back room. Excuse me, my dear Judge. Come with me, Mrs. Elvsted.

MRS. ELVSTED. Oh, if only it were possible!

(*Tesman and Mrs. Elvsted go into the back room. She takes off her hat and cloak. They both sit at the table under the hanging lamp, and are soon deep in an eager examination of the papers. Hedda crosses to the stove and sits in the arm-chair. Presently Brack goes up to her.*)

HEDDA (*in a low voice*). Oh, what a sense of freedom it gives one, this act of Eilert Løvborg's.

BRACK. Freedom, Mrs. Hedda? Well, of course, it is a release for him . . .

HEDDA. I mean for me. It gives me a sense of freedom to know that a deed of deliberate courage is still possible in this world,—a deed of spontaneous beauty.

BRACK (*smiling*). H'm—my dear Mrs. Hedda . . .

HEDDA. Oh, I know what you are going to say. For you are a kind of specialist too, like—you know!

BRACK (*looking hard at her*). Eilert Løvborg was more to you than perhaps you are willing to admit to yourself. Am I wrong?

HEDDA. I don't answer such questions. I only know that Eilert Løvborg has had the courage to live his life after his own fashion. And then— the last great act, with its beauty! Ah! that he should have the will and the strength to turn away from the banquet of life—so early.

BRACK. I am sorry, Mrs. Hedda,—but I fear I must dispel an amiable illusion.

HEDDA. Illusion?

BRACK. Which could not have lasted long in any case.

HEDDA. What do you mean?

BRACK. Eilert Løvborg did not shoot himself—voluntarily.

HEDDA. Not voluntarily?

BRACK. No. The thing did not happen exactly as I told it.

HEDDA *(in suspense)*. Have you concealed something? What is it?

BRACK. For poor Mrs. Elvsted's sake I idealised the facts a little.

HEDDA. What *are* the facts?

BRACK. First, that he is already dead.

HEDDA. At the hospital?

BRACK. Yes—without regaining consciousness.

HEDDA. What more have you concealed?

BRACK. This—the event did not happen at his lodgings.

HEDDA. Oh, that can make no difference.

BRACK. Perhaps it may. For I must tell you—Eilert Løvborg was found shot in—in Mademoiselle Diana's boudoir.

HEDDA *(makes a motion as if to rise, but sinks back again)*. That is impossible, Judge Brack! He cannot have been *there* again to-day.

BRACK. He was there this afternoon. He went there, he said, to demand the return of something which they had taken from him. Talked wildly about a lost child . . .

HEDDA. Ah—so that was why . . .

BRACK. I thought probably he meant his manuscript; but now I hear he destroyed that himself. So I suppose it must have been his pocket-book.

HEDDA. Yes, no doubt. And there—there he was found?

BRACK. Yes, there. With a pistol in his breast-pocket, discharged. The ball had lodged in a vital part.

HEDDA. In the breast—yes.

BRACK. No—in the bowels.

HEDDA *(looks up at him with an expression of loathing)*. That too! Oh, what curse is it that makes everything I touch turn ludicrous and mean?

BRACK. There is one point more, Mrs. Hedda—another disagreeable feature in the affair.

HEDDA. And what is that?

BRACK. The pistol he carried . . .

HEDDA *(breathless)*. Well? What of it?

BRACK. He must have stolen it.

HEDDA *(leaps up)*. Stolen it! That is not true! He did not steal it!

BRACK. No other explanation is possible! He *must* have stolen it . . . Hush!

(Tesman and Mrs. Elvsted have risen from the table in the back room, and come into the drawing-room.)

TESMAN *(with the papers in both his hands)*. Hedda dear, it is almost impossible to see under that lamp. Think of that!

HEDDA. Yes, I am thinking.

TESMAN. Would you mind our sitting at your writing-table—eh?

HEDDA. If you like. *(Quickly.)* No, wait! Let me clear it first!

TESMAN. Oh, you needn't trouble, Hedda. There is plenty of room.

HEDDA. No no, let me clear it, I say! I will take these things in and put them on the piano. There!

(She has drawn out an object, covered with sheet music, from under the bookcase, places several other pieces of music upon it, and carries the whole into the inner room, to the left. Tesman lays the scraps of paper on the writing-table, and moves the lamp there from the corner table. He and Mrs. Elvsted sit down and proceed with their work. Hedda returns.)

HEDDA *(behind Mrs. Elvsted's chair, gently ruffling her hair)*. Well, my sweet Thea,—how goes it with Eilert Løvborg's monument?

MRS. ELVSTED *(looks dispiritedly up at her)*. Oh, it will be terribly hard to put in order.

TESMAN. We *must* manage it. I am determined. And arranging other people's papers is just the work for me.

(Hedda goes over to the stove, and seats herself on one of the foot-stools. Brack stands over her, leaning on the arm-chair.)

HEDDA *(whispers)*. What did you say about the pistol?

BRACK *(softly)*. That he must have stolen it.

HEDDA Why stolen it?

BRACK. Because every other explanation *ought* to be impossible, Mrs. Hedda.

HEDDA. Indeed?

BRACK *(glancing at her)*. Of course Eilert Løvborg was here this morning. Was he not?

HEDDA. Yes.

BRACK. Were you alone with him?

HEDDA. Part of the time.

BRACK. Did you not leave the room whilst he was here?

HEDDA. No.

BRACK. Try to recollect. Were you not out of the room a moment?

HEDDA. Yes, perhaps just a moment—out in the hall.

BRACK. And where was your pistol-case during that time?

HEDDA. I had it locked up in . . .

BRACK. Well, Mrs. Hedda?

HEDDA. The case stood there on the writing-table.

BRACK. Have you looked since, to see whether both the pistols are there?

HEDDA. No.

BRACK. Well, you need not. I saw the pistol found in Løvborg's pocket, and I knew it at once as the one I had seen yesterday—and before, too.

HEDDA. Have you it with you?

BRACK. No; the police have it.

HEDDA. What will the police do with it?

BRACK. Search till they find the owner.

HEDDA. Do you think they will succeed?

BRACK *(bends over her and whispers)*. No, Hedda Gabler—not so long as I say nothing.

HEDDA (*looks frightened at him*). And if you do *not* say nothing,— what then?

BRACK (*shrugs his shoulders*). There is always the possibility that the pistol was stolen.

HEDDA (*firmly*). Death rather than that.

BRACK (*smiling*). People *say* such things—but they don't *do* them.

HEDDA (*without replying*). And supposing the pistol was not stolen, and the owner is discovered? What then?

BRACK. Well, Hedda—then comes the scandal.

HEDDA. The scandal!

BRACK. Yes, the scandal—of which you are so mortally afraid. You will, of course, be brought before the court—both you and Mademoiselle Diana. She will have to explain how the thing happened —whether it was an accidental shot or murder. Did the pistol go off as he was trying to take it out of his pocket, to threaten her with? Or did she tear the pistol out of his hand, shoot him, and push it back into his pocket? That would be quite like her; for she is an able-bodied young person, this same Mademoiselle Diana.

HEDDA. But *I* have nothing to do with all this repulsive business.

BRACK. No. But you will have to answer the question: Why did you give Eilert Løvborg the pistol? And what conclusions will people draw from the fact that you did give it to him?

HEDDA (*lets her head sink*). That is true. I did not think of that.

BRACK. Well, fortunately, there is no danger, so long as I say nothing.

HEDDA (*looks up at him*). So I am in your power, Judge Brack. You have me at your beck and call, from this time forward.

BRACK (*whispers softly*). Dearest Hedda—believe me—I shall not abuse my advantage.

HEDDA. I am in your power none the less. Subject to your will and your demands. A slave, a slave then! (*Rises impetuously.*) No, I cannot endure the thought of that! Never!

BRACK (*looks half-mockingly at her*). People generally get used to the inevitable.

HEDDA (*returns his look*). Yes, perhaps. (*She crosses to the writing-*

table. Suppressing an involuntary smile, she imitates Tesman's intona-tions.) Well? Are you getting on, George? Eh?

TESMAN. Heaven knows, dear. In any case it will be the work of months.

HEDDA *(as before)*. Fancy that! *(Passes her hands softly through Mrs. Elvsted's hair.)* Doesn't it seem strange to you, Thea? Here are you sitting with Tesman—just as you used to sit with Eilert Løvborg?

MRS. ELVSTED. Ah, if I could only inspire your husband in the same way!

HEDDA. Oh, that will come too—in time.

TESMAN. Yes, do you know, Hedda—I really think I begin to feel something of the sort. But won't you go and sit with Brack again?

HEDDA. Is there nothing I can do to help you two?

TESMAN. No, nothing in the world. *(Turning his head.)* I trust you to keep Hedda company, my dear Brack!

BRACK *(with a glance at Hedda)*. With the very greatest of pleasure.

HEDDA. Thanks. But I am tired this evening. I will go in and lie down a little on the sofa.

TESMAN. Yes, do dear—eh?

(Hedda goes into the back room and draws the curtains. A short pause. Suddenly she is heard playing a wild dance on the piano.)

MRS. ELVSTED *(starts from her chair)*. Oh—what is that?

TESMAN *(runs to the doorway)*. Why, my dearest Hedda—don't play dance-music to-night! Just think of Aunt Rina! And of Eilert too!

HEDDA *(puts her head out between the curtains)*. And of Aunt Julia. And of all the rest of them.—After this, I will be quiet. *(Closes the curtains again.)*

TESMAN *(at the writing-table)*. It's not good for her to see us at this distressing work. I'll tell you what, Mrs. Elvsted,—you shall take the empty room at Aunt Julia's, and then I will come over in the evenings, and we can sit and work *there*—eh?

HEDDA *(in the inner room)*. I hear what you are saying, Tesman. But how am *I* to get through the evenings out here?

TESMAN *(turning over the papers)*. Oh, I daresay Judge Brack will be so kind as to look in now and then, even though I am out.

BRACK *(in the arm-chair, calls out gaily)*. Every blessed evening, with all the pleasure in life, Mrs. Tesman! We shall get on capitally together, we two!

HEDDA *(speaking loud and clear)*. Yes, don't you flatter yourself we will, Judge Brack? Now that you are the one cock in the basket . . . *(A shot is heard within. Tesman, Mrs. Elvsted, and Brack leap to their feet.)*

TESMAN. Oh, now she is playing with those pistols again.

(He throws back the curtains and runs in, followed by Mrs. Elvsted. Hedda lies stretched on the sofa, lifeless. Confusion and cries. Berta enters in alarm from the right.)

TESMAN *(shrieks to Brack)*. Shot herself! Shot herself in the temple! Fancy that!

BRACK *(half-fainting in the arm-chair)*. Good God!—people don't *do* such things!

THE END